SCIENCE, SUBMARINES & SECRETS

The Incredible Early Years of the Albany Research Center

DECLASSIFIED WITH DELETIONS

BY:
TAI STITH

©2022
Owl Room Press
Albany, Oregon

SCIENCE, SUBMARINES & SECRETS

THE INCREDIBLE EARLY YEARS
OF THE
ALBANY RESEARCH CENTER

BY TAI STITH

OWL ROOM
PRESS

DECLASSIFIED

Science, Submarines & Secrets:
The Incredible Early Years of the
Albany Research Center

ISBN: 978-1-7351366-4-6

©2022 Owl Room Press
Albany, Oregon

Body text set in Century 731 BT Roman
Additional text set in Splendid 66 and Futura
Cover Text set in Aquilone, Courier and, Harlie WF
Cover photo courtesy Stephen T. Anderson
Cover design and formatting by Rocketship Graphic Design
Historic photographs reproduced with permission from the
U.S. Department of Energy

All rights reserved. No part of this book may be reproduced in any form or by any electronic or mechanical means, including information storage and retrieval systems, without permission in writing from Owl Room Press.

FOR IAN R. STITH
This journey began with you.

Contents

Introduction / Page 11

1. The Power of Albany / Page 15
2. Forward Momentum / Page 32t
3. A Laboratory Takes Shape / Page 57
4. Shifting Sands / Page 73
5. Trial and Triumph / Page 85
6. The Little Laboratory That Could / Page 95
7. The Ghost in the Machine / Page 118
8. Radio Silence and Operation Zirconium / Page 156
9. Called the 'Bureau of Mines' by the Man on the Street / Page 188
10. Separation Anxiety / Page 202
11. Uncommon Miracle Metals / Page 241
12. Submarine in the Desert / Page 279
13. Bright Dreams and Nightmares / Page 301
14. The Hustlers / Page 342
15. A New Hope and a New Era / Page 366

Epilogue / Page 381

Endnotes / page 389

Quote Index / page 395

Bibliography / page 443

RESTRICTED

February 2022

ODP: EHG

Owl Room Press
Albany, Oregon

Subject: Acknowledgements

Dear Readers:

This book is the result of an immense community effort. The energy and enthusiasm of those who worked at the U.S. Bureau of Mines Albany Research Center, their families, neighbors, and friends were the driving force behind this work of nonfiction. Without the continued support and encouragement of the following people, this book would not have been possible.

First and foremost, this book and the images within wouldn't be possible without Stephen T. Anderson. Steve has worked for decades to preserve the history of the U.S. Bureau of Mines Albany Research Center. He has invested hundreds of hours of his own time to digitize original photos and other documentation related to the site, and probably another hundred hours answering my many questions and finding photo for me. Without his knowledge and guidance this book would simply not have come to fruition.

Dennis Emerson was pivotal in introducing me to Albany's metals industry as a whole. Through Dennis I have made key connections with some of Albany's finest minds. I appreciate his energy and continued enthusiasm for the incredible advancements in Albany's metals industry. Many thanks to Dennis and the crew at Albany Regional Museum.

Robert L. Govro was a fountain of knowledge and encouragement during the creation of this book. He took me under his wing and taught me about the early days of zirconium production. He spent hours drawing out the zirconium production process by hand and then described each step to make sure I understood what I was writing about. His spirited descriptions of his time working at the Bureau were nothing short of magical. Bob's enthusiasm was contagious and I hope I captured a fraction of his energy in my writing. Bob is one of the most interesting people I know, and a true gentleman.

I had the pleasure of meeting George J. Dooley III, who graciously offered to be one of my reviewers. I am so thankful for his input on the manuscript and it was a pleasure getting to know this veteran Bureau of Mines Research Director. Because of his help, this book is far more accurate.

Shelley C. Martin, communications & public affairs officer at NETL, graciously provided an abundance of assistance during this entire process. She always responded with quick answers and without her help I wouldn't thave been able to experience the campus as it is today. My deepest appreciation goes out to Shelley for granting me permission to publish historic images from the Bureau's earliest days.

My friend and mentor John R. Bruning has been an inspiration for me since before I made the leap to historical nonfiction writing. As an accomplished author of the genre, John writes with an intensity and passion that I can only hope to emulate.

All my contacts at the Department of Energy were wonderful to work with. Dr. Eric W. Boyle, Historian at the Office of Legacy Management, was very helpful when I asked obscure questions. Many thanks to the FOIA officers who fielded my various requests, and a very special thanks to Cliff Nunn, Chief Counsel at the Naval Reactors Laboratory Field Office, and Don Dahl, Public Affairs Director for the Naval Reactors facility at Idaho National Laboratory, for taking the time to personally contact me regarding the availability of information regarding zirconium, the Mark I reactor, and the U.S.S. Nautilus.

A million thanks to my editor, Lisa Poppleton Farnam, who labored over my many mistakes to help me produce a much more polished book. I am so grateful that our paths crossed at exactly the right time. Lisa's personal knowledge of the Bureau and her meticulous proofreading took this book to the next level.

I rely on the positive energy and continual support from the best group on Facebook, The Historical Significance of the Albany Research Center. This group was one of the reasons I stepped out in faith to begin writing in the first place. If it hadn't been for the tremendous amount of support, encouragement, and information provided by former employees and family members, there simply would be no book. With over 950 members to date, it goes to show that there is a strong interest in the work done at the Bureau of Mines and NETL. The laboratory remains relevant and continues to be one of Albany's most important historical landmarks.

Linda Hogan, owner of Cookie Binge Coffee Shop in Adair Village, kept me supplied with a steady stream of the best coffee and cookies on the planet while writing at her peaceful, happy shop. If you happen to be in the area, try her frosted peppermint shake, spiced Chai latte, or fresh ginger molasses cookies (my favorite!)

A heartfelt thanks to my husband Derek, who has fully supported me while I completed this book. When writing only part time was no longer adequate, I switched to being a full-time writer in order to complete the book in a timely manner. His belief that I could successfully put this incredible story onto paper fueled me through the difficult times.

And lastly, I firmly believe the Lord Jesus put this whole thing into motion and kept it moving forward by providing just what I needed to continue at just the right moment. With no effort on my part, doors were opened (literally), contacts were made, sources were uncovered, and families offered to contribute. These providential events ultimately paved the way to a completed book.

To my readers—thank you for this opportunity for me to share this incredible story that isn't mine, but belongs to the men and women who lived this history.

Very Truly Yours,

Tai Stith

The most beautiful thing we can experience is the mysterious. It is the source of all true art and science. He to whom the emotion is a stranger, who can no longer pause to wonder and stand wrapped in awe; is as good as dead; his eyes are closed.

ALBERT EINSTEIN

The whole history of science has been the gradual realization that events do not happen in an arbitrary manner, but that they reflect a certain underlying order, which may or may not be divinely inspired.

STEPHEN HAWKING

INTRODUCTION

THE CAPTAIN AND THE METALLURGIST
August 1949

A commercial flight touched down in Portland, Oregon during the summer of 1949. Light was draining from the sky that Friday evening as tired passengers disembarked. Most were probably thankful to be one step closer to their destination, but one passenger still had an hour or more left in his journey. The slight man, a U. S. Navy captain, dressed in a gray suit and tie, was no stranger to traveling at odd hours and frequently arrived at his final destination in the middle of the night.

Once on the ground, a group of government officials plus one metallurgist met the captain. Hasty handshakes were exchanged all around and the group headed to a waiting car. The driver took them out of Portland and onto Highway 99E, a lonely stretch of road that connected rural areas along a verdant agricultural valley. If the captain had been looking out the window, he would've noticed a string of tiny towns with names like Canby and Aurora and Woodburn. But he probably had no interest in the pastoral scenery that passed by in low evening light; his focus was wholly on the metallurgist seated beside him.

Conversation filled the backseat; diagrams and documents passed between the metallurgist and the captain. A hush-hush project of extraordinary importance was being discussed between the two, and not a moment was wasted during the car ride. Neither man was known for being lax with his time and both were driven toward a common goal.

The U. S. Navy captain was famous for his abrasive, petulant mannerisms and unorthodox tactics; the metallurgist was a soft-spoken European refugee who had escaped ahead of Nazi occupation. Though the pair seemed to be utterly opposite in every way, there was a common thread between the two: they were both direct and to the point when it came to their work, and they both championed the effort of the individual.

We don't know whether the carload of government employees stopped at a roadside diner to grab a late meal somewhere along Highway 99E; if they had, they would've been quite the sight: a table full of men in suits would have stood out against the hardworking locals. A tongue or two may have wagged behind a counter bar; what is certain is that the reason for the captain's trip would not have been discussed openly in public. Great care was taken to avoid talking about the subject anywhere roving ears could've picked up even a snippet of information. After all, there were great hopes the project as a whole would be a critical and unprecedented success for the United States military.

Aspects of the secret project were being carried out in facilities across the country and the captain was overseeing them all, which meant a great deal of travel. The visits to this particular location in Oregon were described as being "hurried" and were almost always on a weekend when few employees were present at the laboratory.

Whenever the government group finally arrived at their destination—an unassuming, collegiate-looking laboratory on the edge of tiny Albany, Oregon—their credentials were checked by Bureau employees tasked by the Atomic Energy Commission to maintain strict security protocols. These handpicked employees held the highest level of security, called "Q Clearance," and were intensely confidential about classified activity under their watch.

After all identifications were confirmed, the captain, the metallurgist, and the accompanying government officials would have walked down the narrow main road that traveled south through campus. The night was lovely, warm, and clear as the men walked briskly toward the end of the road, loath to lose a single second. The metallurgist came to a stop at a newly completed two-story brick building with ground-to-roofline windows. All were ushered inside.

Once the door latched securely behind them, the captain—Captain Hyman G. Rickover, who had been put in charge of the U. S. Navy's nuclear propulsion program, and the metallurgist, William J. Kroll, a pioneering force behind the development of titanium and zirconium—could finally discuss progress regarding the secret project, knowing they couldn't be overheard by prying ears. The government officials from the Atomic Energy Commission and the Bureau of Mines stood by and listened intently to the spirited conversation between Captain Rickover and Dr. Kroll.

The two men were working together to accomplish a feat never before attempted in the history of humanity. Captain Rickover and Dr. Kroll were making an educated gamble with an obscure metal called zirconium. That gamble could make or break Captain Rickover's insanely ambitious attempt to create the world's first nuclear-powered submarine for a navy that was clamoring to stay ahead of competing nations.

How had elements of a critical military project ended up in a sleepy valley town in rural Oregon? An incredible chain of events that seemed almost providential had been set in motion years before World War II, before the first controlled nuclear chain reaction, but not before visionary thinkers had dreamed of a true submarine that could traverse the oceans completely submerged for an extended period.

For that to happen, a staggering series of engineering and metallurgical successes needed to be achieved, and two of those critical aspects would take place in a short amount of time . . . and both would occur at a little laboratory in Albany, Oregon.[1]

CHAPTER ONE
THE POWER OF ALBANY
August 1940–March 1943

"It is safe to say that the next decade will witness realization of the fondest dreams of the most enthusiastic community builders, who long ago visioned this territory as the center of a prosperous empire."
Albany Democrat-Herald *editorial, August 15, 1940*

Albany, Oregon was a small but respectable town of fifty-six hundred residents at the onset of the 1940s. A bourgeoning First Street skimmed the banks of the Willamette River and featured feed stores, hotels, and shops. Elegant Victorian-era architecture, low swooping bungalows, and Queen Anne-style homes surrounded the central town hub. Smaller cottage-style starter homes dotted other neighborhoods, and past those, farm homes and barns fanned out for miles. Albany was perfectly situated; sixty miles to the west was the magnificent Pacific Ocean, with miles of jagged coastline boasting awe-inspiring vistas. On the eastern horizon, the Cascade mountain range rose in jagged peaks, and beyond that was Oregon's uniquely beautiful high desert.

By August 1940, the small Oregon town was experiencing multiple major industrial construction projects as the area was trying to attract industries that weren't necessarily related to the floundering timber business. Construction in Albany was supported in part by the Linn-Benton Rural Electrification Act (REA). The Bonneville Dam, a hydroelectric facility on the Columbia River two hours to the north, was built in 1938, and the Linn-Benton REA had provided funds to construct an electrical substation on the western end of Albany. Through this substation, affordable electricity would be provided to consumers in Albany and surrounding areas in the Willamette Valley. In the late 1930s, rural farmhouses in the area had been powered by mobile diesel generator units. The switch to a permanent source of electricity would be a welcome change.

Construction on the Queen Street substation began August 2, 1940, on a swath of land formerly belonging to the late Albany resident Maude Henderson. Fields bordered by thick trees hugged the edges of the property, which was a stone's throw from a road that led west out of Albany. An old home on Henderson's land was repurposed by the Bonneville Power Administration as an office, and within weeks, supplies arrived at the much-anticipated substation location. Construction moved steadily along, and by November, areas of Albany and beyond were receiving power directly from Bonneville. This direct line of power would later prove to be a vital detail in Albany's history.

The Grand Coulee Dam, also located on the Columbia River, was being built around the same time and was expected to contribute significantly to the electrical grid once completed. With two powerful hydroelectric facilities in the Pacific Northwest, the government anticipated there would be far more power produced than what could actually be used. Discussions of ways to use that extra power included establishing some sort of new laboratory. Interestingly, there was talk about establishing an "electro-development" laboratory in the region before either hydroelectric station ever began producing electricity. In 1936, the Pacific Northwest Planning Commission (the northwest division of the National Resources Planning Board) had suggested establishing a government laboratory to help

Photo: BPA/Seattle NARA
Powerlines are being constructed at the future Bonneville Power Administration substation on Queen Street. Photo taken Aug 5, 1940.

Photo: BPA/Seattle NARA
Construction begins on the Queen Street substation. Photo taken Sept. 4, 1940.

optimize mineral development in the western United States.

After years of noncommittal discussion, the first definitive action to establish a government electro-development laboratory happened in early 1941 when Oregon Senator Rufus C. Holman introduced a bill that supported the creation of a laboratory to "assist in the mineral industries." There was considerable support for the laboratory from the Portland Chamber of Commerce, Oregon State College (now Oregon State University), and other Pacific Northwest states, Washington in particular. With such vocal support from a variety of locations, the bill passed in December 1941.

The United States Bureau of Mines (USBM), headquartered in Washington, D.C., would be the entity to establish the laboratory. The USBM was created by the Organic Act of 1910, as spinoff from the U.S. Geologic Survey (USGS), after a wave of mining disasters plagued the nation. A 1907 tragedy in West Virginia—the worst in U.S. history—claimed the lives of 362 miners. Just two years later, another 259 lives were lost in a mine fire in Illinois. As part of the Department of the Interior, the USBM's initial purpose was to make mining safer by improving conditions and finding ways to prevent accidents.

Soon after its creation, the USBM's scope expanded to finding and analyzing mineral resources across the nation, as well as evaluating the impact of proposed mining laws and regulations. The USBM was also tasked with the "conservation, production, sale, and distribution of helium for essential government activities," as helium was the non-flammable replacement for hydrogen in dirigibles. In 1913, an amendment to the Organic Act expanded the USBM's scope to include metallurgy and mineral technology.

In the early 1940s, the USBM's focus expanded once again. "After the United States entered World War II, in 1941, the program's objective was shifted to outlining deposits that could be developed immediately by industry," noted a U.S. Bureau of Mines publication. By using the in-depth mineral analyses performed by the two government entities—the USGS and USBM—the newly proposed laboratory could potentially support the United States with wartime material needs.

Initially, Congress allocated $500,000 to build and furnish the proposed electro-development laboratory with the necessary equipment, but almost immediately, the Bureau of the Budget impounded $460,000 of that. The War Production Board announced that it wouldn't provide the necessary materials to construct the facility and that the entire project should be deferred until the war ended. Of course, this was in direct opposition to what the laboratory's supporters believed: creating this facility would support wartime needs for more raw materials. When the funds were rescinded, politicians weren't shy about making their feelings known.

Secretary of the Interior Harold L. Ickes implored the government to work quickly to develop ways to extract and process domestic ores like copper, lead, and zinc while increasing the production of other ores like lithium and beryllium. Little-known ores weren't the only consideration during World War II: the quest to glean as much aluminum from local bauxite was a high-priority concern. At the time, it was estimated that the United States only had two to three years of bauxite ore in reserve.

The scope of the proposed laboratory's work was well defined at the time, but its future location had not been decided. A news blurb dated August 1942 reported that Senator Charles L. McNary of Oregon declared Corvallis, Oregon as an early favorite, citing it had an "inside track" (likely because it was the home of Oregon State College), but that other site possibilities still needed to be explored. It wasn't long until a handful of sites across the Pacific Northwest states started viciously vying for the laboratory. "This was a political plum that everybody really wanted," recalled former Albany Chamber of Commerce president Vince Hurley. What followed was an epic battle that came to a head in 1943.

Somehow, after the Corvallis announcement, there was word that a location in Spokane, Washington, had actually received the go-ahead for the laboratory. But that subterfuge was quickly exposed by an impartial party, and a colossal tug-of-war expanded to over fifty possible sites across other western states, including Montana, Utah, and Idaho.

One tricky detail that steered the entire conversation about the laboratory's establishment was that allocated funds couldn't be used for construction. With the tremendous amount of materials being consumed by the war, there was a stipulation that the future site would already have buildings in place—the closer to move-in ready, the better. Although facilities at several colleges had been offered, those were refused, as the vision for the laboratory was that it would be an entity unto itself. Eventually, the budget was restored to the original amount of $500,000, but finding an existing facility was still the number one priority.

Incredibly, little Albany, Oregon, had one such location: a 47-acre college campus had recently been vacated by its previous tenants. The former home of

Albany College (which had been an Albany institution since 1867) was left empty when the educational institute had moved its operation up to the Portland area and renamed itself Lewis & Clark College. Four substantial and relatively new buildings stood in the southwest corner of Albany, awaiting new tenants.

But Spokane also had something to offer: a former school campus (news reports have called it a high school, junior college, and even a junior high), which had some heavyweight backers: Washington State's Senator Monrad Wallgren and President Roosevelt's very own son-in-law, John Boettiger, publisher of the *Seattle Post-Intelligencer*. In the past, Boettiger had been able to pull strings with his father-in-law to gain favor for his state. On this particular matter, it seems he traveled to D.C. with the express intention of winning the laboratory for the state of Washington.

The small town of Albany had its own secret weapon who wasn't afraid to take on nepotism at the presidential level: a native Texan named Carl "Zeke" Curlee, secretary of the Albany Chamber of Commerce. With a bigger-than-life backstory, Carl Curlee was dubbed the "fireball" of Oregon. Sure enough, he lived up to his nickname and was a key player in one of Albany's most unbelievable tales: in 1942, Carl Curlee, Chamber president Vince Hurley, and others from the Chamber were expecting a Bureau of Mines inspector to be heading up from California, with his first stop being Albany. After stopping in Albany, he was expected to visit the rival site in Spokane. While waiting for his arrival at the station, the trainmaster alerted Curlee and others that no Albany stop was planned that day.

Photo: Lewis & Clark College Special Collections and Archives
The Albany College campus, as viewed from Woodward Hall (Building 2) on May 1, 1931.

Photo: Stephen T. Anderson Collection
From left, Carl "Zeke" Curlee, manager of the Albany Chamber of Commerce, Congressional Inspector Lowell Seaton, Albany Chamber of Commerce President Vince Hurley, and Ralph Cronise, publisher of the Albany Democrat-Herald newspaper, shown here in 1942 recreating the infamous moment the Washington-bound train was flagged down so Inspector Seaton could view the unoccupied Albany College property.

"Like hell it won't stop," Curlee stated. "We'll stop that train." With that, Curlee grabbed a red flag and a flare.

"A bunch of us got out and blocked the tracks," Vince Hurley recalled many years later. "The engineer really had no choice." Sure enough, after the train ground to a halt, Curlee found the inspector and persuaded him to disembark.

"Now that you're here, we want you to look at the site," Hurley later recalled Carl Curlee saying to convince the inspector to travel the two miles from the station to the site. As the story goes, the inspector stayed for half a day and was quite impressed. On campus, four buildings—a collegiate-looking administration building, a lovely multi-storied dormitory, an almost-new machine shop with equipment, and an impressively large brick gymnasium—were ready and waiting to be occupied at the sprawling, lush campus.

"Albany seemed to have just what the Bureau wanted—a large site with buildings ready to move into—and the price was right," recalled a local newspaper article, but "there was still a lot of lobbying left to do."

On January 7, 1943, the general manager of the Portland Chamber of Commerce called Curlee with an urgent message that a decision regarding the laboratory's location was imminent. That conversation was quickly followed by a similar call from P. M. Robinson, head of the Portland chamber's industrial division, who urged the Albany chamber to act fast if they wanted any chance at winning the electro-development laboratory.

With stunning expediency, Carl Curlee left for Washington, D.C. the very next day. His journey wasn't without hardships: upon his arrival, Curlee couldn't

Photo: Stephen T. Anderson Collection
Once Carl Curlee urged Congressional Inspector Lowell Seaton to disembark at the Albany train station, it's highly likely Curlee showed him this photograph of the former college campus. This photo was also part of Curlee's "marketing package" that he presented on January 12, 1942, during the hearing to determine the location of the Electro-development Laboratory.

Photo: Lewis & Clark College Special Collections and Archives
The light-filled stairwell landing in Gray Hall (Building 1).

Collected by VA Hurley

/s/ V A Hurley

We, the undersigned, who are interested in the development of a Bigger & Better ALBANY, hereby subscribe the amounts set opposite our names for a fund to defray the representative of the Albany Chamber of Commerce to Washington, D.C. for his appearance at the hearing before the U.S. Bureau of Mines to be held Tuesday, Jan. 12, 1943, at which time the location of the Electro-Metallurgic Laboratory is to be selected in accordance with an act passed by Congress early in 1942 which carried an appropriation of $500,000 for the erection and equipment of such a laboratory together with a continuing appropriation of $250,000 annually for operation.

#	Name		Amount
1.	Lowell Seaton	Pd	10.00
2.	G. C. Knodell	Pd	10.00
3.	Seth French	Pd	10.00
4.	W. Savage	Pd	10.00
5.	R. E. Nebergall	Pd	10.00
6.	V. A. Hurley	Pd	10.00
7.	W. L. Jackson	Pd	10.00
8.	Rowe	Pd	10.00
9.	The Plamondon Co.	Pd	12.00
10.	MCDOWELL-EAGLES CO.	Pd	10.00
11.	FRAGER FURNITURE CO., ALBANY, OREGON	Pd	10.00
12.	Bank of Albany, ALBANY BRANCH	Pd	10.00
13.	FIRST NATIONAL BANK OF PORTLAND	Pd	10.00
14.	U.S. National Bank	Pd	10.00
15.	Montgomery-Ward & Co. (Taylor)	Pd	10.00
16.	J. C. Penny Co. (Ellingbe)	Pd	10.00
17.	Sweetlands		10.00
18.	Albany Planing Mill	Pd	10.00
19.	Venetian Theatre	Pd	10.00

Photo: Stephen T. Anderson Collection

"We, the undersigned, are interested in the development of a Bigger and Better ALBANY, hereby subscribe the amounts set opposite our names for a fund to defray a representative of the Albany Chamber of Commerce to Washington, D.C., for his appearance at a hearing before the U.S. Bureau of Mines to be held Tuesday, January 12, 1943, at which time the location of the Electro-Metallurgical Laboratory is to be selected in accordance with an act passed by Congress early in 1942 which carried an appropriation of $500,000 for the erection and equipment of such a laboratory together with a continuing appropriation of $250,000 annually for operation."
On additional pages, many more businesses pledged similar amounts in support of Curlee's trip.

25

find a single place to stay and ended up riding in a taxicab for part of the night. The next night he resorted to sleeping in a bathtub at a friend's residence. He complained that the food available in wartime D.C. wasn't as good as anything back home, noting "a great deal of horsemeat is served."

While Curlee was navigating awkward inconveniences on his journey, business owners back home were asked to donate $10 apiece to cover Curlee's travel expenses. Over seventy businesses pledged funds in an incredible show of support, from as little as $5 to as much as $100. The wide variety of backers helped prove that there wasn't just a narrow band of petitioners hoping for the U.S. Bureau of Mines to choose Albany.

Curlee arrived just in time for the hearing led by Secretary Ickes. At 10 a.m., January 12, Curlee and "two carloads of assorted Oregonians" arrived at Ickes's hearing. In a message sent back to the Albany Chamber, Curlee gave details about the meeting:

> At five minutes after 10, Secretary Ickes blasted in like the wind coming out of Cape Disappointment and seated himself at the end of this flatcar-sized table making complaining remarks about the absence of heat in the apartment building he calls home. The hearing was officially opened with Dr. Sayers and Dr. Dean, Director and Assistant Director of the Bureau of Mines, seated at the opposite end of the table, a city block away. Delegations from Washington, Montana, Idaho and Oregon had seated themselves along each side of the table. The Washington and Montana delegations were complete with both senators and congressmen.

They were determined, they were all determined.

    Armed with blueprints, aerial shots, interior photos, and a written offer from its current property owners (Lewis & Clark College) to sell the former college, Curlee did his best to convince everyone that the government simply wouldn't find a better place *anywhere* to land the laboratory. His presentation greatly impressed the attendees, with Oregon Representative Harris Ellsworth praising Curlee's letter-perfect presentation. Ultimately, though, Curlee noted that "Dr. Dean is the man upon whose recommendation the location will probably be chosen. It comes directly in his department."

    Not only was Carl Curlee's pitch spot on, but one particular selling point of the Albany location stood out among the rest: its proximity to Oregon State College, which was recognized as "one of seven accredited colleges in the west with ample libraries, laboratories, etc., in chemical engineering." It also fulfilled the requirement that the facility not be near the city center in case of fire or explosion. The fact that the Bonneville power substation was less than 400 yards away was yet another major plus.

    Despite all the favorable aspects of the old Albany College site, nothing was in the bag yet. Curlee's trip to D.C. was only supposed to last two weeks. It ended up stretching out much longer; Secretary Ickes fell ill with pneumonia after the initial hearing and Curlee felt it was essential to remain present in Washington. He didn't want to return home until he felt quite sure he'd done all he could do to convince everyone that Albany was the only logical choice. After eight weeks in the nation's capital, Curlee returned to Albany with the impression the trip had been a success, and he reported positive feedback all around. But there was still no answer. Everyone waited, expecting an announcement at any time.

Mere days after arriving home, Curlee detailed his trip during a general meeting of the Chamber of Commerce on a Wednesday night and again for the Albany Kiwanis Club on Thursday, March 4, 1943. While he was regaling attendees with tales of what it was like to spend two months in wartime Washington, D.C., Secretary Ickes was in the midst of a monumental struggle as he tried to make the final call. He was still being bombarded with petitions from the concerned parties: "On February 2 and 5, Secretary Ickes received telegrams from E. O. Holland, President of the State College of Washington in Pullman, enhancing the offer made previously, including a promise from the Governor to sell the building of interest."

Oregon Senate Minority Whip Charles L. McNary wrote to President Franklin D. Roosevelt that he was "earnestly desirous" that the laboratory be located in Albany, based on its proximity to the Bonneville Dam. "After succinctly describing the facility, the advantages of the location, and the minerals and metals available, he closes: 'I hope very sincerely that should the issue be referred to you, you will support our cause.' "

Secretary Ickes had been stewing in the quandary that was before him. He invited Oscar L. Chapman, the Assistant Secretary of the Department, to confer with him. On his desk, Ickes laid out all the information given to him regarding possible sites. He examined them, carefully weighing the pros and cons of each. In a written gesture equivalent to throwing up his hands, he confessed to President Roosevelt in a memo dated March 10, 1943, that deciding the laboratory's location was "the worst spot I have been in during the past ten years.

"Last week you referred me to a letter to you from Senator McNary urging that the electro metallurgical laboratory which the Bureau of Mines has been authorized to build should be located at Albany, Oregon. Since the plant was authorized, I have been subjected to an intense barrage from Washington, Oregon, Montana, and Idaho," Secretary Ickes confessed in a memo to the President. "I have held numerous conferences and a public hearing attended by the delegations from the four states. All of this controversy has effectively delayed the establishment of the needed laboratory."

He went on to write that either the Spokane or Albany location would be a fine pick. However, pressure from John Boettiger, the President's son-in-law, held "strong opposition to the location of the plant in Oregon and he has favored Pullman, Washington. There is insufficient land available at Pullman to permit location of the plant there," Ickes decided.

"On the whole, I believe that it will be most advantageous to locate the plant at Albany, Oregon. However, the delegations from the four Northwest states are all bringing every possible pressure to bear in behalf of their own state. One would think there was a king's ransom involved. I can't locate the plant in more than one state," Ickes lamented. "I thought at first that I would ask you to decide the question but then I concluded that that would be a mean and cowardly thing to do," he confessed to Roosevelt. "So I will decide it myself and keep the heat off of you. I am warning you in advance, however, that there may be a bit of a tempest in three different teapots after the decision has been announced."

In a memo stamped with his name and dated March 17, 1943, Franklin D. Roosevelt responded to Senator McNary: "This will acknowledge with thanks your letter of February 8, presenting the many reasons why the Bureau of Mines electro development laboratory should be located at Albany, Oregon.

"The facilities available at Albany appear to be excellent... After careful review of the situation, Secretary Ickes has advised me that of all sites proposed, the Lewis & Clark College property located at Albany, Oregon best meets all requirements for the establishment of the Bureau of Mines laboratory, and that he will make a public announcement of his findings soon. Sincerely yours, Franklin D. Roosevelt."

With a stamp of approval from the President himself, the tiny rural corner of southwest Albany changed forever.

THE WHITE HOUSE
WASHINGTON March 17, 1943

My dear Senator McNary:

This will acknowledge with thanks your letter of February 8, presenting many reasons why the Bureau of Mines electro development laboratory should be located at Albany, Oregon.

The facilities available at Albany appear to be excellent, and the information which you have supplied has been of material assistance in selecting a site that will provide satisfactory and ample housing at a point not far removed from vast resources of power and undeveloped mineral wealth.

After careful review of the situation, Secretary Ickes has advised me that of all sites proposed, the Lewis and Clark College property located at Albany, Oregon best meets all requirements for the establishment of the Bureau of Mines laboratory, and that he will make a public announcement of his findings soon.

Sincerely yours,

FRANKLIN D. ROOSEVELT.

Hon. Charles L. McNary,
United States Senate.

Photo: NARA College Park MD
The memo that sealed the deal: President Roosevelt himself approved Albany as the chosen location for the Electro-development Laboratory.

31

CHAPTER TWO

FORWARD MOMENTUM
March 1943–April 1944
"It was no easy task to bring the laboratory to Albany, but the Oregon community won out over politics."
Albany Democrat-Herald, *March 17, 1943*

Word traveled at lightning speed and states across the Pacific Northwest knew of the laboratory's chosen location on the very day President Roosevelt sent the memo regarding his decision. One particular quote from Bonneville Power Administration's Paul J. Raver had stunning foresight: "Secretary Harold L. Ickes' orders locating the project at the old Albany college campus might prove more important to the future of the Pacific Northwest than the recent establishment of any single war plant in the region, because it will lay the groundwork for a sound and continuous industrial development."

With the decision in place, Bureau of Mines Director R. R. Sayers promised the laboratory's establishment would be "pushed as rapidly as possible," especially because, as Ickes had stressed, "critical minerals which are vital to the nation's war economy" were available in the Pacific Northwest, just waiting to be used advantageously. Despite that declaration, Washington State was still vying for the laboratory.

As soon as Albany had been announced as the chosen location, cries of protest arose from all different directions—just as Secretary Ickes had predicted. In 1941 Congress formed The Special Committee of the Senate to Investigate the National Defense Program—also known as the Truman Committee—to study and investigate the misallocation of war-related resources,

Photo: Stephen T. Anderson Collection

Against tremendous odds, Albany, Oregon was chosen for the hotly debated laboratory. Headlines heralded the good news that would change the little town forever.

and the group wasn't shy about seeking information from the public regarding such infractions. Members of the Truman Committee (of which Washington State's Senator Wallgren was a member) heeded complaints about the Albany location and tried to get the decision reconsidered in spring 1943. But in Albany, no time was wasted in evaluating the grounds and buildings of the former Lewis & Clark property. "The Bureau of Mines proceeded with plans for conversion of the buildings at Albany as soon as the Secretary signed the order in March 1943, although the Government did not acquire title until July," recalled a 1946 report on the site.

Less than a month after Secretary Ickes's Albany decision was confirmed, the first Bureau officials arrived in town to inspect the newly acquired property. A. H. Bragonje, superintendent of the Salt Lake City Bureau of Mines station buildings, and prominent East Coast architect Henry Powell Hopkins of Baltimore, Maryland, arrived on April 14 to analyze all aspects of the former college campus. They spent ten days examining each building, taking measurements and noting what alterations would need to be made before the facility could function as a proper metallurgical laboratory. Unfortunately, just as Bragonje and Hopkins arrived, so did a lawyer representing the Truman Committee.

Rudolph Halley showed up unannounced on campus on April 19, 1943 to prove the property was a poor choice for the planned laboratory. Architect Hopkins refused to entertain Halley's demands to be let in on the details of the site. "I told him that the existing buildings were structurally sound and that with the normal amount of repairs and replacements they could be put in a good condition and that my report . . . would be favorable," recalled Hopkins.

HENRY POWELL HOPKINS
Architect

April 19, 1943

Mr. C. W. Davis
U. S. Bureau of Mines
New Interior Building
Washington, D. C.

Dear Mr. Davis:

    Yesterday, Sunday, a Mr. Rudolph Holley, of the Truman Committee, appeared unannounced on the site, requesting all sorts of information pertaining to the property. He first requested the sum of money it would cost to put this plant in condition for your use. This I told him I was unable to give him until my report was completed and when this information was compiled it would have to be obtained by him directly from the Bureau of Mines. He requested that I give a copy of my report to him direct, which I refused to do. He wanted to know how long it would take me to prepare the drawings and specifications so that work could be started on the buildings. This I told him was a matter of weeks and not months. He asked what I thought about the conditions of the property as being available for our problem. I told him that the existing buildings were structurally sound and that with the normal amount of repairs and replacements they could be put in a good condition and that my report to you would be favorable.

    This man was a lawyer. He had no technical knowledge whatever about the problem he was examining and admitted to me that he was not qualified to pass on building construction, but was here to make a report as to whether the Government was making an economical move and benefiting the War effort in carrying out this project in this manner. I explained to him that I thought it was an economical move and that I would so report to you. He left the premises after being on the site around 45 minutes. This information I think you ought to have.

Very truly yours,

(s)

HENRY POWELL HOPKINS
Architect

Photo: *Report on the Northwest Electrodevelopment Laboratory*
Henry Powell Hopkins' letter regarding Rudolph Halley's unannounced, and unwelcome, visit to the chosen laboratory site.

But Halley was hell-bent on swaying the Department of the Interior. He assessed that "The Albany place is very inferior. The building needs a great deal of work before it would be fit for use. It is also farther away from the minerals and generally much less desirable." He also claimed concern about a lack of strength of the floors and roof, the total cost of remodeling, and the overall functionality of the facility.

A few days later a hearing was held in Spokane. Though attendees denied they were there specifically to dispute Ickes's decision for Albany, it would seem that was one purpose of the meeting. Attendees included Senator Wallgren and seventeen other witnesses from Idaho and Washington who opposed the Oregon location. Also in attendance was Albany's own Carl Curlee.

To address Halley's concerns, the Bureau of Mines ordered additional assessments to measure structural stability on top of calculations that had already been made. But by the time those assessments were completed, work had already begun on the buildings and equipment was being moved into place.

When A. H. Bragonje and Henry Powell Hopkins arrived in Albany, teases of spring were beginning to weave through the small town. Delicate white cherry trees were blooming and dewy, rain-soaked grass freshened the air. Across the vacant former college campus, a few lush evergreens were a verdant green while deciduous trees were still mostly bare.

Photo: Lewis & Clark College Special Collections and Archives
A laboratory on the first floor of Gray Hall (Building 1) during Albany College days. Photo circa 1940.

Photo: Lewis & Clark College Special Collections and Archives
Woodward Hall (Building 2) had a storied past even before it arrived at its final resting place. Photo circa 1931.

As Hopkins and Bragonje entered the campus, the men took note of the stately twentieth century Colonial-style building on their right. Portland, Oregon architect F. Manson White designed the William Henry Gray Hall in 1925 to serve as the administrative headquarters for Albany College. Its brilliant white daylight basement abutment contrasted beautifully against classic red brickwork that adorned the second and third stories. Thin front steps ascended to the front entrance, flanked on either side by metal lampposts with milk glass globes. Large trees surrounded the sides of the building, including a rare Persian walnut on the southwest corner whose branches almost touched the ground.

The building had been left empty when the college moved to Portland, having seen only thirteen years of use, save a brief interlude in July 1941. The War Department had leased the entire abandoned campus from Lewis & Clark College and the Army took over the top two floors of Gray Hall, with access to the east entrance. The upper spaces were converted into drafting rooms for the U.S. Army quartermaster department, likely for the construction of Camp Adair.

Continuing down the concrete path in front of Gray Hall, the two men would've passed the former Woodward Hall, which had served as a women's dormitory at the southwest Albany campus. Although the white abutment and red brick exterior had been constructed to match the administration building, the façade also served to conceal the storied history of the building and its previous use. Hopkins and Bragonje likely would've never guessed that the building had begun as an orphanage at a location across town.

In 1890 a philanthropic group called the Ladies' Aid Society began fundraising to support the construction of an orphanage that would also house a

Photo: Stephen T. Anderson Collection

The only known photo of the Ladies' Aid Orphan Home, standing in the background behind Oregon National Guard soldiers as they practice with a Gatling gun. Photo was taken in 1901, after the building had been sold to Albany College, but before it was moved to the first Albany College site at 9th and Broadalbin.

Photo: Stephen T. Anderson Collection

The former Orphan Home as it was being rolled to its new location at Albany College's Monteith Campus (between Broadway and Liberty streets in southwest Albany). This would be the building's final move.

hospital. Donations were collected from community members, businesspeople, and the Oregon legislature allocated $3,000 toward the project. Architect C. W. Ayer volunteered his services to build the home. The original location of the proposed orphanage was lot #70 of the Goltra Park addition, a location far southeast of the future Bureau of Mines site. M. H. Ellis and S. E. Young donated the lot and a streetcar line out to the home was proposed. The streetcar ran while the orphan home was in operation but was later abandoned.

The orphan home project progressed slowly, drawing the ire of the donors and Albany townspeople, but in March 1892 the Ladies' Aid Society Orphan Home received its first children, then called "inmates." Some children who spent time at the home were not true orphans but were in situations where parents could not provide care. "Often children came to the Home for a short period, perhaps while a parent was ill, or for some reason could not care for them for a few months," noted Beverly Haven, who wrote a detailed account of the Orphan Home meeting notes. Parents were expected to pay $5.00 per month for care, with additional fees paid by Linn County. By the end of its first year, the Orphan Home had admitted nine children.

No photos of children at the home have ever been found. Sad stories about the orphanage dotted the local paper; one article told of two girls who decided to run away and made it as far as Shedd, twelve miles from the orphan's home, before they appeared on someone's doorstep, muddy and tired. They were promptly returned. Another article told about the four Flower children; the two older siblings were sent to a home in Portland and the younger two to the orphan home in Albany when their father left them to fend for themselves when he took a job in another state.

In 1897 there was talk of closing the home. Meeting notes show there was a high turnover rate of house matrons. Low numbers of inmates resulted in drastic pay cuts; one matron simply walked off the job in 1898. For several years the Ladies' Aid Society tried thinking of different uses for the building—a hospital was proposed several times and a home for the elderly was also suggested. In September 1901, after four years of struggles, the home shut its doors. Assets, including cows, were liquidated. The Ladies' Aid Society Orphan Home had operated for nine and a half years with a total of 86 children served, with some children returning more than once.

Finding a buyer for the building proved difficult but the structure was finally sold to Albany College for $250. At the time, the college was near the center of town (currently the corner of Ellsworth Street and Ninth Street; now Central Elementary). Using horses and logs, the structure was moved in two sections over the course of a week. The outer appearance of the building remained the same; the delicate, three-story wooden structure had ornate, wraparound balconies that ran the length of the building. The college christened the building Tremont Hall and it began its life as a women's dormitory.

When Albany College moved to its "Monteith campus," the property on the far southwestern corner of town, Tremont Hall was moved once again. The balconies were stripped off before transport and the bare building was placed on a basement, increasing the number of stories by one. A brick façade was erected to match the administration building. Interestingly, students were very much involved with the construction and groundwork of the new college. While the brickwork was being completed an inscription was unearthed on a cornice. A carpenter who had helped

Photo: Stephen T. Anderson Collection
The already-furnished machine shop, left intact by the National Youth Administration, was just what the Northwest Electro-development Laboratory needed. Photo circa 1944.

Photo: Stephen T. Anderson Collection
Besides Gray Hall (Building 1), Woodward Hall (Building 2), the Hauser Gymnasium (Building 23) and the NYA machine shop (Building 5), there was a boiler room (white building with smokestacks) and a covered, but unfinished, basement (see slight roofline center left) that Henry Powell Hopkins strongly suggested be backfilled. This building later became the basement of Building 33.

construct the orphan's home had penned, "Frank Camp, November 17, 1890. Weather fine, cold in the mornings."

Once completed, the building was renamed Woodward Hall and once again served as a women's dormitory. Sleeping porches were built onto the north side of the building, and the roofline was extended to cover the addition. After Albany College moved up north and vacated campus, wives, mothers, and girlfriends of nearby Camp Adair soldiers were allowed to stay in the former Woodward Hall while visiting their men. While it sounds like conditions were sub-par for a time (lack of heat and hot water were main issues), at least sixty women were staying in the building at once, if not more. Activity during this short period of time could've started a salacious urban legend about the post-college campus; the former Woodward Hall was rumored to have housed prostitutes before the Bureau arrived. Perhaps the steady stream of out-of-town soldiers visiting resident ladies caused neighborhood gossipmongers to jump to conclusions. After the building was used for ladies' temporary housing, the bottom floor of Woodward Hall housed Army personnel, and upper floors were open to the National Youth Administration (NYA), which had a presence at the abandoned campus between 1941 and 1943.

As Bragonje and Hopkins continued to the southernmost end of campus during their preliminary tour of the site, they stopped to inspect a long, white prefabricated shop building typical of the World War II era. The shop was filled with equipment left over from a brief NYA school.

In 1941 the Federal Security Agency entered into a one-year lease with Albany College to use portions of the former campus to train young men for work in defense occupations focusing on machining. Gray Hall was used for office space and Woodward Hall became living quarters for students. Classes required a machine shop so the NYA erected a prefabricated warehouse just south of Woodward Hall. Students helped install the concrete floor and building footings as part of their training.

There were high hopes that the Albany machinist school would churn out high numbers of graduates. By the end of 1941, a total of 52 young men had graduated from the program and moved to Seattle for employment at Boeing. In early 1942, the demand for machinists specializing in aviation sheet metal called for an additional 3,500 workers. A night class that ran from 6 p.m. to midnight was offered on the first floor of Gray Hall and was open to non-NYA participants who did not qualify for Class A draft.

During the last half of the year, attendance at the NYA machining program dropped to 40 attendees. Discussions were held on whether or not to move the school to Eugene—and the building with it, but the Bureau of Mines negotiated to purchase the structure and most of the equipment in it.

After inspecting the machine shop, Hopkins and Bragonje walked across the road to a massive brick building with an unusual geometric roofline and lovely, tall arched windows. The former Hauser Gymnasium was situated on the east side of the campus and had also been used by the NYA as a recreation center.

The gymnasium was constructed in 1930 at the cost of $60,000 by architect F. Manson White, designer of the administration building. During the college days, the Albany campus had focused on basketball, tennis, archery, and baseball, and while tennis courts were constructed outdoors and archery was practiced on the west lawn, the gymnasium was primarily used for basketball. Early interior photos of the gymnasium show it also had a stage.

Hopkins and Bragonje agreed that the expansive structure had loads of potential for the future laboratory and they earmarked it as the "operations building" where furnaces and ore bins would be kept. During the conversion, the barely-used wooden floor inside the gymnasium was taken out and repurposed as the floor of the little machine shop and concrete floors were laid in the new operations building so they could withstand the weight and heat of future furnaces and heavy equipment.

After taking a good look at the empty gymnasium, the architect and engineering supervisor surveyed the only other buildings on campus: in the far northeastern side of the property sat a small boiler house surrounded by stacks of firewood. When constructed for the college the little structure had been strategically placed as far from other buildings as possible in case of an accidental explosion.

Another persistent urban legend about the Bureau of Mines campus was the story of underground tunnels that led to subterranean laboratories. As with most tall tales, this legend has a bit of truth mixed in with exaggerated details: there were indeed tunnels that led from the boiler house to other buildings on campus. But instead of being easily accessible passageways, they were little more than large steam tubes, about four feet in diameter, used for heating campus buildings. In a blueprint drawn by Henry Powell Hopkins in 1943, those tunnels can clearly be seen, connecting the boiler house to each existing building. "Once the Boiler building was not used to supply steam to all the buildings on the site the service lines were capped off," noted longtime Bureau employee Stephen T. Anderson. "The majority of the 4-

Photo: Lewis & Clark College Special Collections and Archives
The former Hauser Gymnasium was the perfect fit for a future Operations building. Photo circa 1930.

Photo: Lewis & Clark College Special Collections and Archives
Main floor of the gymnasium. Photo circa 1940.

foot service tubes were kept in place for maintenance of air lines as well as future needs."

On an interesting note, a weekly report from April 8, 1944 gives captions to five photos provided to detail progress on the campus's conversion. On one caption pertaining to the former Hauser Gymnasium (then being converted to the Operations Building), it says "in the center foreground [of the photo] are piles of dirt taken from the excavation for tunnels and trenches." What those tunnels and trenches were for remains unknown.

The rumor of underground laboratories also had a likely starting point: the last structure visited by Hopkins and Bragonje was nothing more than a mere foundation with a basement, initially built by the college with the intention of becoming a men's dormitory. A roof was thrown up to cover the foundation, and Hopkins saw it as an eyesore. "The entire area is covered over with a wood roof. This should be removed from the premises as it is an unsightly thing to look at as well as a potential hole to collect moisture," he noted in his assessment. But this covered-up concrete basement, as well as the boiler house, weren't a top priority for the construction; the former Gray Hall, the NYA machine shop, and the Hauser Gymnasium would need to be completed first. Hopkins got to work immediately drafting a transition plan for the site.

———•—◂•—•———

By May 1943, it seems that despite the earlier protests raised by other states and the Truman Committee, the laboratory was in Albany to stay. Hopkins had forwarded his detailed conversion plans to the Bureau's regional office in Salt Lake City where they were reviewed by the technical department. "The arrangement of laboratories, shops, and offices . . . appeared desirable in the light of their own experience, and [they] indicated a few structural changes," recalled a 1946 report on the laboratory.

On July 21, 1943, the deed for the college grounds was officially transferred to the United States Government for a purchase price of $134,500. That same month, Dr. Bruce A. Rogers of the Pittsburgh, Pennsylvania Bureau of Mines station made a trip to Oregon to survey the buildings and grounds. Rogers was soon named engineering supervisor of the campus conversion and throughout the process he conferred with Hopkins about nearly every aspect of the project, including what construction materials and laboratory equipment would be needed to complete the facility. By September 1943, a list was ready for submission to the War Production Board (WPB).

Unfortunately, the WPB denied the first proposal for supplies. A second submission was made, this time with a request for fewer materials, copper in particular. The Bonneville Power Administration stepped in to help by offering the Bureau a surplus of copper conductors, leftovers from pre-war production. The amount of machinery needed to start up the laboratory was also reduced, in part because the Bureau was able to retain the equipment left in the machine shop by the NYA.

In October 1943, Dr. Rogers arrived in Albany for good to fulfill the role of director of the laboratory and declared the new institution had an official name: the Northwest Electro-development Laboratory. The day he moved into his office on the second floor of the former Gray Hall, the building was in massive disarray as former college administration offices were being torn asunder to be converted to laboratories by November 1943.

The new director was upfront with the press about expectations for the site's operations: "Dr. Rogers expects this laboratory to work on projects of immediate importance to the war industries, for the present, but said after the war the Bureau will continue to aid in the development of mineral resources in the northwest," the local newspaper stated. The article also noted that Rogers hoped to have an initial staff of 30–40 people who could concentrate their efforts on iron, nickel, and chromium ores.

During the conversion, the local newspaper, the Chamber of Commerce and area service clubs kept Albany residents apprised of every bit of activity at the once-quiet former college campus. What once was a community eyesore—tall weeds and unkempt grounds had residents complaining loudly to the city about the formerly abandoned college campus—was now the talk of the town and the subject of multiple newspaper articles per month, and a bustling hub of activity. Henry Powell Hopkins arrived back on campus in early October 1943, accompanied by a mechanical engineer, contractors, and Guy Jolivette, of the Portland, Oregon contracting firm Reimers & Jolivette.

With construction plans coming together, there were high hopes that the laboratory would be in operation before the end of the year. However, on November 18, 1943, the War Production Board refused "very emphatically" to approve the purchase of new materials for the Northwest Electro-development Laboratory, once again stating their position that the site would have little to no immediate contribution to the war effort. Despite the Bureau's requests for a minimum amount of materials to get started, the WPB refused to give up any materials for electrical use and it was soon feared that laboratory operations wouldn't begin until the war was over.

Dr. Rogers wasted no time in calling Washington. After a "direct telephone conversation" with the head of the Bureau, the government started scouring other agencies for the needed materials. The effort was rewarded with success and another much smaller request was filed with the WPB.

While construction noises were still emanating from the former college campus, the Bureau attempted to assemble a skeleton crew of employees. But just as with materials and equipment, finding qualified staff for the very specific roles needed at the laboratory was extremely difficult. "Because of the shipyards in Portland and war industries elsewhere in the northwest, in addition to nearby Camp Adair, the supply of skilled men had been drained away," noted a later report. The government began pulling employees from other Bureau of Mines stations across the nation to fill positions, Salt Lake City and Pittsburgh in particular.

Frank Stellmacher was the very first employee hired at the Bureau; when he arrived the only other person on campus was Dr. Rogers. There may have been no other soul more perfect for the job of site caretaker than Frank. When he was five, the young boy moved with his parents to Albany from Wisconsin, to a home located on the future Bureau property. He attended Albany College as a young man and had been working as the groundskeeper at the college for several years before being brought on by the government. In November 1943, 65-year-old Stellmacher was hired to act as caretaker of the old heating plant, as well as maintenance man and groundskeeper on the campus that he was already so well acquainted with.

During his years at the Bureau it was said that Stellmacher greeted everyone with a salute and a kindly "how are you;" his habit of saluting may have had something to do with his veteran status. In 1898, he was an army sergeant during the Spanish-American War and later served as a first lieutenant in the Quartermaster Corps in World War I. During the 1920s, he worked for the State of Oregon as a Fish and Game Commission director of research, and in the 1930s, he inspected schools and other public spaces for fire dangers as a member of the State Insurance Commission. After that job Stellmacher was hired by Albany College to tend to the buildings and grounds.

The second employee of the Northwest Electrodevelopment Laboratory was Mrs. J. E. Monteverde of Pittsburgh. Though her name was consistently published as Mrs. J. E. Monteverde until her death in 1977, the first female hire was a 45-year-old widow and mother of two teenage boys. Josephine Muldowney Monteverde temporarily moved from Pittsburg to Albany to become the chief of laboratory staff. She was expected to assemble a skeleton crew when she arrived in November 1943. Her office was likely in Building 2— the brick-clad, former college dormitory—which had temporary offices for incoming staff while Building 1 was being finished.

At the end of November 1943, it seemed that public frustration began brewing about the laboratory's delayed progress. Though there was much support for the site, locals were growing impatient and wondering why the government would put effort into creating a new facility, then fail to equip it. As the weather worsened and the days grew shorter and colder, December brought heartening news to all involved with

Photo: *The Bureau Bugle*
Frank Stellmacher was the first employee to be hired by Director B.A. Rogers. Stellmacher had a lifelong connection to the property for which he was hired to take care of.

Photo: Stephen T. Anderson Collection
Parts of the former Hauser Gymnasium were dismantled as it was readied for its new role as the Bureau's Operations Building. Here, the wooden gym floors have been removed and preparations are being made for the floors to handle heavy equipment.

the Northwest Electro-development Laboratory: the War Production Board had given the nod to begin diverting materials to furnish the facility and had also approved all remodeling as outlined by Henry Powell Hopkins. At the rail station only a mile and a half away, carload after carload began delivering much-needed machinery, woodworking tools, and electrical equipment. On December 17, Dr. Rogers stressed that one laboratory facility on campus was almost completely finished, possibly to reassure the public that construction was actually progressing. By the end of December, Dr. Rogers hoped the laboratory would be open for business within the next three months.

As the new year rolled around, forward momentum seemed to double. A. H. Bragonje was named the superintendent of construction just as Hopkins arrived back in Albany to begin working with Reimers & Jolivette on the final aspects of conversion. Mrs. Monteverde was joined by Edith Olsen, also of Pittsburgh, who was placed in charge of the entire staff.

H. J. Kress of Lebanon, Oregon, was placed in charge of the former NYA machine shop. By the end of January 1944, the number of staff at the not-yet-operational facility totaled five people. In February, Bureau employees from Salt Lake City were moved to Albany to fill in laboratory positions. Claude W. Sill and John M. Fenton were hired for the chemistry lab and Donald T. Holmes became the ore lab supervisor.

A weekly report from April 8, 1944 outlined the overall construction progress that had happened up to that point: in Building 1 (then called "Laboratory 1"), a good deal of electrical work had been completed, plumbing lines below the ground floor were completed, and water lines were being installed on the first and second floors. Concrete work was being done on the floors and loading platforms. The former NYA machine

Fig. 6. Interior of Operations Building during construction showing brick wall of electrical vault going up on north side. April 1944.

Photo: Stephen T. Anderson Collection
More transformations occurred across campus, turning former college buildings into a functional electro-development laboratory.

Photo: Stephen T. Anderson Collection
The ore dressing area in the Operations Building. Photo circa 1944.

shop had been renamed the "service building" and half of its electrical work had been completed, and a brick wall was being constructed within that would partition off the woodworking area of the shop.

The former Hauser Gymnasium from the college days, now renamed the "Operations Building," was undergoing an extensive transformation. Brick walls were being erected throughout the interior, including a 22-foot-high enclosure that would eventually house a 1000 kVA (kilo-volt-ampere) transformer. Some construction on the operations building had been put on hold because some materials had failed to arrive. Despite that, the tone of the report indicated overall progress was moving along at a satisfactory rate.

No new personnel had been hired during that particular week in April, although the report noted that a local man with cabinetry skills had been recruited for a job in general woodworking, indicating that some residents benefitted directly from the presence of the not-quite-finished laboratory.

Just as hints of spring were starting to weave their way through Albany once again, seven officials from the Bureau of Mines paid a visit to the Northwest Electro-development Laboratory. The group, comprised of key Bureau employees from across the western states, were acting as an advisory committee for the new facility. The seven men were shown around the campus by Dr. Rogers and the press reported that the visitors were pleased with the progress of the reconstruction of the former college grounds.

Just a little over a year had passed since the controversial decision had been made to place the facility in Albany, and there were high hopes operations would begin in earnest very soon. The Bureau advisory committee suggested the laboratory could start limited operations in June—but the exact projects to be undertaken were still being discussed. The committee raised ideas about possible future directions, including investigating high nickel-alloy steel and experiments on chromium-containing ores. Experiments with aluminum were mentioned as a possible direction but the advisory group left Albany without any solid plans, as any work done in the future was dependent on one factor: the ability to find and hire qualified personnel.

CHAPTER THREE
A LABORATORY TAKES SHAPE

April 1944–November 1944

"This laboratory will prove of great value to the Pacific Northwest and I am anxious to see that it is provided with proper staff and equipment for effective work in developing resources of this territory." —Congressman Harris Ellsworth, August 1944

"We are starting a little laboratory out in a farming town in Oregon. If you would like to move that far, the Bureau of Mines would like to have you work on this interesting possibility." — Letter from Dr. R. S. Dean to Dr. William J. Kroll

Not long after the early April visit, Bureau officials presented a strong case for the Albany site before house appropriations committees in Washington, D.C., as they outlined the proposed scope of work that would be beneficial during both wartime and beyond. Of course, ore development for copper, zinc, nickel, chromium, manganese, magnesium, and aluminum was at the top of the list.

One glaring omission was any mention of zirconium. Thus far, the little-known ore, which could be found in Coos County beach sands in the form of zircon had been overlooked—or so it would have seemed to the general public. Behind closed doors, however, a meeting and an inquiry had set in motion a series of events that would prove critical to the Northwest Electro-development Laboratory. A few months prior to April 1944, Dr. R. S. Dean, the assistant director of the U.S. Bureau of Mines, had met with a prominent metallurgist from Luxembourg.

The son of an iron-master at a blast furnace and grandson of an iron-ore mine operator, William Justin

Kroll was steeped in metallurgy from a young age. "A far away picture still remains in my mind, when, as a child, in the darkness of a cold morning I was taken out of bed to light a new blast furnace with a bunch of cotton, impregnated with burning kerosene and fastened to the tip of a long pole," recalled Kroll. In his youth Kroll received a classical education at a distinguished high school called the Athenium. Kroll spoke German, English, French, and Luxembourgish and was taught Greek and Latin in school. Classes in physics and chemistry aided the young Kroll in his eventual career choice. William and his five brothers all chose professions in metallurgy or engineering.

Kroll's education at the Technische Hochschule in Charlottenburg, Germany was supervised by metallurgy professor Walter Mathesius. Kroll's thesis work dealt with preparing elemental boron, which was the catalyst for his rare metals research. Ferrous metals faded away as Kroll became enchanted with learning about the uncharted metals: titanium, beryllium, uranium, and zirconium were little-known metals with few known uses.

While employed for two years by German lead refinery Metallgesellschaft, the young metallurgist worked on using a calcium-lead alloy to draw bismuth out of lead. After being refined by an American company, the process became known as the Kroll-Betterton process and was widely used.

Kroll was thirty years old when he moved to Vienna, Austria, where he established a scrap-recovery plant whose main purpose was to recover minute amounts of tin, silver, and gold from recovered copper. "Two years spent in building a metallurgical plant—

Photo: Stephen T. Anderson collection
Dr. Kroll stands amongst the equipment in his home laboratory in Villa Lecerc in Luxembourg, circa 1934.

Photo: Stephen T. Anderson collection
Villa Lecerc, on the corner of Merl Street in Luxembourg, circa 1934.

including a reverberatory furnace, converters, shaft furnaces, bag houses, and electrolytic cells—prepared him for a lifetime of developmental work on the whole field of nonferrous metallurgy. It also left him with many pleasant memories, because his dark eyes take on a certain fire as he reminisces of the wine, women and the good food of old Vienna," wrote Earl T. Hayes in *A Biographical Appreciation*.

The metallurgist's next move was back to Germany, where he was hired by a foundry in Baden Baden. There he helped develop a magnesium-base alloy, which was later used in World War II. After 13 years away from his hometown, Kroll returned to Luxembourg and purchased a sprawling building on the corner of Belair Street.

In the basement of his grand Villa Leclerc manse in Luxembourg, Kroll established an unauthorized home laboratory. The 32-year-old metallurgist hadn't been granted permission to run the facility and neighbors who were privy to Kroll's activities vehemently disapproved. "In the beginning, my neighbors didn't trust me an inch and in the cafes of Merl Street they said I one day would blow Villa Leclerc up together with the whole neighborhood," recalled Kroll "The roses, however, that I grew in abundance in my front garden—say it with flowers—cooled feelings down."

Kroll kept punishing hours at Villa Leclerc. "Whoever in the thirties made his way home in the middle of the night past the brightly illuminated windows of Villa Leclerc in Belair Street and inquired about what was going on there, was told that there lived an engineer named Kroll, an inventor who was at work night and day," noted one passerby.

The years at Villa Leclerc were fruitful and full of discovery. Kroll employed three people—a secretary, a laborer, and a mechanic—and during the years in that location he worked on a wide swath of metallurgic techniques that resulted in successful ideas and patents that would send a ripple across the metallurgical field. His work with beryllium was particularly influential, and despite suffering from beryllium poisoning, Kroll's work led to "an agreement with Siemens and Halske for the work in the broad field of 'rare metals,' " wrote Hayes. Kroll's development of high-purity calcium as a reducing agent led him to producing thorium, uranium, zirconium, and most notably titanium, as a sponge or powder form.

Commercially producing pure titanium wasn't a new concept, as the Hunter process had been developed in 1910, but it had drawbacks which prevented it from being an ideal mass-production method. The Hunter process used sodium as a reduction agent and it was deemed dangerous, expensive, and inefficient. After Kroll transitioned to focusing on titanium and its alloys in the early 1930s, it was only a matter of time before he figured a way to substitute less-expensive magnesium for sodium as a reduction agent. Magnesium was also easier to remove from the titanium once the process was finished, creating a more commercially viable technique. At Villa Leclerc, Kroll succeeded in producing a rolled sheet of titanium. It was time to introduce the strong, lightweight, corrosion-resistant metal to the world.

Twice Kroll traveled to the United States, first in 1932 and then again in 1938, with hopes of exciting interest in the metal, but to his great disappointment he wasn't successful either time. Upon moving to United States in February 1940—the same year he was awarded a patent for his work on titanium—Kroll tried once again to tout the characteristics of the metal that he'd worked so diligently on. After courting Union

Carbide, Westinghouse, General Electric, and others, he found there was simply no commercial interest in high-purity titanium, despite its low density, high strength, and excellent corrosion resistance.

Even if industry in the United States wasn't quite ready for titanium, the government had had the metal on its radar for some time. Before Dr. Reginald S. Dean was appointed as the assistant director of the U. S. Bureau of Mines, he held the position of head of the metallurgical division in Tucson, Arizona. Dean was aware of titanium work being done in the Netherlands, and in 1938 decided to set two of his metallurgists onto exploring commercial production of titanium. In 1941, one of those metallurgists, Frank S. Wartman, considered the metal's potential: "With physical properties similar to those of wrought iron, and only sixty percent as heavy, it would be an interesting structural material if it could be prepared cheaply." It is interesting to note that the only commercial zirconium production in the world was also happening in the Netherlands; the Phillips Lamp Company in Eindhoven was creating zirconium through the laborious and expensive van Arkel method.

In 1942 the Bureau's titanium exploration was established at the newly opened Salt Lake City station. At first, small batches of 15–20 grams were made. By 1944, titanium was being produced in fifteen-pound batches. The research then transferred to the Boulder City, Nevada Bureau of Mines station, where 100-pound quantities were made.

The more metallurgists worked with the metal, the more they were convinced that Kroll's process was the clear winner: "A critical survey and small-scale test of virtually all known methods of producing the metal were made. The method devised by Kroll appeared to be the best adapted to immediate commercial production," noted a technical paper authored by the Bureau of Mines. "However, for scale-up to occur, significant metallurgical research had to be done," noted Kathleen L. Housley, author of *Black Sand: The History of Titanium.* "When it came to titanium, nothing had ever been, or would ever be, easy. It was for this reason that the Bureau had contacted Kroll."

Kroll was working as a consulting engineer for Union Carbide and Carbon Research Laboratories in Niagara Falls when a meeting between him and Dean took place in Washington, D.C. At that point, Kroll was still hoping titanium would take off as a commercial success and had begun feeling around once again for interested parties. "In the summer of 1944 I made a call to the U.S. Bureau of Mines, Wash. D.C., to inquire about the status of titanium research in the laboratories of this institution, which had taken up titanium reduction as an investigation project. On this occasion I suggested to Dr. R. S. Dean, then Assistant Director, that I would be in a position to produce zirconium in a similar way [to titanium]," Kroll recalled.

While Albany's Northwest Electro-development Laboratory was still struggling to acquire enough equipment—not to mention staff—to start operations, Assistant Director Dean had the foresight to take note of Kroll's extensive metallurgical knowledge. It was known that titanium and zirconium were very similar, and during their first meeting, the two discussed Kroll's method of producing malleable zirconium. If anyone in the world would know how to investigate transforming the zircon from Oregon sands into a useful, malleable metal, it would be Kroll. Such a discovery—a superbly corrosion-resistant material produced on a commercial scale, and the industry that could result—would be an incredible boon for Oregon . . . *if* it could actually be achieved.

Up until the 1930s, zirconium was known as a dull, brittle silver metal with few uses. It was too soft to be used as a structural metal and when finely ground it was too flammable to be used as much else except as a powder used for early flash photography. Just as with titanium, there was no immediate demand for such a material, even if it could be improved into a super strong metal. Times were changing, though, and the U.S. Bureau of Mines was in the position to make zirconium relevant.

No evidence suggests an agreement was made to use Kroll's services after the meeting in Washington D.C, and in late April 1944 Dean lamented to Dr. Rogers, director of the Albany laboratory, that he feared he may have missed his opportunity. "It would appear that the manufacture of metallic zirconium has been gotten under way by the Foote Mineral Company. I am quite sure that this was done by arrangement with Dr. Kroll. This takes away some of the advantage of the Bureau in working on zirconium, but there are doubtless certain aspects of the problem which we can study."

That very day Dean penned a letter of inquiry to Kroll, who was still consulting at Union Carbide. He described the newly established Northwest Electro-development Laboratory in Albany and explained why they had zirconium in their sights: "One of the problems of considerable local interest is the utilization of the beach sands which contain zircon. We had the idea of undertaking a demonstration of the manufacture from these sands and some studies of its uses." Dean admitted that the work at Foote Mineral Company may have rendered local research unnecessary, but "there are doubtless still some things to be done in perfecting the method of manufacture and developing the fabrication and use of the metal." He concluded by asking Kroll if he would be available on a consulting basis for the Albany laboratory.

All the while this was being considered, there wasn't a single mention of zirconium to the press or even during the presentation to the appropriation committee for funding, quite possibly because there was no real guarantee the Bureau would be able to secure Kroll's services, or if they were, be able to pay for them.

Dr. Rogers was correct in asserting that Foote Mineral Company of Pennsylvania had begun working with zirconium, though there's no evidence Kroll was involved. Foote also dealt with other rare metals such as thorium, beryllium, and uranium. "It was primarily these rare metals which fascinated us," said H. Conrad Meyer of Foote Mineral Company. "We'd handle the common ores if our customers really insisted, but our heart wasn't in it. We wanted to be specialists in the rare metals." During World War II those at Foote were privy to a rumor that Germany had successfully developed a zirconium-steel alloy for bulletproof armor "three times as strong as the best armor plate," said Meyer. But the rumors later proved to be false; the alloy in question was difficult to make, dangerous to work with, and entirely too expensive.

But Meyer and Foote Mineral Company were so enamored with zirconium that the metal's wild behavior did not deter the fledgling business from diving headlong into learning how to produce it. With help from Drs. Anton van Arkel and Jan de Boer of Holland, Foote learned to produce pure zirconium using a method called the crystal bar process, or the iodide method, which was entirely different than Kroll's proposed method.

As the anticipated June 1944 opening date of the Albany laboratory drew near, top officials from Washington, D.C. traveled to Albany to assess progress at the new laboratory. Though no agreement had yet been made with Dr. Kroll to assist in future zirconium development, Dr. Dean and administrative officer John Morris conferred with Dr. Rogers about what other metallurgical laboratories were working on around the country. "They are pleased with the work that is being done here and expressed their confidence in its future success," the local press reported.

The month of June came and went and still the laboratory had not begun operations. Staff was still being assembled and with that came the need for housing, which was already in high demand in the area. The lack of available homes and apartments was a recurring theme during the early years of the Northwest Electro-development Laboratory; Rogers pleaded numerous times for Albany to consider increasing housing of all types for incoming employees, who often had families and even extended family moving with them to the West Coast.

One such transplant was Mark L. Wright, who transferred from Salt Lake City to head the analytical laboratory in Albany. His wife and young son were able to find a house on Takena Street, just blocks from the laboratory's campus. Dozens of future employees would also find housing within walking distance of the campus as new subdivisions were gradually overtaking farmland on that edge of town.

As the cool late spring transitioned into longer, warmer days, there were once again high hopes that the facility would officially begin operations on July 1, 1944. However, material shipments didn't arrive as expected and the grounds were still being prepped for use. Though delayed, some orders that had been placed actually ended up costing less, so that financial surplus was used to improve the roads between buildings on campus. Details about the buildings themselves were also being ironed out: in July, Rogers conferred with the Bonneville Power Administration to see if electricity could be used for heating instead of resurrecting the wood-fired boiler house that had been left over from the Albany College days.

 Electricity itself was the foundational component behind the concept of the Northwest Electrodevelopment Laboratory but getting the pieces and parts to come together was no easy task. By the end of July 1944, the biggest electric arc furnace in the country was ready to be shipped from Pittsburgh to Albany, but no transformers had been received at the laboratory, so even if the furnace had arrived there would be no way to power it. But the public was assured, once again, that forward momentum was occurring: within a weeks' time, the first ore shipments from Coos and Curry counties would be received at the laboratory, "with which investigations are being made for the recovery of chromium, zirconium, etc."

 Thus, the first public mention of zirconium was declared in the *Albany Democrat-Herald* on July 29. At this point Kroll had still not been secured by Dean and the Bureau started searching for someone to immediately pursue the exploration of zirconium at the laboratory. Coincidentally, two years prior Oregon State College (located just a town away from Albany) had reopened its school of mining and had hired thirty-year-old Albert W. Schlechten to head up the department. Dr. Schlechten and his wife Eleanor had moved from

Minneapolis, Minnesota to fulfill the appointment at the college. Schlechten came well-qualified: he was a graduate of the Montana School of Mines and had received his doctorate degree at the Massachusetts Institute of Technology.

In July 1944, Dr. Schlechten was recruited by the Bureau of Mines to investigate zirconium at the Northwest Electro-development Laboratory. Dwindling enrollment at Oregon State College motivated Dr. Shlechten's decision to join the Bureau and he was warmly welcomed to the new facility: "Dr. Rogers regards him as a valuable addition to the staff and is especially pleased in view of the fact that it is difficult to obtain good men since so many are frozen to work in connection with the war effort," the local paper noted. Despite this, more key staff would arrive at the laboratory in the next few months, including chemist Raymond H. Moore, who would join Mark Wright in the analytical lab. Like much of the staff before him, Moore was transferred from a Bureau laboratory located at the University of Maryland in College Park.

By fall, most construction work at the Northwest Electro-development Laboratory had been completed and buildings were starting to be used for their purpose. The former Gray Hall administration building—now Laboratory Building No. 1—naturally became the location of most of the office staff. The third floor housed a large chemical laboratory that would work well for analyzing ores for various experiments, and interestingly enough, a large laboratory on the first floor from the college days had been partitioned off to create smaller rooms. A service elevator—painted a hue of green with a peculiar diamond-shaped chicken-wire window—was installed to handle transport of heavy equipment. Additionally, power, water, and waste lines were established for the

Photo: Stephen T. Anderson Collection
One of the earliest photos of the newly formed Northwest Electro-development Laboratory. Analytical lab, circa 1944.

Photo: Stephen T. Anderson Collection
Electric transformer installation at the Operations Building, circa 1945.

laboratory, and transformers were installed outside to provide a power supply. Equipment purchased for Laboratory No. 1 included a Baird spectrograph and x-ray apparatuses, furnaces and their temperature controllers, and supplies for the chemical laboratory.

Just south of Laboratory No.1, the massive red brick building with the decorative roofline had been transformed from a barely-used college gymnasium to a fully equipped Operations Building. Sump pumps were needed to drain the basement, which had leaked badly and filled with rainwater. The gleaming wood gym floor with painted lines had been carefully pried up and set aside. A vault had been installed to house a massive transformer, and floors were reinforced to handle the incredible weight of future machinery. A gantry crane was built to hoist equipment around the space, a service elevator was added, and two electric furnaces—the biggest one able to contain one ton of metal—plus a high-frequency furnace and a significant amount of ore dressing equipment, were all purchased for the Operations Building.

Across from the Operations Building, the newly christened Service Building received the repurposed gymnasium floor, which covered its existing concrete slab. Leftover machinery from the National Youth Administration days was positioned diagonally across the hardwood floors. While other buildings had been receiving a somewhat steady stream of supplies and equipment for months, the Service Building was already well-equipped: "The machines acquired from the National Youth Administration's shop were sufficient to provide for metalworking," recalled notes. A separate woodworking area had been divided off from the main floor with a brick wall, and the heating system was updated. Diffuse sunlight gleamed in through wall-to-wall windows and the lighting system was updated with ample drop lighting above workstations.

Lester Miller was one notable employee on campus at the time. "Pop"—as he'd been dubbed early on by another Bureau employee—had assisted contractors Reimers & Jolivette in converting the former college campus into the government laboratory before beginning his government employment on August 23, 1944. Miller had a generous amount of previous experience with building upkeep when he worked at nearby Camp Adair, overseeing 40 buildings at the former cantonment. He continued on at the Bureau as a painter when he was brought on late that summer to help maintain those first buildings on campus.

As early fall transitioned into cold, crisp days with early evenings, a subtle shift was taking place. While finishing touches were underway and the final pieces of equipment and supplies were awaited, the Northwest Electro-development Laboratory, quietly and without much fanfare, transitioned from a campus under construction to a functioning laboratory.

Photo: Stephen T. Anderson Collection
Equipment installation in the basement of Building 2.

Photo: Stephen T. Anderson Collection
Machine shop (Building 5), circa 1945.

CHAPTER FOUR

SHIFTING SANDS

October 1944–December 1944

"One problem of considerable local interest is the utilization of the beach sands which contain zircon. We had the idea of undertaking a demonstration of the manufacture of zirconium from these sands and some studies of its uses."

—Dr. R. S. Dean, assistant director of the U.S. Bureau of Mines

The last quarter of 1944 was a critical turning point for the fledgling laboratory in Albany as seven key directions were outlined for the facility to begin working on. The first project was electrometallurgy of Pacific Northwest iron-nickel-chromium ore, which did not start immediately. Neither did the next project, treatment of Scappoose high phosphorus iron ore. Lack of qualified, available employees was still a primary issue plaguing the little laboratory, but one project had just enough staff to get rolling: production of ductile zirconium from Oregon black sands, and by extension, studying the concentration of the products from those same sands.

For the "concentration of the products in the black sands of Oregon" project, two general guidelines were initially established: to obtain good samples of valuable elements in beach sand, including chromite and zircon, and "the hope that some improvement in procedure might be found which would make the concentrates produced at Coquille [Oregon] of still better grade than that attained in the Defense Plant Corporation's operations," as stated in a report from that time. In other words, the zircon concentrate that served as feed material for the project needed to be refined even further.

Three other projects—magnesium pilot plants and research, electrometallurgy of zinc and lead, and conversion of quartz to vitreous silica—received some equipment and staff, but only the magnesium project was touched on in 1944.

The Bureau of Mines station in Pullman, Washington had been working on magnesium studies when operations were suddenly assigned to the new laboratory in Albany in October 1944. With only the chemical laboratory and the ore-dressing building up and running, new transfers E. Don Dilling and William F. Hergert were to "work on equipment for producing metallic magnesium from northwest magnesite deposits," the local paper reported. A month prior, equipment had arrived in Albany for this magnesium pilot plant research, which was intended to be a continuation of a project that had been undertaken at a Ford Motor Company plant in Dearborn, Michigan.

Magnesium was a highly sought-after material during World War II, as it was an essential ingredient in some aluminum alloys used for aircraft construction. Magnesium was also used in ammunition, flares, and incendiary bombs. It was also a dangerously flammable material to work with; the Albany station had actually inherited the project and some of the necessary equipment because of a fire at Ford's Dearborn magnesium plant. Aspects of the project to be worked on in Albany included working on the second production phase, called distillation.

Despite the newly assigned magnesium project, zirconium studies were the laboratory's primary concern. Initially, Dr. Schlechten, the former Oregon State College professor and metallurgist, was named as chief of the project and Leland Yerkes, a chemical

Photo: Stephen T. Anderson Collection
Equipment installation in the basement of Building 2.

Photo: Stephen T. Anderson Collection
The magnesium project, inherited from Ford Motor Company, was one of the first tasks undertaken by the Northwest Electro-development Laboratory.

engineer, assisted Schlechten as they began preliminary studies in late 1944. Forty-six-year-old Yerkes was hired on December 1, 1944, and moved into a two-story cottage-style home directly across from the old Albany College tennis courts.

Assistant director of the Bureau R. S. Dean had maintained contact with Dr. Kroll over the summer, and in October, correspondence between the two men confirmed that Kroll had resigned from his consulting position at Union Carbide on July 1, though he still maintained a residence at the Red Coach Inn at Niagara Falls, New York. There were a few key details to be resolved before Kroll could accept an assignment with the government, however. The metallurgist wanted to make sure that any work he performed at the Bureau would still remain his property, and in a letter to Dean, he emphasized that "any ideas I have regarding processes for making malleable zirconium would remain my property and that patents would be applied for, where the practical development has proved them sound." Kroll also mentioned that because of the knowledge he'd gained just before leaving Luxembourg, he was confident that he would be "making malleable zirconium within six months with little assistance," upon arriving at the laboratory in Albany.

Issues of travel, moving Kroll's possessions, and salary expectations were also discussed through correspondence. Kroll had been receiving $5,000 a year while working half-time at Union Carbide and would be agreeable to working under similar conditions, though he noted "I did however work practically full time," and thus had received some of his inventions as compensation from Union Carbide.

Dean replied that Kroll's proposals seemed entirely reasonable but Dean would need to forward Kroll's requests to the Bureau's legal department for confirmation. After this point, Dr. Rogers, the Albany director, began corresponding with Kroll directly. On November 18, 1944, Rogers expressed to Kroll that the Albany lab was "most anxious to begin the work [on zirconium]." Even though all the details hadn't been worked out with Kroll's employment and move, Rogers requested a list of necessary equipment—down to the tiniest detail—that Kroll would need to begin his research on zirconium.

While quick correspondence was bouncing between Drs. Kroll, Dean, and Rogers, one thousand pounds of zircon had been obtained by the Bureau and was being experimented on by former OSC professor Schlechten, Rogers, and chemist Yerkes. The three were trying to solve preliminary problems in turning zircon into malleable zirconium, but their efforts didn't yield the results they were hoping for. Letters regarding Kroll's anticipated employment with the Bureau continued.

In keeping with the sense of urgency, Kroll promptly responded on November 22 with a list that included where the very specific parts and chemical supplies could be ordered. A month later, on December 22, 1944, Dr. Dean was able to give Kroll some excellent news: "I am glad to inform you that the Secretary of the Interior approved your appointment on December 19, 1944, as a Consulting Metallurgist . . . I suggest you proceed immediately with plans to start work at Albany at the earliest possible date."

Dean informed Kroll that a salary of $8,000 per annum had been approved, and additionally Congress had also approved a $55,000 appropriation for work on the production of zirconium. A "small supply" of necessary government forms were sent along for Kroll to fill out, including a "travel order, book of transportation requests, identification card, a copy of the travel regulations and a supply of travel voucher forms for preparing your expense accounts."

On the second day of 1945, Dr. Rogers provided an update on the equipment and materials that Kroll had requested. Rogers requested more information "on the type of vacuum gauges to be obtained, and notes they 'shall be glad to have as much additional information as you can send us previous to your arrival here. No item is too small to mention, as we might well overlook it. As you are aware, this Laboratory is just being started up and is not well stocked at the present time. Consequently, some small item that has been overlooked might delay our work considerably.' "

William J. Kroll arrived in the small community of Albany, Oregon on January 16, 1945. The slight man who stood at no more than 5'9" was impeccably dressed in a suit, vest, tie, and hat. It was noted by more than a few employees that the Luxembourg native was never sloppily dressed for any occasion.

Kroll set up his office on campus but established his home elsewhere. Perhaps it was the ever-present housing crunch in Albany that caused Kroll to choose the nearby town of Corvallis as his residence, or maybe it was the proximity to Oregon State College, or it could have been that Kroll seemed to favor hotels as lodging—whatever it was, the metallurgist chose the seven-story Hotel Benton in Corvallis as his living quarters.

The resplendent seven-story hotel where Kroll made his home was a little over ten miles from where the Northwest Electro-development Laboratory was located. In 1945, it was considered the social hub of

Photo: Author's Collection
Kroll's first home in Oregon, the Hotel Benton in Corvallis, Oregon.

Photo: Author's Collection
A current photo of the former Beaver Hill Separations Plant near Coquille, Oregon.

Corvallis and several notable names had, or would later, pass through the establishment. Shirley Temple, John F. Kennedy, Richard Nixon, and Ronald Regan all made stops at the tallest building in the downtown area during its heyday. Perhaps living in a hotel afforded Kroll the luxury of being able to focus entirely on the work he was so dedicated to. Before moving to Albany, Kroll had given Dean an estimate of just six months to produce malleable zirconium, so it's no surprise that just weeks after his arrival, Kroll planned his trip to the coastal lumber town of Coos Bay to obtain sand containing zircon. But, of all the sand in Oregon, how did Kroll know exactly where to find sands with the highest zircon concentrations?

It had been known for quite some time that beach sands of the Pacific Northwest held incredible potential: in 1852, enough gold was discovered along the Oregon coast to attract significant attention; one town was even rechristened Gold Beach because of how much of the valuable metal was found there. Some of these areas were productive for a short time, and a U.S. Department of Geology and Mineral Industries report cited that "the extraction of several millions of dollars of gold and platinum from some of the old workings," had been achieved.

Beside gold and platinum, it was noted that the Oregon sands contained other curious components that could have possible future potential. In 1897–1898, Dr. David Day, chief of the Department of Mineral Resources of the United States, spent considerable time panning for platinum and gold on the beaches of rivers and seas. He came away with a curiosity regarding the fine, glittering black sand and "concluded the troublesome black sand was worth investigation."

In 1905, Congress appropriated $25,000 for Day to initiate a study regarding the sand. In 1905, Day and

Dr. Richards sampled over two hundred locations along Oregon's coast and found that many samples "indicated the presence of zircon in substantial amounts," though at that point in time, the two men were once again looking for platinum deposits.

The 1905 Lewis and Clark Exposition, held in Portland, Oregon, became the nexus of their research: a public pavilion was erected, and in that facility, Day began his work. Miners from any part of the country were invited to mail in four-pound samples for testing. Day and his team were soon flooded with over one thousand sand samples to treat at the pavilion. "This shows a greater general interest in the matter of obtaining additional useful values from black sands than had been expected," observed a 1905 article in *Mining and Engineering World*.

Finding a way to separate out all the elements in the sand proved to be a success after some trial and error. Day's team found several ways to tease each of the mineral components from the sand, and "the interesting minerals proved to be magnetite, chromite, ilmenite, garnet, monazite, and zircon," noted Dr. Robert H. Richards, in the 1906 *Technology Quarterly*.

One tool called a "Wilfley table" initially separated out mineral components. Heavier minerals were sifted away from the lighter ones by way of a jerking motion, another way was to use a Wetherill magnet, which had six magnetic poles. Five different ampere levels separated the minerals; a level of 0.2 amperes would lift out the magnetite, followed by 0.8 amperes to lift out ilmenite and chromite (chromite being another mineral of great interest in Oregon later on), 1.75 amperes to lift out garnet, 1.90 amperes to lift out hypersthene (a mineral having no value at the time), and 3.50 amperes to lift out heavy monazite (from which thorium is derived). Zircon would be the only remaining mineral after all else was removed.

Also housed in the pavilion was a little electric steel furnace, "as novel as any instrument employed in this investigation by the United States Geological Survey, and is more striking and spectacular," Richards noted. With "boundless enthusiasm," the crowds at the public pavilion watched as the furnace was cranked up, fed cold sea beach sands, and an hour later, "white-hot steel was tapped from it."

Day and Richards's preliminary studies paved the way for further studies of Oregon's black sands, and interest in the sands' composition never really subsided after the 1905 Lewis and Clark Exposition. Studies continued through the decades, and beginning in 1938 the Oregon Department of Geology and Mineral Industries (DOGAMI) focused on potentially commercially viable chromium deposits in the sands, as well as the concentration of ilmenite, from which titanium is derived. The study also recorded concentrations of other minerals within the black sand, taking careful note of where the deposits were located along the Oregon coast.

In the summers of 1942 and 1943, Dr. William H. Twenhofel, a University of Wisconsin researcher, conducted another painstaking survey of Oregon's shorelines, from Coos Bay to the mouth of the Columbia River, again cataloguing the locations of deposits and percentages of minerals. In a roundabout way, the search for other minerals provided a wealth of information on zircon, and because of these studies, Dr. Kroll learned that Oregon's sands were a source of zircon.

The journey from the Willamette Valley to Coos Bay was a picturesque 142-mile drive. Kroll left the relatively flat oak savannah and drove over the evergreen-laden coastal range, down the Pacific Coast Highway (now Highway 101). Once on the coast, Dr. Kroll was treated to stunning wind-whipped views of the vast Pacific Ocean. The narrow, cliff-hugging serpentine highway that runs from Newport then continues south to Coos Bay would have provided a first-class view of stormy winter seas that are typical for January. One has to wonder what the native Luxembourgian thought of his first trip to Oregon's wildly rugged coastline.

Kroll's journey took him through a town of a little over 5,000 people—just about the same size as Albany—that had been known as Marshfield up until 1944. The coastal enclave had been fairly isolated until Highway 101 was completed in 1926, better connecting the Marshfield area to other coastal towns. During the early 1940s, growth and new industry were booming, and the citizens of Marshfield voted to change the town's name to Coos Bay.

By the time Kroll made his first visit to the newly christened town, the lumber industry was no longer the only economic driver; with the advent of World War II, the government's needs for chromium and the area's black sand deposits had spurred two businesses—Krome Corporation and Humphreys Gold Corporation—to construct chromium plants just south of Coos Bay. Krome Corporation constructed its facility along Seven Devils Road and the Humphreys facility was closer to Bandon, but there was a third and lesser-known plant that was the metallurgist's ultimate destination.

Once on Highway 42, heading southeast away from Coos Bay and toward Coquille, Kroll took a sharp right-hand turn off the main road, then took another hard turn onto a gravel drive. Across a single railroad track his journey would end.

Tucked into a forested hillside directly in front of him loomed a giant multi-leveled corrugated tin building built by Southwest Engineering Company to be a government-owned separation facility. Public confusion about this third location endured, especially when it came to what it was actually called, and who ran the operation. Whether the details were intentionally obscured or not isn't known, but interestingly enough, it was sometimes referred to as the Krome Corporation by the local newspaper, probably because the lion's share of materials to be processed came from Krome Corp. For lack of a proper name, however, the facility was usually described by its location, often just called the "Defense separations plant at Beaver Hill."

At this hulking facility, tailings from the two local chromium plants were further refined through magnetic separation into three different grades: two chrome products and a tailing rich in zircon. It was that last item that Kroll was seeking. After he'd obtained a load of the concentrated tailings, the metallurgist headed back to Albany, eager to prove that he'd be able to produce malleable zirconium in six months' time, just as he'd confidently promised the assistant director of the U.S. Bureau of Mines, R. S. Dean.

CHAPTER FIVE
TRIAL AND TRIUMPH

"The atmosphere when he [Dr. Kroll] was here was just blazing with ideas and enchantment, and the work put out was fantastic."

—H. Andrew Johansen

It was no secret that Dr. William J. Kroll had a penchant for subterranean laboratories. In his luxurious Luxembourg manse he'd performed his crucial titanium experiments in the reinforced basement laboratory. Later on, Kroll would construct another fortified, lower-level laboratory in the basement of his Corvallis home. But in Albany in January 1945, the 56-year-old consultant and his team—Drs. Schlechten and Yerkes—chose the basement of the oft-overlooked Building 2 as the headquarters for the new direction of zirconium work they were about to delve into.

The brick-clad building that had started its life as an orphan's home was finally coming into its purpose. Despite being cast aside during Henry Powell Hopkins's early campus assessment and passed over for any renovations, the former Woodward Hall went from a barely used building to a critical location on the Northwest Electro-development Laboratory campus.

Kroll established his office in one of the third-floor corner rooms in Building 2. While the room was plain, its two windows (one facing west and the other facing south) allowed ample daylight to stream onto his desk. But the critical work of creating zirconium would take place in the former dormitory's basement, where the lab equipment that Kroll had specified to Dr. Rogers would be assembled.

Before any experiments could begin again, Kroll and Schlechten knew they would need to know what work had already been done collectively on zirconium, so they executed an exhaustive study of what had already been written regarding the metal. The three men at the Bureau weren't alone in their quest for large quantities of malleable zirconium; three companies in the United States were attempting to produce commercial-grade zirconium at that time: Foote Mineral Company, Titanium Alloys Manufacturing Co., and the Metal Hydrides Co. Despite that, there wasn't a great deal of information readily available on the obscure metal.

After Kroll returned to Albany with a great deal of zircon sand, an assistant further refined the tailings by tabling and magnetically separating them, causing the zircon percentage of the tailings to increase. Using this higher-concentration product, Kroll, Schlechten, and Yerkes got to work on producing metallic zirconium.

The process of taking the reddish-brown zircon sand and making it into a malleable metal involved a bit of heat, chemistry, and time. It was like being in a kitchen where the entire aim of the process was to produce a pure ingredient—in this case, zirconium—a semi-lustrous, dark gray metal that Dr. Kroll asserted could be pounded and shaped, but only when it was free from impurities.

The funny thing about this "kitchen" was that most of the ingredients were incredibly dangerous, and if not handled carefully, they had potential to kill. One of the chemistry ingredients Kroll needed—chlorine—was highly poisonous. Kroll and company also noted that small particles of zirconium could spontaneously ignite if exposed to air, or even explode if pounded underwater. And everything in this "kitchen" was heated to wildly hot temperatures. Additionally, some of the "cooking" couldn't even take place in the air we breathe—some processes needed to happen in a hydrogen atmosphere and others in an inert gas or a vacuum. Suffice it to say, the "cooking" was a little finicky.

In the beginning of the process, they added ingredients to the heated zircon sand for the purpose of drawing away impurities. Different ingredients draw away different impurities, and then those ingredients had to be drawn away from the zirconium as well, for they became impurities too. Anything that wasn't zircon was an impurity which had to be dealt with eventually.

In the cold basement of Building 2 during the last half of January 1945, Kroll got to work. The basement didn't stay cold for very long, however: the first step in creating metallic zirconium was to make a carbide and heat it to around 3,600°F in a carbon resistor furnace—a high temperature by any standard. (By comparison, silver melts at 1763°F and gold at around 1948°F.) The carbide mixture was made by combining the refined zircon sand (which contained about 14% silicon) with carbon, and between two and twenty-four pounds of the mix could be heated at a time. The run sizes were limited by the capacity of the small furnace. This first step wasn't absolutely necessary, but in small-scale tests like these they found if silica was mixed in, a lower furnace temperature was needed to start the self-sustaining reaction that was necessary to continue the process.

The next step was called chlorination, and naturally, the device used for this step was called the chlorinator. Its purpose was to introduce hot chlorine gas to the carbide mixture from the previous step. A vigorous self-sustaining, heat-producing chemical reaction resulted, and it was so effective that temperatures could quickly climb to almost 2,200°F, even in the tiny apparatus Kroll was using. If needed, the reaction could be slowed by adding a little more zircon sand.

The final product of chlorination was a mixture of zirconium chloride (by its very nature, zirconium loves chlorine, so it was happy to soak up all that gas coming in) and silicon chloride. The process that made this mixture possible was called sublimation.

Sublimation is a fairly simple concept. Think of an icy pond that is exposed to sunlight; the ice (a solid) can sublime into vapor (a gas), skipping the liquid stage (water) altogether. The stunning thing is that some metals can do this too—though at extremely high temperatures.

While the resulting products were zirconium chloride and silicon chloride, it was desired that only zirconium sublime. Remember, as ingredients were added, it was necessary to take some out once their purpose had been served, and at this stage, it was silicon's time to go. Kroll and his colleagues realized that by keeping the condenser (a part of the chlorinator apparatus) heated, they could collect almost all the zirconium chloride—and almost none of the silicon chloride.

The chlorinator was designed to run continuously. For these early runs, Kroll and his associates mixed up a large initial batch of carbides—almost eighty pounds—but the first batch of carbides fed into the chlorinator only weighed about eleven pounds or so. As the zirconium carbide mixture decreased, the heated chlorine gas could be turned off and up to six pounds of carbide was mixed in to continue the process. Once every twenty-four hours, the condenser (where the sublimated condensation gathered) was emptied of the chloride product. Of the zirconium "charged" (run through the chlorinator), 94.6% was recovered in the chloride.

Even though plenty of crude zirconium chloride resulted from that step, there were still "ingredients" that had to be drawn out. Up to .5% of iron and trace amounts of chromium, silicon, and aluminum were still present. Recall that anything that wasn't pure zirconium was an unwelcome guest (impurities would lead to brittleness and make malleability difficult in the final product) so the next step was designed to eliminate iron and chromium.

In a furnace made of sheet nickel, the third step would be to sublime everything again, but this time in a hydrogen atmosphere. About fifteen pounds of zirconium chloride was put into a little nickel "boat" which was pushed into the heating chamber of the furnace. Hydrogen was then continuously blown over the boat, and the resulting product would have an iron content of only 0.05% rather than 0.5%. But, this process wasn't without its drawbacks; there was an enormous 8.7% loss of zirconium in this step alone. Kroll and his associates chalked it up to the "inadequate capacity of the condenser."

The fourth step, called reduction, had been perfected by Kroll for reducing titanium, but it was his job at the Albany Bureau of Mines station to adapt it to zirconium. A reduction run involved placing magnesium metal and zirconium chloride into a special container and putting those into a reduction furnace. An ingenious lid system was devised for the reduction furnace: molten lead-antimony would form a seal as it cooled and hardened, then the air within was sucked out to create a vacuum. Helium was filled back in and heating coils were turned on, which would liquify the metal seal as well as the magnesium within.

After the magnesium liquified, a separate heater was turned on to vaporize the zirconium chloride. Those vapors circulated downward and mixed with the magnesium, reducing them to solid metal. If extra pressure built up inside, it could easily blow out the molten seal. If pressure inside the furnace was less than atmospheric pressure, helium was added through a valve in the side of the furnace so air couldn't be drawn in through the molten seal. Air was the enemy in this step; any addition of nitrogen or oxygen would contaminate the materials inside.

The resulting product was a combination of metallic zirconium, magnesium chloride, and magnesium, which was left over in the lower pot of the reduction chamber. A typical run would take ten hours to complete and 93.8% of the zirconium was recovered as metal. A little zirconium was left in the residue from the procedure, and even less in the distilled salts, resulting in about a 3% loss of zirconium.

Product losses during the process was inevitable during these first experiments, but Kroll and his associates were always looking for ways to improve their gains. Their goal was to model a process to create commercial amounts of zirconium at the lowest possible cost, and maximizing the amount of zirconium produced in each run was vital. They analyzed the content of the residues, and figured that at least one of the losses could've been avoided by more carefully regulating the furnace's temperature: at one point in the reduction step, high temperatures caused excess pressure in the furnace and resulted in zirconium chloride fumes "bubbling out" of the molten metal seal.

At this point, there were new "ingredients" that had to be eliminated before pure metallic zirconium could be achieved: magnesium chloride, magnesium metal, and hydrogen were pesky particles that needed to be drawn out through vacuum distillation. Other methods had been tried, but they'd proven to be rather unpredictable and downright dangerous. Leaching and grinding zirconium to recover it from the magnesium and hydrogen wasn't preferred, as oxidation was a problem and the grindings had a nasty habit of catching on fire.

The distillation furnace was another vertical stainless steel cylinder which held the reduction pot from the previous step. To begin the run, the reduction pot was placed in the furnace, the furnace was closed, and after a good vacuum had been obtained, heating coils were left on until the interior reached about 1472°F.

Kroll, Schlechten, and Yerkes observed a number of runs and realized a shortcut that could speed up the process: they figured that if they turned the reduction pot upside down, the magnesium chloride would simply run out, leaving the zirconium behind because they noted that the "zirconium metal adheres tightly to the inside of the pot and will not fall out." An average run would take six hours.

Although it was beneficial that the zirconium grabbed onto the sides of the pot during that step, it created a bit of a problem for the next. Chipping away at the zirconium metal to recover it wasn't ideal because it increased the risk of fire. The metallurgists found that slowly pressing a beryllium-copper chisel into the zirconium would help loosen it from the pot. Even still, the risk of spontaneous fire was a constant threat. Kroll and his associates also figured a suitable work-around: "If fires are started, a snuffer is placed over the pot and helium gas is blown in through a pipe."

At this point in the process, Kroll, Schlechten, and Yerkes observed that some runs contained less than 1% of the impurities magnesium, magnesium chloride, and hydrogen. But in other runs, they found those impurities to be deeply embedded in the zirconium. If this were the case, an interim step would need to be taken: degassing in a different type of furnace. The metal with impurities would be put into a high-frequency furnace under a vacuum, and after a few hours, the magnesium chloride would be removed.

At this stage in the process, Kroll and his associates would have a collection of zirconium pieces that were porous and irregular. The dull gray chunks looked much like metallic lava rocks, and just as rough, and it was coined "sponge" because of its appearance. Though the material was a far cry from the sand they'd started with, further refining still had to be done to have an ingot that could be shaped or forged.

The final step was to take those rough chunks and remelt them in a vacuum arc furnace. This apparatus, a water-cooled furnace with a thirteen-inch inner height, was custom fabricated by Yerkes in the machine shop that had been left by the National Youth Administration. During this step, the pieces of zirconium metal were placed on a water-cooled electrode, then air would be pumped out and replaced with pure helium. The power was turned on, resulting in an arc of electricity going straight to the chunks of metal. Contact with the arc would melt the metal until it formed a single piece.

Like everything else in this process, this step wasn't without its dangers: the furnace operator had to view the melt from above, peering down through one of two glass windows, to determine the position of the electrode and quality of the arc. "Considering the high degree of potential danger viewing these melts directly, it is amazing that no critical accidents occurred," Bureau scientist later recalled. There were stories about Kroll himself being burned when his small furnace blew up, though his injuries weren't severe. As for the danger, "he just brushed it off as one of the hazards of research," noted Stephen T. Anderson.

The melted metal, considered an ingot at this point, would then be turned over and slightly melted again to smooth the other side. These hardened pools of melted zirconium were aptly called "buttons," as they were bright, smooth and round, and about 2–3 inches in diameter. A button melt would take about two minutes.

The hardness of these final buttons was of great importance. Hardness was measured on the Brinell scale, where the higher the number, the more energy it would need to deform or shape it. Gold has a Brinell hardness of 188–245 MPa (Megapascal Pressure Unit). The buttons melted by Kroll and associates were as low as 192; they determined that any zirconium ingot under 300 MPa could be forged, rolled, cut, machined, or swaged (forcing metal into a die to change its dimensions), although Kroll and his peers demanded even better results from future experiments. "It is expected that future work will make it possible to produce zirconium metal with lower hardness than that obtained so far," Kroll, Schlechten, and Yerkes concluded in their first technical paper. "This will require the elimination of all possible sources of contamination . . . .Difficulties can be eliminated, or at least minimized, by perfection of the equipment, the operating procedure, and the raw materials."

But these first zirconium experiments by Kroll, Schlechten, and Yerkes proved that using Kroll's method of reduction—using magnesium instead of sodium (as in the Hunter process) could indeed create zirconium pure enough to be malleable. With continued tinkering and scale-up, zirconium could be produced commercially in great quantities at an affordable price.

All the seemingly unrelated circumstances in the Pacific Northwest and in the little town of Albany, Oregon, had coalesced. The plentiful power from Bonneville and Grand Coulee dams, the presence of mining colleges in the Western states, and the availability of a vacant college campus in Albany secured the location of the Bureau's premiere station. The stunning foresight of one very knowledgeable assistant director, Dr. Dean, plus the availability of the father of titanium, Dr. Kroll, combined to create a potent synergy in the fledgling laboratory. The age of zirconium had arrived.

CHAPTER SIX

THE LITTLE LABORATORY THAT COULD
May 1945–July 1947

"This laboratory was built during the war and like everything else it was confronted with difficulties with the obtaining of materials and equipment as well as personnel. The difficulties, however, have been overcome and the Albany laboratory is now not only the largest but one of the finest in the United States. When this laboratory was established the only Albany that most people knew about was Albany, New York. Now they are beating a path to Albany, Or., from all over the country."

—*Dr. R. S. Dean assistant director of the U.S. Bureau of Mines, March 1946*

It's very unlikely that the neighbors who lived in the little cottage-style homes across the street from the Northwest Electro-development Laboratory had any idea that a tremendously complex—not to mention dangerous—process was happening just a stone's throw from their homes. The local papers had sporadically touted the past accomplishments of Dr. Kroll, but his zirconium work was generally described in vague layman's terms. The ambiguity may have been purposeful, as there was already an air of proprietary secrecy about the laboratory.

While Drs. Kroll, Schlechten, and Yerkes were making tremendous headway with their zirconium work, the little laboratory in the rural southwest corner of Albany was beginning to grow. In the months since Kroll arrived, the laboratory's focus had solidified. "It is the purpose of the Bureau management to produce a finished product out of the raw material to be of marketable value that will be handled by some commercial organization," the local press reported in early 1945.

Though the laboratory was in its infancy, the U.S. Bureau of Mines validated its potential. In May, Albany's site was named the headquarters for the northwest division that included Washington, Oregon, Idaho, and Montana. Not one, but two positions would now report directly to Washington, D.C. Dr. Rogers, the current director of the Albany site, would head up the metallurgical division. S. H. Lorain and his team, of Moscow, Idaho, would be transferred to Albany to head up the new mining investigations department.

Other activities at the laboratory included the magnesium project inherited from the Ford Motor Company in October 1944, which had been started early on but stalled out for lack of manpower and equipment. A delivery of much-needed machinery allowed the project to enter its second stage, which was distillation of the magnesium. With the war still raging, magnesium was still being produced for military needs and progress on the project was considerable, and it continued to receive ample funding through 1946.

There were around thirty employees at the Northwest Electro-development Laboratory during the spring of 1945, with more on the way. Director Rogers was concerned for future employees and once again implored Albany to consider solving the housing crisis. "I am greatly worried over the problem of providing living quarters for all the families that will come here, and we are hoping that a number of new homes of the better class will be constructed in the vicinity of the laboratory to take care of these people," he remarked in May.

One key position was filled by young Martin Farlee in 1945, who was placed in the shop crew as an electrician. Farlee already had substantial electrical know-how; he took electrical engineering classes at Oregon State College and had earned a position as an Electronic Technician in the U.S. Navy. Mart—as his fellow employees called him—started working for the Bureau in Boulder City but upon his move to Albany, quickly became intimately familiar with the electrical systems of every building on campus.

Along with the growth of the laboratory came discussion about what would happen once the war was over. After all, its establishment had been touted as a wartime necessity for taking advantage of critical mineral resources located in the western states. Strategic materials—or raw materials often used for wartime purposes—were of utmost importance. Once demand for strategic materials had lessened or ceased, how would the laboratory segue to fill other needs? Naysayers—specifically Rudolph Halley, the Truman Committee lawyer who had vehemently opposed the Albany site from day one—resumed questioning the suitability of the Northwest Electro-development Laboratory, even as growth was steady and progress was building.

World War II ended on a warm late summer day in September. Fair skies and eighty-degree weather accompanied the news that the Japanese had surrendered. In the local paper, the Red Cross reminded workers to remain at their jobs and there was a call for "turkey pickers" to register at once, as local poultry farms were still sending food to soldiers overseas. The war may have ended, but the Armed Forces still needed support.

That same month Kroll gave a presentation about the ongoing zirconium work that he had been working on with his associates, and his presentation may have birthed another unanswered question about possible classified work performed in Albany.

A persistent and long-standing story about the Albany Bureau was that it had somehow been involved with atomic bomb development for the Manhattan Project. Experimentation for the bombs dropped on Nagasaki and Hiroshima began in 1939; the Albany Bureau had a skeleton crew and began operations in the fall of 1944, and Fat Man and Little Boy were dropped on Japan in August 1945. Given the timeline, there is a possibility that Kroll may have had a role in uranium reduction for the Project and beyond, either at Union Carbide, the Bureau, or both.

While working in his home laboratory at Villa Leclerc, Kroll worked on producing malleable uranium using high-purity calcium as a reducing agent. Close friend and Bureau associate H. Andrew Johansen noted that during the invasion of Kroll's home town, "the first thing the Nazi troops did in going through Luxembourg was to go to his laboratory, and they took only one thing. He had been involved in purifying uranium. He had 20kg of purified uranium. That's the only thing they took."

As soon as Kroll arrived stateside in 1940 he was employed by Union Carbide in New York, where he worked until he was hired by the Bureau. At Union Carbide, Kroll worked on a variety of projects, one of which was the separation of uranium oxide with calcium. "Much of Union Carbide's involvement in the Manhattan Project dealt with the processing and enrichment of uranium," notes the Atomic Heritage Foundation.

Possibly the most compelling evidence that suggests Kroll may have worked on uranium for the Manhattan Project is found in a 1945 *Albany Democrat-Herald* article. While speaking at a Kiwanis club gathering, Kroll gave an account of his life and work. While working at Union Carbide, "...he played a vital part in perfecting a process for the reduction of uranium, the element from which the atomic bomb is made."

With this admission, and the fact that the Manhattan Project's official end came in 1946, there's a glimmer of possibility that Kroll could have further consulted on uranium reduction while working at the Albany Bureau, supported by a single reference in a recent Department of Energy history document, which stated,

> Metallurgical properties of uranium were unknown before the Manhattan Project. Most of the early uranium metallurgical research was accomplished from 1942 to 1943 at various research facilities including the University of Chicago Metallurgical Laboratory (known as the "Met Lab"), Iowa State College (now the Iowa State University) in Ames, Iowa, DuPont's Chambers Dye Works in Deepwater, New Jersey, Princeton University in New Jersey, and the Albany Research Center in Albany, Oregon.

The same document also lists the Albany Bureau as being one of four laboratories to work on uranium chemistry and metallurgy during the years 1942–1946 as part of the Manhattan Engineer District, without giving further details. With the Albany laboratory getting into full swing in fall 1944 and the Manhattan Project ending in 1946, there's certainly a possibility that some sort of early uranium research occurred. Unless we find further documentation, the Manhattan Project mystery will remain just that.

While laboratory neighbors may not have fully understood the complex experiments that were being performed at the former college campus, at least they could see things were looking more refined. As warm summer days ripened into equally pleasant fall afternoons, a Portland-area contractor installed an entire irrigation system across seventeen acres on the property. Local garden store owner Floyd C. Mullen was contracted to tend to the expansive lawns and beautify the property. Mr. Mullen was tasked with planting 750 "ornamental plants and shrubs" in addition to the trees that had been planted before Albany College had established its Monteith campus, when a substantial nursery business had occupied the corner of Queen and Broadway Streets at the turn of the century.

  In 1883, New York state native Albert Brownell traversed the country and landed in Albany, Oregon. Albany Nurseries was established at that time, on the corner of property that would later house Albany College, and the Northwest Electro-development Laboratory after that. Mr. Brownell's botanical enterprise was no small operation; he shipped trees across the United States and to Canada. The breadth of varieties sold at the Albany Nurseries was staggering; one recollection lists "fruit trees, shade and ornamental trees, evergreens, hardy flowering shrubs, roses, clematis, wisteria, etc. They also offered weeping trees including cutleaf birch, camperdown elm, teas' weeping mulberry, weeping mountain ash, killmarnock, and new American weeping willow." It is believed several treasured trees at the site date from Albany

LOOKING SOUTH FROM QUEEN AVENUE

Photo: Stephen T. Anderson Collection
One of the earliest known photos of southwest Albany shows the Albany Nurseries business, which occupied the corner of current Broadway and Queen SW.

Photo: Stephen T. Anderson Collection
A variety of trees were already on campus when the Bureau arrived; more would be planted later on by Floyd C. Mullen and others. Photo circa 1948.

LOOKING NORTH FROM SITE OF ADMINISTRATION BLDG

Photo: Stephen T. Anderson Collection
A view of the Albany Nurseries property around the turn of the century.

FROM QUEEN AVENUE LOOKING SOUTHWEST. PRESENT SITE OF ADMINISTRATION BUILDING IS JUST PAST NURSERY BLDG

Photo: Stephen T. Anderson Collection
The Albany Nurseries shop is seen to the right of the home.

Nurseries days, including a beloved Persian walnut, whose branches now gracefully skim the ground to the south of Building 1.

At the end of September 1945, Albany director Rogers traveled to Washington, D.C. The topic of discussion during his one-week stay most likely had to do with the postwar operation of his laboratory. Upon returning, Rogers mentioned to the press that new projects were discussed and there were plans for remodeling more buildings on campus. Interestingly, on the very same day, there was an article about potential peacetime uses for atomic power.

"Speaker Says Atomic Power May Be Harnessed for Industrial Use Soon," the headline read. The speaker was physicist Dr. Eric Peterson, a new hire at the Albany laboratory, who presented to a local Rotary group. In a fascinating case of foreshadowing, the article went on to say that the development of peacetime atomic power may be "a long time in the making," but the forces unleashed by scientists could quite possibly be used for "industrial and other economic use."

While Drs. Kroll, Schlechten, and Yerkes continued to quietly work on continually refining the zirconium process and coming closer to perfection with every run, the Albany laboratory ran into yet another bout of heated opposition. In spring 1946 a Washington State senator urged a house appropriations committee to consider moving the Albany laboratory closer to mining activities near Spokane, Washington. In a case of political déjà vu, politicians lobbed a barrage of accusations at the Albany laboratory, spurred by the recent rearrangement which closed the Spokane site and awarded Albany the position of regional office. "I can find no excuse for the regional office being located so far from the mining areas," lamented Senator Hugh B. Mitchell (D).

"Senator Mitchell, who never misses a chance to take a shot at the Albany laboratory, has repeatedly charged that progress toward placing the plant in operation has been unnecessarily delayed," quipped a mid-March editorial in the *Albany Democrat-Herald*. In a show of high regard for the laboratory and its employees, U.S. Bureau of Mines Assistant Director Dean fought back.

"This laboratory was built during the war and like everything else it was confronted with difficulties in the obtaining of materials and equipment as well as personnel. The difficulties, however, have been overcome and the Albany laboratory is now not only the largest but one of the finest in the United States. We feel that we have done a good job."

Assistant Director Dean continued to summarize the laboratory's ongoing work, including pioneering the process for producing zirconium on a commercial scale. "While this metal was discussed only in terms of grams and ounces a few years ago, about a ton of it has been produced at the local laboratory," he explained.

The first technical paper authored by Drs. Kroll, Schlechten, and Yerkes was published in April 1946 in the wake of Senator Mitchell's relentless campaign against the Albany laboratory and its thirty-plus employees. The paper, titled *Ductile Zirconium from Zircon Sands*, outlined the work that had begun as soon as Kroll had arrived back in Albany with zircon sands from Coos County. Schlechten presented the collaborative work in a national meeting of the Electrochemical Society in Birmingham, Alabama.

Photo: Stephen T. Anderson Collection

Dr. William Kroll with an early zirconium research furnace in the west side basement of Building 1. Photo circa 1947.

The initial success of the malleable zirconium project sent a ripple across the state. Naturally, Coos Bay had high hopes that this brand-new metal could replace the chromium industry that had shriveled before the war had even ended. Zircon sand was still being sourced from the Oregon coast for Albany's projects and a surplus of suitable buildings were empty and waiting for a new industry to boost the coastal town's sagging economy. "There is more than a possibility that it [zirconium] will be a household word in Coos County in the years to come," stated one article that explained Albany's zirconium process in surprising detail, "We have the assurance of the Albany scientists the method is practical and could be done in Coos County."

The statewide buzz about zirconium continued into May, when Dr. Twenhofel, the University of Wisconsin geologist whose 1943 field study pinpointed zircon sand locations across Oregon, once again published a bulletin regarding the "origin, composition, and economics of black sand" from the Columbia River all the way down to Coos Bay. Talk of a possible new zirconium pilot plant in Albany further fueled hopes that coastal communities would benefit from the new metal.

While discussions of a new industry were being bounced around, the location of Albany's laboratory was still being challenged in the political arena. Miners across eastern Washington, Idaho, and Montana were pleading for Bureau headquarters to be restored closer to actual mining operations. Secretary of the Interior Julius A. Krug maintained that "headquarters is just as effective in Albany as it would be in Spokane, Moscow, or Helena," much to the chagrin of miners. By August Krug had changed his tune and began urging the creation of another new laboratory, comparable to

Albany's in size and function, somewhere else in the Pacific Northwest.

Throughout 1946 the Bureau of Mines' Albany laboratory was continually in the public spotlight across Oregon—either for zirconium progress or regarding the squabbling over its location. During the year Drs. Kroll, Schlechten, and Rogers spent a considerable amount of time speaking at service clubs and to the press. Throughout all this coverage, a subtle change was happening. The government facility was becoming less commonly referred to as the Northwest Electro-development Laboratory and more as just "the Bureau laboratory" or "the U.S. Bureau of Mines at Albany."

With the changing of fall leaves came waves of adjustment for the Bureau laboratory. In early September, Dr. Dean resigned from his role as assistant director of the U.S. Bureau of Mines to become an independent consultant and metallurgical engineer in Washington, D.C. A local editorial speculated that the ongoing conflict about the Bureau of Mines' Albany location and pressure from Washington State may have "made life rather unpleasant for him." Press releases across the country avoided any such speculation regarding his resignation but instead touted Dr. Dean's impressive history with the Bureau, highlighting how "under [his] direction, the Bureau's laboratory facilities were expanded from a few minor installations . . . into a group of the finest metallurgical laboratories and pilot plants."

The loss was felt acutely in Albany, where Dean had worked overtime to secure Kroll's consulting position and had personally visited the lab several times. "Dr. Dean maintained an intimate knowledge of all that went on within his various laboratories. He could enter the Albany laboratory and call most of the scientists and their assistants by their first names and know exactly what experiments and processes they were working on," recalled the local paper.

More change was happening in Albany, as well: Schlechten took his leave of Albany for a lucrative position as a Professor of Metallurgical Engineering at the Missouri School of Mines. Another blow came when Rogers requested a leave of absence from the Bureau in November. The reason he gave was that he was aiming to finish a book on physical metallurgy that he'd been working on for years; one must wonder if the strain of continual political discord played a role in his departure.

It was always evident that Director Rogers had cared deeply for the laboratory and its employees. From constantly lobbying for more housing to defending the site's existence over and over, it was clear that through the challenges Rogers and his fairly small staff had become a tight-knit group. In an elegant gesture of appreciation, Rogers hosted a dinner party for his entire staff at The Hub restaurant in Albany. "Places were marked for 42, with seating arrangement according to the date each entered on duty at the Albany station," noted an article on the event. "After the program, in which each person took part, Dr. Rogers expressed his appreciation for the whole-hearted cooperation of the entire staff in developing and maintaining the Northwest Electro-development Laboratory." In turn, his employees presented him with a wristwatch. It was a fitting end to a year full of adversity and achievement, which seemed to confirm that the little laboratory in Albany was outpacing everyone's expectations.

With the sudden absence of a few key employees, the U.S. Bureau of Mines laboratory in Albany found itself in a period of growth and transition. The man to replace Dr. Rogers was 43-year-old Stephen Matheson Shelton, a native of South Carolina who had just the right combination of education, experience, and leadership ability to prosper the fledgling laboratory.

In his youth, Shelton attended the Citadel in Charleston from 1919–1926, then attended Yale University to study metallurgy. After receiving a Bachelors of Science in Metallurgy, he attended George Washington University, where he earned a Masters of Science in Chemistry while attending night school. During the day, Shelton began his work in government service at the U.S. Bureau of Standards, then transferred to the Reno, Nevada Bureau of Mines station in 1935. He moved to stations in Missouri, Maryland, and Washington D.C. His career with the Bureau of Mines was briefly interrupted by his military service, where he spent time doing aerial photography with the United States Army Air Force in the European theater, and he earned a Bronze Star for bravery under fire.

After World War II came to an end, Shelton returned to the Bureau and conducted metallurgical investigations in South America and Mexico, eventually traveling the globe as a consultant to the Philippines Bureau of Mines. In 1947, Shelton was officially named the director of the metallurgical division in Albany. He moved to the West Coast with wife and children in tow.

Photo: *Bureau Bugle*
New director of the Northwest Electro-development Laboratory Stephen Matheson Shelton had the right combination of knowledge and experience to lead the fledgling laboratory into a new era of zirconium production.

Photo: Stephen M. Shelton family collection
Stephen Matheson Shelton

The position in Albany was a perfect fit for Shelton: he had experience heading up several Bureau stations including the Mississippi Valley station in Missouri, as well as the entire eastern division of the Bureau in College Park, Maryland. Not only did he have leadership experience, but Stephen Shelton possessed several curious similarities to Dr. Kroll. Shelton had also achieved early metallurgical successes; by the time he was thirty-three, he already had a patent submitted in his name for developing a process of electrolytic extraction of metallic manganese. One purpose of this process was to obtain high-purity manganese of a quality that hadn't been previously achieved—just as with Kroll and his zirconium.

In January 1946 Kroll traveled back to Coos Bay to address the Chamber of Commerce at the stately Chandler Hotel. There he discussed the possibility of a local industry stemming from his work with zirconium, though he was very careful not to make any promises. Kroll mentioned that there were plans for a scale-up in zirconium production to as much as 40 lb. batches, but he and his team were encountering daily setbacks as they adjusted to larger runs.

In the second published paper from the laboratory, Kroll described refinements to the initial zirconium process. Improvements included using a reduction furnace (with a few adjustments) as the vessel for zirconium chloride purification, instead of performing the step in a separate furnace. That refinement alone reduced the Brinell hardness of final zirconium ingots from 197 BHN (Brinell hardness number) in the earlier tests down to a stunning 156 BHN. A lower BHN number meant a more malleable metal, which equaled a better overall product.

A subtle public relations shift happened in 1947 as the Northwest Electro-development Laboratory began to have a more noticeable presence in Albany. Tours of the facilities began and among the first groups to see the campus were farmers' unions, the Albany Junior Chamber of Commerce, and the University of Oregon chemistry department. Kroll also took a more public role with speaking engagements; he gave a lecture at the University of Oregon (forty-six miles away in Eugene, Oregon) on the topic of alkali metals.

Social connections, within the laboratory and after hours, began to develop. The payroll had swelled to about fifty employees, and the tightly knit crew that had been assembled under Dr. Rogers's keen leadership began to form their own groups. The Wives' Social Club began and later in the year, the Bureau of Mines Wives' Bridge Club began to meet at the home of mining director Lorain; those were the first of many social groups that would have their origins at the laboratory.

A new face that graced the 1947 employee roster was 31-year-old Eleanor Abshire—friends and family called her Ellie—a slim, dark-haired transplant from North Bend, Nebraska. As a child, adventurous Eleanor "grew up on a farm in Nebraska, and she spent most of her youth riding horses, hunting, and fishing. Housework and cooking never appealed to her," recalled niece Molly Perry. As a teen Eleanor worked as a reporter for her high school newspaper, which was printed weekly in the *Ocala Evening Star*. While attending college she began writing for the *Colfax County Call* in 1937, where she covered news specific to her hometown. She also studied business administration at Midland College for three years.

After working for the newspaper, Eleanor began "practice teaching" at a local school and earned her initial elementary certificate in May 1939. The next school year, she was hired in District 66 for her second year of teaching. After students happily fled the school house in June, Eleanor and a few other female friends started taking group trips to the West Coast, with California being the main destination—but future trips included jaunts up to Oregon. For the first time, the twenty-something Eleanor got a glimpse of what the Pacific Northwest had to offer: breathtakingly wild forests, rolling golden fields of ryegrass and wheat, and more prime fishing spots than one could imagine. Oregon pulled at Eleanor's heart and at the same time, she realized that elementary teaching didn't. After a year of teaching in a one-room schoolhouse Eleanor vowed it was time for a change.

Upon returning to Nebraska after one of these trips, young Eleanor pleaded with her parents to consider moving to Oregon. In the early 1940s the Abshire family put their family farm on the market. Eleanor purchased a home for her parents on the corner of 9th Avenue and Broadway Street in Albany, well within walking distance of the future Bureau laboratory. Eleanor and her family would be neighbors to Mart Farlee (the Bureau's electrician) and his family.

The Abshire's move to Albany happened just as Camp Adair was being established close to Corvallis. Like many young women at that time, Eleanor sought out a job at the cantonment and was hired as a medical secretary. Luck would have it that there were plenty of fishing opportunities just in that area and Eleanor wouldn't leave home without a fishing pole in her trunk.

Photo: Stephen T. Anderson Collection
Head librarian Eleanor Abshire found herself in the Bureau's center of knowledge.

Photo: Stephen T. Anderson Collection
"A regional library maintained at the Albany station contains about 1,300 books and 10,000 pamphlets and reports, as well as a wide variety of scientific periodicals. A complete file of all published information on zirconium is being assembled. In addition, a classified section is provided for restricted documents relating to A.E.C. contracts and activities within the region." –from Bureau of Mines Field Operations Region II 1953 handbook

When the war ended and Camp Adair was disassembled, Eleanor was hired at the Bureau as the site's librarian. When the slim brunette arrived to work on June 19, 1946, she ascended the grand front staircase in Building 1, then turned left down the main floor hallway where a nicely sized room with ample windows graced the southern end of the building. Sunlight gleamed off the speckled tile floors as she surveyed the room: library shelves and a desk waited for Eleanor, but not much else other than a few years' worth of technical papers, metallurgical tomes, and journal articles, all waiting to be arranged into a useful order. There was an increasing need for a technical library that could be referenced by Bureau employees, but also any member of the public who needed to view material on a certain subject.

With Eleanor Abshire's arrival at the Bureau, some order would finally be bestowed on the knowledge that had already been gained, as well as the knowledge that would be learned in the future. Eleanor Abshire and the Bureau's library would soon become the center of knowledge for the site, and Eleanor would go on to author two books, the *Bibliography of Zirconium* and the *Bibliography of Hafnium*.[2]

In the summer of 1947, Drs. Kroll and Yerkes were outgrowing the cramped basement of Building 2, and they needed bigger equipment to produce larger runs of zirconium. A budget for a zirconium pilot plant was proposed. They estimated a need for $140,000; in June that budget was granted with an excess $4,000—the equivalent of $1.6 million dollars in 2020.

Days after the pilot plant budget was approved, Kroll took a leave of absence and returned to his native Luxembourg. He needed to assess the state of his former home and laboratory, which had been carefully but quickly packed away before Kroll had fled to the States. In his absence, Travis Anderson, a former supervising engineer from the Rolla, Missouri Bureau laboratory, was named Kroll's temporary replacement. Luckily, Kroll returned to find his home and laboratory almost untouched.

Just as Kroll was leaving for Europe it was announced that the first shipment of Florida sand had arrived in Albany for the zirconium project. Zircon concentrate was still being used from Coos and Curry counties, but it's likely that Kroll and his associates had long been searching for sands with an even higher zircon percentage to start with. But if the Florida sand was found to be superior to what they'd been using, it would effectively quell any hopes for zirconium processing facilities in Coos Bay.

Considering everything that had happened up to this point, it was particularly interesting that the Bureau had known to hone in on a little-known metal with few practical applications. The assistant director of the Bureau himself had found and hired a metallurgist—Dr. Kroll—whom the government believed could make quick work of creating a commercially-viable process of production. A laboratory had been established (despite raging controversy) in a location close to the concentrated sand product needed to create metallic zirconium. And plentiful funding for the coming year—to a tune of $4 million dollars in 2020 dollars—guaranteed that the Albany laboratory's work would continue into 1948.

But once larger quantities of pure zirconium were produced, who would need tons of the dull, gray stuff? And why did there seem to be such a driving force behind the development of zirconium, which was even more obscure than its sister metal, titanium?

CHAPTER SEVEN

THE GHOST IN THE MACHINE
1947–1948

"The type of research engaged in by the [Albany] Bureau of Mines is entirely creative in character and is aimed at bolstering the productive capacity not only of this area but of the nation."

—Walter Underwood, Albany Chamber of Commerce manager, October 1, 1947

The activities of the U.S. Navy in the early 1940s were running a curious parallel course to operations at the Bureau of Mines in Albany and in 1947 those courses would collide to create an orchestrated effort to produce not one, but two materials that were critical to an entirely new engineering masterpiece.

Whether by design or grand coincidence, government discussions regarding the possibility of nuclear-powered submarines had been going on since before a single atomic bomb had ever been developed. Those theoretical reactors that would propel the first true submarines would need structural materials that could withstand an unimaginably demanding environment, such as the engineering world had never encountered before.

In 1938—the same year that Kroll first traveled to the United States to tout the wonders of titanium—German scientists Otto Hahn and Fritz Strassmann had succeeded in doing the (previously assumed) impossible: breaking apart the nucleus of an atom by bombarding it with neutrons. "So much energy had been released that a previously undiscovered kind of process was at work," noted a history of the Manhattan Project by the U.S. Department of Energy.

The experiments by Hahn and Strassmann had caught the imagination of physicist Ross Gunn at the Naval Research Laboratory in Washington, D.C. While others in the Navy were considering all the ways this newfound energy could be made into a weapon, Gunn was formulating ways that nuclear power could be used to propel the world's first true submarine.

At the time, submarines were diesel-powered vessels that could travel quickly on the surface but could dive only for limited amounts of time because of their reliance on batteries for underwater propulsion. Once underwater, submarines were sluggish and inefficient. Special care had to be taken to conserve as much battery power as possible by monitoring the speed and distance traveled at depth. Once depleted, the batteries could take up to six hours to charge using the diesel motors—at the very least, an unfortunate inconvenience during wartime. Gunn hypothesized that all of those limitations could be eliminated if submarines could be designed with nuclear propulsion. A submarine propelled by atomic power would be the world's first true submarine in the sense that it would really only need to surface for infrequent maintenance and for the needs of its human crew.

The idea of a nuclear-powered submarine was bounced around for several years but gained little traction, but the concept never fully went away, mostly because of the persistence of those at the Naval Research Laboratory (NRL). In November 1944, just as operations were starting up at the Bureau of Mines in Albany, a committee met at the NRL and nuclear propulsion was discussed, and the final report from the meeting suggested postwar development of naval nuclear propulsion.

In August 1945, right before the Japanese surrender, a Navy study group proposed that the next decade would be the proper time to pursue "revolutionary developments" in propulsion. Recommendations across the board were made for all naval vessels, but it was suggested that submarines would need the most revamping because of their severe limitations.

After the devastation of Hiroshima and Nagasaki, the reality of atomic power couldn't be hidden from the public. More decisive conversations were had within the Navy about the possibility of nuclear submarines. "One of the most obvious potential uses of this new form of energy was for ship propulsion, a fact which the Navy could now proclaim in public," noted a Department of Energy history of the Nuclear Navy. Ironically, now that nuclear propulsion was a legitimate consideration for the Navy, the massive demobilization that occurred after the end of the war made *any* new shipbuilding a hard sell. The Bureau of Ships canceled the construction of almost 10,000 ocean-going vessels, resulting in almost a billion dollars in reductions. Some wondered if atomic bombs had rendered any seagoing vessel obsolete. If the Navy wanted to pursue the development of a nuclear submarine, they would have a monumental task ahead—not only technologically, but convincing everyone else that it was a worthwhile cause.

The Office of Research and Inventions was established in May 1945 in order to help increase the Navy's research and development capabilities, acknowledging the importance of scientific discovery to aid military technology. This new office was now responsible for the Naval Research Laboratory. In-depth discussions continued for months about the feasibility of nuclear submarine propulsion, proposed timelines, and basic logistical questions dealing with information sharing and security concerns.

In spring 1946, just a month before Kroll and his associates had published their first paper on zirconium, a cooperative effort was suggested to create an "experimental power reactor" that wouldn't be specifically for the Navy's use, but that could benefit multiple parties. "By making this a cooperative effort involving the Manhattan Project laboratories, American industry, and the armed forces, each group would soon have the basic technology needed for specific applications," noted an Atomic Energy Commission's report on the Nuclear Navy.

The Navy suggested that a comprehensive study on nuclear propulsion should begin immediately. It also proposed that a group of officers be assigned to Oak Ridge National Laboratory in Oak Ridge, Tennessee, where the experimental reactor project would take place. Possible candidates were thoroughly reviewed and discussed. A handful of extremely talented and qualified men were also suggested to lead the group of trainees, and at the top of the list was Captain Hyman G. Rickover.

At forty-six years old, Captain Rickover was qualified to command a submarine and had been promoted to an "Engineering Duty Only" officer. EDO officers were usually specialists in a particular field, and Rickover had excelled in his position as head of electrical engineering at the Bureau of Ships in Washington. What set Captain Rickover apart from others—and what made him particularly suited for the Oak Ridge job—was his tenacity and thorough, relentless pursuit of absolute perfection.

Rickover distinguished himself as head of the electrical section through distinctively different tactics that produced results. "He had assembled in his section a group of the best officers and civilian engineers he

Photo: Wikimedia Commons
Captain Hyman G. Rickover was known to be petulant, demanding, and always aiming for absolute perfection—which turned out to be a winning combination during the creation of the world's first nuclear submarine.

could find," wrote Hewlett and Duncan in *Nuclear Navy*. "He personally sifted through battle reports and inspected every battle-damaged ship he could reach to see for himself how electrical equipment performed under combat conditions. Working with his staff, he decided what changes in equipment were required. Then through close supervision of contractors he saw to it that the equipment was produced on time and, more important, to the required specifications."

Rickover's tireless work paid off handsomely: he exposed severe limitations and weaknesses in the fleet's electrical systems and made critical redesigns across many different systems. However, for all his accomplishments, there was a catch: as much as Rickover was known for his successes, he was also known for his unapologetically direct approach and petulant mannerisms. "He could speak with devastating frankness," wrote one author, who noted he had an "almost obsessive view of his responsibilities." *TIME* magazine later quipped, "His passage leaves a boiling wake of lacerated egos…"

Rickover's personality was so abrasive that even though he was a near-perfect technical fit to head the group of trainees at Oak Ridge, the Navy decided that the trainees wouldn't report directly to him. Instead, Rickover was assigned as a deputy to the director of operations from the Manhattan Project, Colonel Walter J. Williams.

While Rickover initially lacked technical knowledge about nuclear sciences, he wholeheartedly believed in the Navy's mission to utilize atomic power for submarines. "Our purpose was to see how nuclear energy could be used to propel ships," Rickover recalled about his first year at Oak Ridge. "It was obvious that a nuclear-powered submarine could revolutionize naval warfare."

His trademark enthusiasm made up for any deficiencies and before long he subtly began asserting his direction for a more organized, efficient group of Navy trainees. In true Rickover fashion, he dedicated every molecule of his time to internalizing what he and others would need to know to create a nuclear reactor—and he insisted others in his group do the same.

By the end of 1946 Rickover asserted that building a nuclear reactor for an oceangoing vessel was still five to eight years away because of several significant hurdles, the first being safety. A nuclear-powered submarine had to be safe for its operators. Having a reactor on board meant that certain amounts of radiation would be present, and only proper shielding would protect those aboard a vessel. Brand-new methods would need to be devised to create a safe operating environment.

Other "severe" requirements for a submarine's reactor were outlined by Rickover: "It had to be compact so that it would fit into a submarine hull. It had to operate when the ship was rolling or pitching, or at an angle when it was diving or surfacing. It had to be safe and reliable. It had to be rugged to meet military demands. Finally, it would have to be operated by young sailors—men who were not scientists or engineers, but who would be carefully trained."

He predicted another need that might hamper development: obtaining proper materials. "Metals that would withstand high temperatures were available, but to meet reactor specifications they would have to have a low attraction for neutrons and be capable of resisting prolonged and intense neutron bombardment," noted *Nuclear Navy*.

One metal that fit the bill for extreme temperatures was titanium. In 1938, the Salt Lake City Bureau of Mines station launched an investigation into titanium by performing a small-scale test to look into every known way to make the metal. The work at the station confirmed that Kroll's method was best suited for making large quantities; in 1942 commercial production methods were tested, which eventually resulted in 15-pound batches of titanium. Later, prompted by wartime needs, work was transferred to the Bureau of Mines station in Boulder City, Nevada. The very metal that Kroll had unsuccessfully touted to private industry not once but three times hadn't escaped the notice of the Bureau of Mines in Nevada.

By 1947, the Boulder City station had four years of experience and experimentation with Kroll's method (patented in 1940) for reducing titanium. Their extractive plant could hypothetically turn out 100 pounds of titanium a day, but O. C. Ralston, assistant chief of the Bureau's metallurgical division, felt that commercial production would likely be as far as five years away. At this time, Ralston also "began what was to become an increasingly regular process of soliciting funds from the military and the Atomic Energy Commission (AEC) to continue work," noted a historical evaluation of the laboratory.

Even so, there was evidence that the Navy was beginning to search for metals that would perform well in extreme environments. In the spring of 1947, Ralston penned a letter to the Navy and the Bureau of Aeronautics regarding their "fundamental alloy studies." In the letter Ralston assured the Navy that the Bureau was the largest producer of malleable titanium and zirconium in the United States and would continue to "give the Armed Forces top priority on all shipments . . . [We] will assure you of a continued supply of all Bureau metal products."

In that same correspondence, Ralston mentioned that the Bureau was already supplying all the Navy "cooperators," including the Naval Research Laboratory—without financial compensation. Although the project under consideration was regarding materials testing and production for a jet aircraft, much detail was given on the Bureau's extensive knowledge of both titanium and zirconium, with Dr. Kroll being the foremost authority on the latter.

While all those involved in the classified submarine propulsion project continued to navigate the unfamiliar waters of creating a nuclear reactor in 1947, projects at the Bureau in Albany were given unprecedented public exposure that year. The laboratory staff had grown to about eighty employees, and more were on the way as locals answered job postings that had been pinned to local bulletin boards.

Work being performed at the Northwest Electrodevelopment Laboratory was prominently touted in the steadily growing midvalley town. Real estate agency Tripp & Tripp even created a window display featuring seven areas of study. Of course, the zirconium project headed by Kroll, Schlechten, and Yerkes was shown, along with the project inherited from Ford Motor Company (carbothermic reduction of magnesium), as well as the production of steel and ferroalloys, production of vitreous silica (a chemically stable refractory glass), electrometallurgy, high phosphorus iron ore treatment, and the mineral dressing unit. Each display had illustrations and flowsheets that explained the processes, plus mineral specimens.

Tours on campus continued into 1947. In August, U.S. Senator Wayne Morse visited the campus and was guided by Henry L. Gilbert, a chemical engineer that

Photo: family of Henry L. Gilbert
A young Henry L. Gilbert on his horse, Buck, possibly in the west hills around Corvallis, where he grew up.

Photo: family of Henry L. Gilbert
Family photo of Henry Gilbert with wife Georgia and children Betty and William.

127

had been hired by the Bureau in Albany a year before. Gilbert—who looked like he could've starred alongside Clint Walker or Roy Rogers on the silver screen—almost seemed out of place alongside the furnaces and other metallurgical equipment.

With parents who loved the outdoors, Gilbert spent his younger years fishing and exploring the Metolius River near Sisters, Oregon. In high school he spent time riding his horse while dressed in full western garb. His experience on horseback came in handy while working summers at the Southworth Ranch in Central Oregon in his college years. Simply put, "he was a cowboy with a degree in Chemical Engineering," recalls son William Gilbert.

Like Kroll, Henry Gilbert had strong family ties to his chosen profession. He'd graduated from Oregon State College in Corvallis, just as his father before him. His family was so prominent that the chemical engineering building had been named in honor of Henry's father, chemistry department chairman E. C. Gilbert.

During the tour, Henry Gilbert and Kroll's temporary replacement, Travis Anderson, demonstrated some parts of the zirconium reduction process for Senator Morse. It was reported that the politician was favorably impressed with the immense progress the Bureau had accomplished in the two years since his last visit to Albany.

Senator Morse was also shown several demonstrations that dealt specifically with Oregon ores; one project in particular was a Bureau project that was trying to produce charcoal from Coos County coal—another connection with the small coastal town that had provided the concentrated raw materials for the first zirconium experiments. Local coastal papers buzzed with continued anticipation that industry might be increased to the area, and interestingly, a singular mention of a new element that may have had some readers scratching their head at the unfamiliar word: *hafnium*.

On September 16, 1947, a shockingly detailed editorial in *The World Newspaper* touted a "Hint of a New Super-Metal," which was also derived from Oregon beach sands. Aside from those quite familiar with the periodic table, it's likely few people drew many conclusions from the article, but with curious transparency the article went on to mention that the "next step in the zirconium process . . . would be to separate the new metal hafnium from its association with zirconium in order to make possible another industry based on a new super-metal."

Hafnium—a silvery-gray metal just like zirconium— had only been discovered in 1923, just twenty-four years prior. It was such an elusive and difficult element to study that it was the second-to-last element (with a stable nuclei) to be added to the periodic table. Hafnium shared so many similarities with zirconium that they were described as the most similar elements on the entire periodic chart.

That hafnium's existence—not to mention its partnership with zirconium—was described to the press seems rather incredible because of what was concurrently happening with the Navy's research on the other side of the country. Engineers and scientists had been earnestly seeking ideal materials to use inside nuclear reactors. Cladding—the metal surrounding the cylindrical fuel rods inside a reactor—was an early, specific focus. Stainless steel, beryllium, aluminum, and zirconium were all frontrunners in the search for suitable cladding materials; aluminum had been used in early experimental reactors (then called "piles") but had proved unsuitable for newer, high-temperature designs like what would be needed in a submarine.

What Rickover, the scientists, and the engineers were all searching for in regards to a naval nuclear reactor was nothing short of a miracle metal; Rickover needed a metal which would "withstand corrosion at high temperatures for long periods of time, which would maintain its integrity in an environment of intense radiation, and which would not absorb neutrons needed for the nuclear reaction," the admiral later recalled. "Furthermore, if the Navy was to have a fleet of nuclear ships, the metal had to be one which could be produced in quantity and at reasonable cost."

All the metals that were being investigated had drawbacks and zirconium had several significant black marks against it: its cost was still prohibitive (around $270 a pound then; about $3,200 in 2020 dollars) as it had never been produced in great quantities. Dr. Kroll and his associates had managed to turn out 25 pounds of zirconium in March 1947 and were later able to scale it up to 75 pounds.

Worst of all for zirconium, scientists who had been running tests at Oak Ridge found that zirconium had a nasty habit of absorbing neutrons, thereby slowing a nuclear reaction—exactly the opposite of what Rickover needed for cladding.

But since zirconium could resist corrosion in water at high temperatures, scientists began focusing on *why* zirconium had such an affinity for neutrons. Perhaps if that could be ironed out—and if commercial quantities could be made cheaply— the dull gray element that the Bureau of Mines in Albany was working to refine might just work.

In late 1947, scientists at the Massachusetts Institute of Technology (MIT) and at Oak Ridge turned their focus to the small quantities of hafnium that occur in zirconium (up to 5%, although zircon from Oregon beach sands usually has a much lower percentage of hafnium, usually between .4% and 1%.

Professor A. R. Kaufmann of MIT came to determine that the trace amount of hafnium (he determined 2% in his studies) in zirconium was "just enough to ruin it," director Stephen Shelton recalled later. "He reached the conclusion that if you could separate the hafnium from the zirconium you would have a very good material."

At about the same time in late 1947, Oak Ridge physicist Herbert Pomerance also focused on zirconium's undesirable behavior by devising something called a "pile oscillator" that could move test materials in and out of a reactor to measure the thermal cross section of elements. Pomerance was also able to confirm that hafnium was indeed the ingredient that was spoiling zirconium's chance at becoming a legitimate frontrunner for cladding material.

With this, the scientists made a stunning discovery: for all their shared similarities, it turned out that hafnium and zirconium had one major dissimilarity that would define their uses from here on out. Zirconium was virtually transparent to neutrons, allowing them to pass through, while hafnium had the exact opposite effect of absorbing neutrons. Incredibly, scientists had two potentially formidable materials that now needed to be evaluated for use in nuclear applications.

Naturally, the next step would be to separate the two deeply entwined elements, but given the incredible similarities between the two it would be easier said than done. At that time "there was no known way of separating this hafnium and zirconium," Shelton noted later. A Report of Investigation issued by the Bureau elegantly surmised of hafnium and zirconium, "so intimate is the association of these two sister elements and so similar are their chemical properties that only complex chemical or metallurgical treatment can break the bond between them."

The Atomic Energy Commission wasted no time in assigning this difficult problem to one of the rising stars in the science world. Chemist Glenn T. Seaborg, who had recently codiscovered the element plutonium with Edwin McMillan, was more than qualified to work on the zirconium-hafnium problem. Seaborg was fresh off his last assignment of heading up the plutonium work for the Manhattan Project from 1942–1946 while at the University of Chicago's Metallurgical Laboratory and "was responsible for determining how to extract and isolate plutonium from uranium. His work was developed into industrial processes for producing plutonium at Hanford, WA," notes one biography.

In experiments most likely in late 1947 or early 1948 at the University of California Radiation Laboratory (UCRL) in Berkeley, Seaborg coauthored a classified document describing one plausible method of drawing hafnium out of zirconium. Although the test sample was very small, the authors were quite confident that it would work on a larger scale, illustrating the "applicability of the method to produce significant amounts of pure hafnium and zirconium." The sensitivity surrounding this paper—and other nuclear work performed under the umbrella of the AEC—was highly classified at the time; Seaborg's paper on hafnium-zirconium separation wasn't released to the public until 1979. That's why the mention of hafnium's separation in *The World Newspaper* was so peculiar, given the circumstances.

Secret or not, once hafnium was ferreted out as the culprit to zirconium's neutron-absorption problem, it became a frontrunner of all the materials considered for a submarine reactor. In December 1947 a nuclear engineer at Oak Ridge National Laboratory suggested using zirconium to Rickover. Sam Untermyer brought up the silvery metal to Rickover and sold him on the properties that would make it an excellent candidate for the hellish environment it would need to endure: it would stay strong when subjected to intense heat and it seemed to have good corrosion resistance.

"Why haven't we heard about this before?" asked Rickover.

"We always though it was a neutron absorber," replied Untermyer. "But recently Herb Pomerance, in the physics group here, discovered that zirconium almost always contains about 2 percent hafnium, another element that is very hard to separate from zirconium. Pomerance has now obtained some zirconium without much hafnium in it and discovered that pure zirconium should be practically transparent to neutrons."

Rickover was stunned at how well zirconium seemed to check all the boxes. "At once I decided to choose zirconium for the naval reactor," Rickover later wrote.

Like everything having to do with creating a naval reactor from scratch, there would be monumental hurdles ahead, particularly in producing pure, hafnium-free zirconium in significant amounts—*and* at an affordable price. "At the time of the decision," Rickover noted, "there was no assured source of zirconium, no estimate of how much would be needed, no certainty that any known of conceivable process could produce the required amount, and no specifications for the nuclear, mechanical, or corrosion qualities the metal had to possess." And despite the immensely quick work separating the conjoined elements, Rickover added one more possible complication: "It was also possible that removing the hafnium could destroy the other qualities that had made zirconium worth investigating in the first place."

Despite the uncertainties that still swirled around the use of zirconium, a direction was definitively chosen. "So at that time I would say that the zirconium industry was a gleam in Captain Rickover's eye," Albany Bureau director Stephen Shelton later remembered, "but we started in."

———•◀▶•———

As 1948 rolled around, Oregon was experiencing a postwar period of unparalleled growth. It was the number-one fastest growing state in the nation—having experienced a staggering population gain of 49%—and housing shortages were severe. Even before 1948, the housing situation in Albany had been difficult; with such a boom in population, finding a home could be a daunting task.

The partially rural area to the north of the Bureau of Mines campus was morphing away from two-story barns and orchard trees and into proper streets of tiny, tidy cottage-style homes with neat postage-stamp front yards. People were clamoring for more housing, and proximity to the Bureau of Mines was a top selling point.

A larger parcel of farmland to the south of the Bureau was sold and the Fir Oaks Charter of 1948 paved the way for a new luxury subdivision. The charter stipulated that each lot was to be a minimum of a half acre and sell for a price no less than $12,000. At that time, the average home price in Oregon was around $8,500, making the Fir Oaks homes a rather exclusive and very expensive area to buy a home, which might be one reason the neighborhood was soon nicknamed "mortgage row." To relieve already-crowded schools, three additional elementary schools were also proposed, including one directly across from the Bureau.

As Albany was expanding, so was the scope of the laboratory. The two divisions of the Albany station—metallurgy, headed up by Shelton, and the minerals division, led by Lorain—were acquiring new capabilities at a rapid-fire pace. The metallurgical staff had grown to about 70 employees, which included 24 professional chemists and metallurgists. Also included in the staff were clerks, machinists, groundskeepers, construction workers, and others.

It is possible that it was around this time that a small fleet of beach cruiser-style bicycles were purchased for employees to use while at work. Neighbors to the site grew accustomed to seeing white-coated laboratory technicians and coverall-clad craftsmen pedaling from one side of the campus to the other. It wasn't unusual to see groups of bikes clustered under eaves at the entrances to each building during working hours; staff would be allowed to claim a beach cruiser and ride it for the duration of their employment.

New to the minerals division in 1948 was petrographer Harold Hess, who was hired at the Albany station to analyze geologic samples for uranium content. Domestic uranium was actively being sought by the government because of recent events: with the success of nuclear weapons, there was a high demand for the silvery, lightly radioactive metal. At the time nearly all of the world's supply of ore came from Canada or the Belgian Congo. As soon as uranium was classified as a strategic material at the beginning of World War II, it was carefully controlled in the United States, even to the point where the well-known ceramics company Fiesta Ware was forced to stop using uranium to add vibrancy to their orange glazes after the government confiscated their stock. The AEC hoped that a good domestic source for uranium could be found—and prospectors hoped they'd strike it rich by finding that source.

The U.S. Atomic Energy Commission was so keen on finding domestic ore that a $10,000 "bonus" ($108,000 in 2020 dollars) was publicly offered to any prospector who could produce twenty tons of ore from a new mine. The bounty excited a buzz among prospectors in Oregon, and it was thought that an even wider swath of potential miners might join the search if more information was available on radioactive ores. Although the AEC was able to distribute informative pamphlets to ore seekers, it would be about a year before the AEC and USGS would publish a book on the subject.

For the Oregonian looking to prove whether he or she had struck it rich with their potential uranium sample, there were only a few options to verify their find. A news article in the *Medford Mail Tribune* suggested a few home tests, one of which was placing the sample next to undeveloped film for several hours. If the ore specimen was radioactive it would impart its own image on the film. To conclusively prove that an ore sample was what the AEC was actively seeking, one could now take or send it for analysis to the minerals division at either the Bureau of Mines in Albany or Boulder City, Nevada.

Uranium wasn't the only radioactive substance on campus in Albany in 1948. Thorium, a more abundant naturally occurring radioactive material (NORM), was also reportedly worked with in some capacity. In some respects the earliest work done with thorium is one of the enduring mysteries of the Albany

Bureau. The Department of Energy states that beginning in 1948 thorium was machined and alloyed on site, but the details of that work seem to be either lost to history or still locked away as still-classified Atomic Energy Commission documents.

In 1948 high-priority national concerns continued to be intimately interwoven with the Bureau's purposes. "President Truman cautioned Congress today that 'much remains to be done' to develop low grade ores as a dependable source of strategic metals until new high-grade deposits are discovered and asked [to] increase appropriations for work on strategic metals," noted a paper from the state's capital. In that vein, an overall increase of $1.5 million in funds ($15 million in 2020 dollars) were requested for projects focusing on experimental mining and metallurgical research on strategic metals.

O. C. Ralston, assistant chief of the Bureau's metallurgical division, took the opportunity and continued to tout the achievements of the Bureau on a national scale, to the military and beyond, in hopes of receiving additional funding. Information about the Bureau's work with both titanium and zirconium had been presented to the Bureau of Ships, and although funds wouldn't immediately be available from that department, the Navy encouraged further materials development for future naval applications.

In December 1947 zirconium was suggested to Captain Rickover as a metal to consider. Just five days into January 1948, Albany director Shelton sent a memo to O. C. Ralston alerting him that A. R. Kaufmann—the Massachusetts Institute of Technology (MIT) scientist who had recently discovered that hafnium was the element that effectively ruined zirconium for nuclear use—was requesting a visit to the Albany laboratory. Kaufmann had also hinted that he wanted to bring along a member of the Atomic Energy Commission. Shelton approved the trip and about a month later, the *Albany Democrat-Herald* reported that an "A. R. Kaufman, J. E. Glen, and Frank J. Graceio"—all of New York—were guests at the Hotel Albany.

Despite the discrepancy in the spelling of the last names, this was A. R. Kaufmann from M.I.T, along with two employees (Frank J. Giaccio's last name was also misspelled in the press) of the Atomic Energy Commission's New York procurement office. "With normal sources of supply unavailable, the procurement of zirconium was complicated and time consuming," explained Lawton Geiger of the AEC. "It was originally the responsibility of the AEC's Division of Production, which delegated it to the AEC's New York Operations Office . . . which sought suppliers for the combined requirements." Mr. Kaufman and the two AEC officers were likely visiting to scope out Albany's ability to produce larger quantities of zirconium.

While proposed budget increases were being approved, there were issues with supply availability. On March 16, the press reported that the Bureau of Federal Supply, a division of strategic and critical materials, had been withholding a stockpile of chrome concentrate (the leftover zircon sand from chromium production used by Dr. Kroll and associates to produce malleable zirconium) at a plant in Coos County. The Albany Bureau needed this material more than ever to continue commercial zirconium production studies, which had become increasingly important since Rickover's declaration for zirconium for the nuclear navy project.

By the March 30, the Coos Bay Chamber of Commerce had received word from Representative Harris Ellsworth that an agreement had somehow been reached between the Bureau of Supply and the federal

Bureau of Mines. Fifty tons of the wartime-era stockpile was released to the Albany laboratory for continued zirconium work.

Coos County had been vying for the Bureau's business since the beginning—at the very least, to deplete zircon sand leftovers from the defunct chromium industry, or in a best-case scenario, to convert the abandoned chromium facilities into zirconium processing plants. However, it may have been at this time that other sources of zirconium were being seriously explored by the Albany bureau, if not to secure supply, perhaps to find a concentrate with an even higher percentage of zirconium content.

Just as in the early days of the Northwest Electro-development Laboratory, Representative Ellsworth continued to offer significant support to Albany and beyond. Oregon's explosive population boom meant more power was needed across the state, particularly for the Willamette Valley and southward to Coos Bay. He suggested more than three million dollars would be needed to create new power lines to serve the most in-need area of the state. Along with this increase, Ellsworth urged additional budget increases for the Bureau laboratory in Albany for several ongoing projects: "to permit development of a pilot plant for the smelting of phosphorus for the recovery of vanadium; complete construction of a pilot plant to determine the best commercial method for producing zirconium; continue study of vacuum metallurgy; work on electrolytic extraction of magnesium and construct an electrochemical laboratory building."

Ellsworth's support wasn't in vain. What started as a small lab struggling to stand on its own was now a player in two top-priority projects of national importance. The minerals department had seemingly taken a backseat to metallurgy since the early days of the laboratory, but was now participating in the nation's hunt for domestic uranium. And the metallurgy department, with zirconium on the radar from the very beginning, was now coming into its own. The end to which Kroll and his associates had been striving—producing commercial amounts of the dull gray metal—was paired with a high-demand need at the exact right time: the creation of the world's first nuclear submarine.

The ghost in the machine had been silently and delicately weaving together the timeline of the nuclear Navy's submarine project and the Bureau's zirconium production up to then. But would zirconium be the "Cinderella metal" everyone hoped it would be, and would Rickover's gamble for choosing the metal prove to be a wise choice?

Even though Dr. Kroll and his peers had a promising start on developing zirconium for commercial purposes, they weren't the only ones who knew how to produce the silvery-gray metal. When Rickover made the decision to use zirconium for nuclear propulsion, there were two main ways of producing it in malleable form.

At the Albany laboratory, Kroll's method (known as the Kroll process) used magnesium as a reducing agent to produce airy, sponge-like pieces of metal that would be melted again to make solid ingots. Although Kroll was making great strides toward the commercial product for general use, the zirconium crafted in Albany wasn't greatly corrosion resistant for use in the extreme conditions found within a nuclear reactor. "It is ironic to reflect that, of . . . titanium, zirconium, and hafnium, only zirconium shows this exaggerated sensitivity to hot water corrosion resistance with respect to purity and structure," author Benjamin Lustman would later recall.

Long before Kroll's work, the de Boer process was used to produce malleable zirconium. Developed in the 1920s, the de Boer (or van Arkel, or crystal bar) process used a hot tungsten filament to "grow" metallic zirconium. The resulting raw product was much different than the dull sponge produced at the Bureau. Zirconium produced by the de Boer process created thin rods of shiny, silvery-gray crystalline metal whose facets reflected gleaming light.

Although the de Boer process was slow, expensive, and only created small amounts of malleable zirconium, its one advantage was that it had unmatched purity. Even so, the resulting metal was sometimes fickle and inconsistent. In 1948 the only commercial producer of de Boer-process zirconium was the Foote Mineral Company in Philadelphia and the cost topped out at $235 per pound, with only about eighty-six pounds being produced that year.

Captain Rickover wasn't the only one investigating zirconium and its uses. In a paper declassified in 2002, Ohio State University's cryogenic laboratory prepared a thorough investigation of zirconium for Air Materiel Command at Wright-Patterson Air Force Base. The document was prepared for anyone working with zirconium, titanium, hafnium, or thorium, because "no general review of zirconium and its compounds has appeared."

"The use of Zr in industry, up to the present time, has been on a rather small scale," the report began. "Efforts are now being made by the U.S. Bureau of Mines ... [unreadable] ... cheaper methods of production, and so far they appear to be fairly [unreadable]. Should the cost of zirconium decrease sufficiently, its use as a [corrosion?] resistant metal may become important." Clearly, the Air Force was also

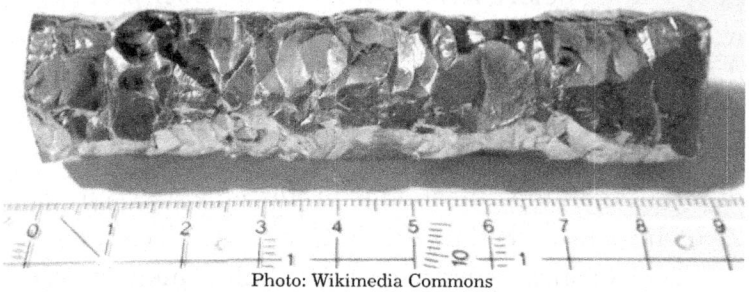

Photo: Wikimedia Commons
A sample of zirconium created by the crystal bar (or de Boer/van Arkel) method.

Photo: Stephen T. Anderson Collection
The first model of a zirconium vacuum arc furnace at the Albany Bureau. Circa 1948.

interested in the same characteristics that had endeared zirconium to Rickover.

Faced with two possible methods of creating zirconium, Rickover had a decision to make. Would the ultrapure, but wildly expensive, lustrous de Boer zirconium fit the bill, or could Kroll's humble sponge be tweaked enough to perform perfectly within harsh environments?

Ultimately, the decision wasn't made during 1948, though work on zirconium in Albany was about to get a massive boost, and the Atomic Energy Commission most definitely had a hand in the changes that were about to occur. "We are soon to be favored with AEC money and a job for them that we want to fill with the best possible metal," O. C. Ralston wrote to Shelton that spring. "Therefore, quick action is necessary in order that we avoid building the wrong kind of melting furnace on a larger scale."

In a paper published that year by the senior Dr. Kroll, silver screen lookalike Henry Gilbert, Travis Anderson, Leland Yerkes, and H. P. Holmes, the group describes scaling up from a mere sixty pounds to a whopping 300 pounds of zirconium a day. This dramatic increase was due in part to better equipment, including a purification unit that could hold nearly 200 pounds of raw zirconium chloride and a new graphite resistor vacuum furnace that could hold ten pounds of zirconium at a time.

While the equipment in the first miniature zirconium pilot plant may have gotten an upgrade, their location hadn't changed, although it had expanded. What began as a small operation confined to the basement of Building 2—the former Albany College women's dormitory—was now a much larger affair. During the college years, the entire four stories of the northern side of the brick building was expanded to include a sleeping porch for the residents. When Kroll and his associates needed more room, they used all four stories on the former sleeping porch to create a pilot plant that could produce much larger amounts of zirconium.

To truly satisfy the requirement for commercial production standards, something much larger would need to be built—something in the way of a standalone building dedicated only to zirconium production. Up until then, only a few new structures had been built at the Northwest Electro-development Laboratory. A few small buildings from the former Camp Adair found new life at the laboratory, as the Army cantonment had been shuttered two years prior and buildings were shipped across the state and repurposed.

But all of that changed during the spring of 1948. As the horse chestnut trees along the west of campus were blooming in shades of pink and white, ground was being broken on the first significant new building to be constructed on campus since the college days. Building 26, or the Zirconium Pilot Plant, was about thirty percent finished by mid-March and there were high hopes for a speedy completion. Despite the Atomic Energy Commission's keen interest in the metal, construction on the new pilot plant was hampered by a less-than-robust budget. "If we receive the requested appropriation for the coming fiscal year we would be able to complete the pilot plant during that time," Regional Director Shelton wrote to O. C. Ralston, "If A.E.C. is in a hurry for zirconium (and apparently they are), we could rush completion of our pilot plant and possibly have it in production within six months."

A tight budget didn't deter the spirit of those at the Albany laboratory, however. With a true "can-do" attitude that was prevalent at the Bureau, employees of all kinds rolled up their sleeves and got to work—even the scientists, who were generally professionally dressed in a dress shirt and tie. "The building was constructed by station personnel," recalled one employee, "scientific types, wheeling and pouring cement, etc."

In July, the AEC placed an order for 50 pounds of zirconium. As the Building 26 Zirconium Pilot Plant wasn't even close to being finished, Kroll's enlarged zirconium plant in Building 2 produced the metal, which was to be sent straightaway to Battelle Memorial Institute. Battelle was—and still is— a private, nonprofit science and technology laboratory located in Columbus, Ohio. Battelle was involved in a significant number of government contracts and this wouldn't be their only involvement with the nuclear Navy for this project. The day after the zirconium order was placed, the Bureau of Ships shelled out $50,000 to help cover the cost of improving "high temperature strength properties of zirconium."

It wasn't all work and no play for the employees of the Bureau of Mines during the summer of 1948, however. On the evening of Friday, June 18, after a perfectly-pleasant 73-degree day, Bureau employees and their families gathered on the laboratory grounds for one of the first recreational events: an outdoor picnic.

Children wearing summer frocks had the run of the Bureau grounds: soft grasses that were still green from late spring rains were perfect for running along barefoot and the enormous variety of trees made it a perfect place to play tag. One particular tree that grew next to Building 1 was considered a favorite among neighborhood kids and employee children alike because of its enormous, sprawling low branches that were perfect for climbing on—and if you were daring enough—for bouncing on. The Persian walnut had "branches so wide you could walk out on them for miles, it seemed to a little kid," recalled one Bureau family member, Monika Niebuhr-Sims. "When we were kids . . . those branches weren't touching the ground, but low enough to jump on," she recalled.

While evening light filtered through the lush canopy of the walnut tree, alive with children crawling through its branches, the adults below gathered around buffet-style tables. The adults in attendance brought along a sandwich and another dish to be shared. After everyone had piled their plates with food, ice cream and drinks were provided by the Bureau's recreation association. With ice cream cones still in their hands, children gathered to compete in a variety of contests, and prizes were handed out to the winners. Men gathered to play softball or a round of horseshoes and women from the Bureau's bridge and pinochle clubs chatted on the lawn.

After the sun dipped below the western sky, an azure night sky brought temperatures dipping into the mid-50s. Ladies pulled on shawls over their cotton summer dresses. Neighborhood kids mingled with employee's kids to organize a game of hide-and-seek as darkness fell. Meanwhile, next to Building 2 and across from the construction of the new zirconium pilot plant, adults gathered for the night's final activity: dancing on the tennis courts left by Albany College.

The courts were illuminated just enough by the last blush of dusk and whatever extra lighting could be found. Strands of music from the likes of Doris Day and Buddy Clark, Nat King Cole and Dinah Shore wove across the tennis courts and along the park-like campus. Ladies in full, mid-calf skirts and matching jackets danced with men in dress shirts and trousers. Just like the dance that night, things at the Northwest

Electro-development Laboratory were now in full swing.

Just days after employees were dancing on the tennis courts that radiant June night, an article was published in the *Wall Street Journal* regarding Albany's zirconium production efforts. With this, the little Albany laboratory was thrust into the national spotlight.

"A metal of princely price is being reduced to commoner status—to benefit industry, medical science and national defense," wrote correspondent Vernon S. White. "Its rarity has put a price tag of around $250 a pound on zirconium up to now . . . if zirconium demand should rise to 10,000 tons a year, production cost might be pushed down to $5 a pound." The article revealed that the Bureau had produced 1,500 pounds of zirconium in the past year—the most malleable zirconium that had ever been produced.

A plethora of possibilities were touted for the novel metal: better, tarnish-free silverware for the modern housewife, medical-grade zirconium for implants, and use as a liner in harsh chemical environments were all listed as current or future uses. The correspondent followed with a very thorough and informative history of zirconium processes, including a very precise description of Kroll's process of reducing zirconium.

"None of the Albany-produced metal has been sold," White concluded. "It has been furnished in various amounts to firms experimenting with its uses. These include General Electric, Westinghouse, Union Carbide, Foote Minerals, the U.S. Naval research lab at Anacostia, Md., and one French and one Dutch surgical equipment supply firm." Interestingly, the article also revealed that in addition to the AEC's interest, the Air Force was looking at zirconium for use in jet engines.

The local newspaper in Albany reprinted the article a week after its original appearance in the San Francisco edition of the *Wall Street Journal*, and with it likely came the first hints that government-sponsored projects were in the works at the Albany laboratory. From this article, Coos County residents realized that projects at the Bureau were forging ahead with "undiminished vigor," and that the government contracts might cause the long-hoped-for zirconium industry to boost the coast's economy. "We may be on the verge of a new industry, one about which a few people have dreamed for many years," noted *The World Newspaper*.

However, it was now known that there were other locations with better black sand; sand that had higher zircon concentrations than what was available in Coos County. Locations abroad including Australia and Brazil, plus domestic sources in Texas and Florida, offered zircon sands with potentially better ratios. Because possible ore competitors had been disclosed, the editorial suggested a "heads-up" attitude for interested Coos County residents so they wouldn't lose out on a potential zirconium industry boom.

As July rolled around, construction on the Zirconium Pilot Plant was continuing at a steady, though still under funded, rate. It was anticipated that part of the budget for 1949 would be needed to finish the work, with final construction complete sometime in the first half of that year. The brick building with enormous roof-high windows rose two stories above ground, measuring 30 by 60 feet. "The final window pane had been installed on July 22, the roof interior had been painted, and the main beams of the mezzanine were in place as well as some of the major pieces of equipment," recalled a report on the laboratory. "The small chlorination building behind the plant was operational, and the carbiding furnace in Building 23 was working." Although much progress had been made, there was still much to be done. Concrete floor still needed pouring, and—most concerning of all—the design of the furnaces needed to be finalized. Kroll and his team were working continuously to find the best possible solutions.

Coinciding with this stage of construction was an upgrade to the existing Bonneville Salem–Albany transmission line No. 2, which would "reinforce the overloaded circuit furnishing Colombia river power to . . . the Bureau of Mines at Albany," among other customers.

The pilot plant wasn't the only project receiving upgrades; on a less pressing note, the old Albany College tennis courts that had just hosted the Bureau's first dance were due for an upgrade. While the Willamette Valley weather was at its finest, volunteers from the Bureau worked to set up nets and backstops not only so that their own tennis teams could practice, but also that members of the public could enjoy additional courts. Previously, only two other public tennis courts had been available, one at Eleanor Park and the other at Henderson Park. After effort from Mark Wright and the Bureau "tennis division," there were now an additional two courts open to Albany residents.

It was a cool and cloudy early fall afternoon when newly appointed national U.S. Bureau of Mines director Dr.

James Boyd touched down at the Corvallis airport on a Tuesday in September. Boyd was visiting the Albany laboratory as part of a West Coast tour that included stops between San Francisco and Juneau, Alaska. The middle-aged man had formerly been the dean of faculty at the Colorado School of Mines. That day Boyd was met at the airport by Shelton, who drove him to Albany.

Shelton and Boyd had much to discuss as they walked the grounds of the Northwest Elctro-development Laboratory. Boyd surely visited the mineral dressing department and chemical analysis labs. The pair probably spent a good amount of time inspecting and discussing the ongoing construction on the Zirconium Pilot Plant.

While zirconium production was always a key project from the late 1940s on, it's important to understand that there were many other less-publicized projects that were occurring at the laboratory at any given time. "The zirconium project . . . has sometimes tended to overshadow the other important phases of work being carried out at the Albany station," the local media correctly asserted. On his tour, Boyd would have heard about the electrolytic zinc project, work with high phosphorus Columbia County ore, and the beginnings of ductile chromium work at the Albany site.

A topic at the forefront of Shelton's mind was the ongoing search for a reliable, high-quality zircon concentrate. With a brand-new Zirconium Pilot Plant—the likes of which had never been built before—the Bureau in Albany was going to need a mind-boggling amount of concentrate. In October, Oregon State College and the state Department of Geology and Mineral Industry once again initiated a study on Oregon's black sands.

A report on Oregon's black sands hadn't been penned since University of Wisconson researcher Dr.

Twenhofel began sampling black sands up and down Oregon's coast, beginning in 1938 and finishing in 1943. On October 7, 1948, Shelton attended a meeting at the Tioga Hotel in Coos Bay. In attendance were Congressman Ellsworth, Dr. F. W. Libby, director of the state Department of Geology and Mineral Industries (DOGAMI), state representative Ralph T. Moore, and several Oregon State College department heads, as well as interested locals. During the meeting it was agreed that after data had been collected it would be compiled into an informational booklet to be published by the college. The end result of the project would be publication of a comprehensive collection of all available information regarding Oregon's black sands.

Interestingly, it was noted during the meeting that a chunk of necessary information was mysteriously missing, "undoubtedly lost forever," noted one article. Records from the Krome Corporation—one major provider of zircon concentrate—were gone. Efforts were being made to recover the data, but meeting attendees offered little hope they'd be found. Although local powers were focusing on possibly resurrecting Coos County's chrome production, updated information about Oregon's black sands would benefit future projects at the Northwest Electro-development Laboratory.

By the fall of 1948, the Albany Bureau was steadily gaining employees. Robert L. Govro was one of those new hires. Fresh out of the Navy, twenty-year old Govro was mailing a letter at the Albany post office one October afternoon when he noticed a job posting for the Albany Bureau of Mines tacked to a bulletin board. "I walked over and looked at the bulletin board and . . . I took one of those sheets and filled it out and sent it in. They called me in for an interview," Govro recalled. He

Photo: Robert L. Govro
Robert Govro and his sweetheart Beverly, right around the time Robert was hired at the Bureau.

was quickly hired and was assigned a position in the chemistry lab. Though he received an entry-level paycheck, the job meant the world to the young man—and his high school sweetheart, Beverly.

"On the second day I was hired," Govro said, "I called Bev, who was down in Eureka [California] and said, 'Bev, we can get married! I got a job!'" Govro was part of a wave of new employees at the laboratory; around the time he was hired there were about seventy people on campus.

Radiant fall leaves scattered across the lush green lawn at the Albany campus. A blustery wind heralded the changing season. A single request dated September 17, 1948, may have had a hand in steering vital events at the Albany Bureau. On that day director Shelton received a memo from O. C. Ralston that read:

> Would you kindly prepare for demonstration purposes cylinders of zirconium and nickel, respectively, 1-7/16" dia. and 1-1/2" high. Kindly send the specimens to this office for transmittal to Capt. H. G. Rickover, Bureau of Ships.

This one request was the catalyst for a significant contract awarded the Albany Bureau by the Bureau of Ships in March of the following year, which had a hand in catapulting the local laboratory into Rickover's nuclear propulsion project. Just a few weeks later, Ralston contacted Shelton again asking him to hurry up with the order. One can almost sense Rickover breathing down Ralston's neck, demanding to know where his zirconium samples were:

EXPEDITE PREPARATION OF DEMONSTRATION CYLINDERS (1-7/16" DIA. AND 1-1/2" HIGH) OF ZIRCONIUM AND NICKEL AS REQUESTED IN MY MEMORANDUM OF SEPTEMBER 17. SEND SPECIMENS TO THIS OFFICE FOR TRANSMITTAL TO BUREAU OF SHIPS.

According to a history of the site, the specimens had slightly different measurements than requested but were shipped out nonetheless on November 26.

As 1948 drew to a close and people across the nation were preparing to celebrate Christmas, readers of the December issue of *Popular Science* were given a tease of another new metal, newly available in commercial quantities: titanium. Immediately following an in-depth article about how the year's new mechanical toys worked was a full-page article titled "New Strong, Light Metal Is Extracted."

"How to extract titanium from its ore was the long-puzzling problem that the U.S. Bureau of Mines recently solved by treating compounds in a furnace with molten magnesium," the magazine explained. Of course, it was Dr. Kroll's initial work on titanium that influenced work at the Boulder City Bureau of Mines station, finally resulting in commercial production at a duPont plant in Newport, Delaware. The plant was able to churn out 100 pounds of titanium per day. "Titanium's strength and lightness promise to make it rival aluminum and magnesium as a material for airplane wings, pontoons, and cables . . . when manufacturers awaken to its possibilities, mass production may follow," wrote the article.

Two miracle metals were on the cusp of changing the face of science and technology, and both were a result of Dr. William Kroll and his associates at Albany's Bureau of Mines. What once had been a little laboratory that clamored to find enough employees was now a place one could read about by picking up a national newspaper or magazine . . . and the best was yet to come.

CHAPTER EIGHT
RADIO SILENCE and OPERATION ZIRCONIUM
January 1949–December 1949

"Even though it was impossible at that time to determine with any certainty the amount of zirconium needed for the nuclear submarine project, there was little doubt that the figure would be substantial."
—Lawton Geiger, Atomic Energy Commission

"Science is eyeing zirconium these days with the realization that the new wonder metal, produced in big quantities only at Albany, is almost certain to play a major role in the U.S.'s fast-moving scientific development."
—Charles De Ganahl, Albany Democrat-Herald

Even before the Albany Bureau of Mines began operating in earnest, the local press had been abuzz with information regarding its establishment, operations, and politics thereof. Despite the proprietary nature of the work that occurred on campus, there seemed to be a free exchange of information with the public regarding the laboratory's achievements. The Northwest Electro-development Laboratory was very much the talk of the town and a pivotal point of interest for Albany, which had doubled in size since 1940 to a robust population of about 10,000 people by 1950. The laboratory itself had grown to over eighty employees.

But come January 1949, all of the almost-weekly blurbs about the laboratory ceased. There were no mentions of employee picnics, the ladies' card club meetings, or even Kroll's progress with zirconium, which previously had been thoroughly covered many times over on the local and national scene. News about the laboratory went nearly silent for the duration of 1949.

It's likely that only a select few employees at the Albany Bureau knew the true extent of the Atomic Energy Commission's interest in zirconium during the last half of 1948 and into 1949, and if there wasn't already a culture of proprietary secrecy about work carried out at the Albany Bureau, it would certainly begin soon. Information about projects would be on a need-to-know basis, and those employees working on sensitive projects would have to refrain from speaking about their work.

In this post–World War II culture, secrecy about government work wasn't viewed as fodder for conspiracy but instead was considered an employee's patriotic duty. It was very common for a Bureau worker of the "Atoms for Peace" era to never speak of the work they did—not to coworkers, not to friends, and especially not to family. Even within the walls of the laboratory, a worker would usually know only enough about what he or she was working on to be able to complete the job without ever knowing the end result. Knowledge about AEC or military-sponsored projects went to the grave with many an employee. The exception to this rule was when a project would be publicly announced by the press, but even then, an employee might only be able to confirm that they were part of the project, and specifics were forbidden.

Though a sullen hush had fallen over Albany's laboratory, the town's residents who took the daily paper may have come across something intriguing on a chilly, wind-whipped day in February. "Big Atom Plant to Test Devices" the first-page header read. "A multimillion-dollar atomic plant was in the works, and one of the first projects on the docket was "an engine to propel ships with power extracted from splitting atoms." The plant was planned for an unnamed western state, to be announced sometime within the next few months as a facet of a larger, $3.5 billion dollar ($38 billion in 2020 dollars) atomic project that would focus on four "revolutionary" reactors. "One of them will be a land-based prototype of an atomic engine theoretically capable of driving a warship 'tens of thousands of miles' without recharging," noted the article. The same facility would also manufacture a breeder reactor and an atomic aircraft engine.

Back in Albany, the first post-war public open house was held during early spring with the promise that attendees could view the lab in full operation. "A Century of Conservation" was the theme for the whole-day event, to celebrate the accomplishments of the Bureau of Mines. As trees across the laboratory grounds were bursting forth with bright green foliage and blossoms, hundreds of people (between 600 and 1200 by some reports) strolled along perfectly manicured paths.

Beside the original five-and-a-half buildings, (Administration in Building 1, Kroll's office and small zirconium pilot plant in Building 2, the machine shop, the Operations Building in the former Hauser Gymnasium, the old boiler building and the sunken basement building) only a few additional shacks, garages, and storage sheds had been constructed, plus an electrolytic tin plant on the southernmost end of campus.

The most noticeable activity across the whole site was the construction of the new Zirconium Pilot Plant, and it's likely many a visitor gazed at the half-completed brick building with two-story high windows. Another attraction was Kroll's smaller pilot plant in Building 2, which was actively churning out ten-pound blocks of zirconium that day. Visitors "saw the complete operation [from] processing of the zirconium sands to the final job of rolling the finished sheets," recalled one news blurb.

Children flocked to the basement of Building 1 where the petrographic laboratory was located. Hundreds of rock samples were on display for all to see, and one favorite demonstration was how a Geiger counter worked. A lab-coat-clad geologist would wave the counter's wand past a sample of uranium, and gasps of surprise would ripple through the crowd of kids and parents as crackling clicks would erupt from the detector. Another stop on the tour included an area where experiments with ductile chromium was being worked on. Yet another laboratory had a demonstration of how the Albany bureau was using material from Montana to devise cheaper methods to produce zinc.

Since the Albany Bureau's beginnings, researchers needed parts and equipment that literally didn't exist anywhere else in the world. Photos from that era show metal placards affixed to house-made equipment that read, "Designed & built by U.S. Bureau of Mines, Albany, Oregon," with the date proudly displayed on the bottom.

The custom equipment was crafted in the humble machine shop left over from World War II days and on that spring day, visitors entered its wide rolling warehouse doors to see a wood-floored room bathed in sunlight. Lathes and other machining tools were mounted in rows at a diagonal slant. Skilled craftsman, clothed in overalls and hats, worked at each station and the high, curved ceiling allowed the sounds from the machinery to dissipate. The workmen were busy creating some of the custom equipment necessary for the Zirconium Pilot Plant; after all, there wasn't anything like it in the world.

Photo: Stephen T. Anderson Collection
Custom equipment was constructed on site by skilled craftsmen.

Enlargement of the placard on the above equipment: "Designed & Built by U.S. Bureau of Mines, Albany, Oregon Dec. 19??"

That day, visitors learned that while the laboratory had sourced fifty tons of black sand concentrate from Coos Bay, a shipment from Brazil had also been received, signaling that a better grade of zircon sand was being sought out; possibly with better nuclear qualities.

It was also revealed that day that the Atomic Energy Commission had funded thirty percent of the work done at the laboratory that year, and to date $100,000 had been spent on such work at the Albany Bureau. But no hints were given to the nature of that work, though recently declassified documents reveal that other AEC offices were collaborating with Albany's Bureau on other nuclear-related projects.

In May 1949, as part of the nuclear submarine effort, the Y-12 plant of Carbide and Carbon Chemicals Corporation at Oak Ridge, Tennessee began work on a tricky but vital aspect of the nuclear propulsion project. From data that had been collected at MIT, Oak Ridge, and the University of California Radiation Laboratory, the scientists at Y-12 began researching the best way to separate hafnium and zirconium on a large scale. Eventually the facility would begin producing hafnium-free zirconium oxide feed material that would be sent to Albany to create the initial zirconium sponge.

In the fall of 1949, representatives from the Hanford AEC office traveled to Albany to confer with Dr. Kroll, Director Shelton, and E. T. Hayes regarding the possibility of a titanium-boron alloy for control rods within a reactor. Control rods were tubes that were lowered or raised within a reactor to moderate the reaction; lower the rods and a reaction would slow, pull them up and a reaction would increase. The Albany men weren't able to directly assist the visitors from Hanford office, as none of them had worked on titanium-boron alloys, though Kroll and his associates knew that the Battelle Laboratory had a contract to study titanium alloys and their characteristics. Further, though Hanford requested the Albany Bureau to be involved in their investigation, their involvement was deferred to the College Park, Maryland station, where all the Bureau's titanium studies were now being conducted.

As the Zirconium Pilot Plant was nearing completion, Dr. Kroll and "cowboy chemist" Henry Gilbert had been rigorously testing different methods of working with zirconium to ensure the absolute best possible commercial production adaptation. In a paper titled *Melting and Casting Zirconium Metal,* Kroll and Gilbert used not one but three different types of furnaces (a high-frequency furnace, an arc furnace, and a split-tube graphite-resistor furnace) for melting.

"The melting and casting of zirconium and titanium present many difficulties owing to their high melting point and chemical activity," the authors stated. "These two factors restrict the means of heating, the furnace atmosphere, and especially the crucible and mold materials." Although the paper was almost exclusively about zirconium, the authors included titanium because of its similarity.

Kroll and Gilbert stressed that every single detail made a world of difference when it came to melting zirconium. Crucible materials were dependent on what type of furnace they would be used in, unless it

Photo: *Bureau Bugle*

"I have wanted to be only one thing, and that is a good metallurgist," said Chief of the Physical Metallurgy Branch E. T. Hayes in 1953. In high school, Hayes worked as a miner in Idaho. His employment with the Bureau of Mines began in 1938 at College Park, Maryland. He then moved to the Salt Lake City station where he was an assistant metallurgist. He was transferred to Albany in March of 1948.

Photo: Stephen T. Anderson Collection

Henry L. Gilbert with an arc furnace.

was an arc furnace; in that case, the metal could be directly melted on a water-cooled copper block, though that would only produce a small cake of zirconium. When using a copper crucible, it had to be "intensively cooled" to prevent the zirconium from accidentally alloying with its crucible. Zirconia (zirconium dioxide) and alumina (aluminum oxide) crucibles were "rapidly attacked" by molten zirconium and titanium, but "the discovery made at the Albany Station of the U.S. Bureau of Mines two years ago that titanium, zirconium, thorium, and probably hafnium may be melted satisfactorily in gas-free graphite was of considerable importance, as it at once opened the road for melting large quantities of metal," wrote the metallurgists.

The two scientists had also confirmed that the best oxide they'd yet found for melting zirconium was "thoria," or thorium dioxide. It didn't noticeably harden zirconium or titanium (hardening was undesirable and would indicate a more brittle, and less malleable product) but unfortunately, it wouldn't likely be used for commercial production, as "it is rather expensive and now difficult to obtain," Kroll and Gilbert noted. In later years, a mysterious, unnamed oxide known only as the "Y-12" oxide would be used.

The paper went on to describe various tweaks to the melting process over time, and how furnaces had been modified by Kroll and others in different ways to achieve better results. A question remained about electrodes, however. Electrodes were rods of metal that electricity flowed through to create an arc of intense heat that in turn would melt the metal within. Kroll and Gilbert noted that the largest electrodes commercially available would only "permit fusion of ingots up to perhaps 6 inches in diameter." For large-scale production, an entirely different type of electrode would be needed. "tungsten electrodes may have to be bundled," they suggested, or perhaps a tantalum carbide electrode could be created.

In Albany, the split-tube carbon-resistor furnace had won its way as the preferred method of melting zirconium. "This very successful and cheap method of melting is used for all zirconium produced at the Albany, Oregon station . . . a three-phase model of this furnace has been found quite successful and offers several advantages," the paper noted. In a vacuum, this type of furnace could melt fifteen pounds of zirconium in twenty minutes with fifty-five kilowatts of power.

Kroll and Gilbert concluded that for commercial zirconium only a graphite crucible would suffice, but the type of furnace used would depend on what end result was desired. "Experiments indicate that all three types of furnaces [arc, high frequency, and split-tube graphite resistor] have distinct advantages and disadvantages," they agreed.

A separate declassified paper published a few years later by the Atomic Energy Commission revealed their interest in how the Bureau's melting techniques affected the quality of zirconium produced. The quantities produced by Kroll and associates were still small and the AEC proposed that the zirconium melted at Bettis Atomic Power Laboratory was the front runner product, though the zirconium made at the Bureau with the special "Y-12 oxide" needed more investigation. "Some of the early products were melted at the Bureau of Mines and also at M.I.T without encouraging corrosion results. It is believed that these failures resulted from the fact that the reduction operation was carried out on too small a scale and with improper control and that the impurity content of the product was therefore too high. A later sample of sponge which was produced on a larger scale by the

Bureau of Mines is presently being tested by the Bureau after melting in argon by the arc technique. Results to date make this sample appear very promising."

Another issue was how to crush large amounts of zirconium that needed to be fed into the furnaces or to be extruded. To date, the crushing had been performed by using hand tools, making for a tiresome job that simply wouldn't work for creating commercial quantities of zirconium. Mechanical means of crushing were soon investigated.

As all logistical factors—construction, equipment manufacturing, and zirconium production—were coming together in Albany, Rickover and his submarine team were forging ahead, though it had been a slow and disjointed process at first. But early on Rickover had insisted that instead of developing the reactor in a linear fashion, work would proceed with multiple aspects being worked on simultaneously. He saw it as the only way to achieve success in a reasonable time frame.

One critical question at this point was what type of reactor system to use: water-cooled, gas-cooled, or liquid-metal-cooled. Making this decision was a vital step, as whichever cooling system was chosen would determine nearly everything else about the reactor's design. "Until the coolant had been selected, everything else about the system was up in the air: radiation shielding, pumps, heat exchangers, even the pipes and valves," explained Theodore Rockwell, who had worked closely with Rickover. Argonne National Laboratory was fervently researching which system would be best suited within the confines of a submarine, but Rickover was already leaning toward one design in particular: the water-cooled system.

In 1949, the Atomic Energy Commission established the Bettis Atomic Power Laboratory specifically to meet the needs of Rickover's Naval Reactors Group, including possible zirconium production. "Even though it was impossible at that time to determine with any certainty the amount of zirconium needed for the nuclear submarine project, there was little doubt that the figure would be substantial," recalled Lawton Geiger, who had been hired as the manager of the Pittsburgh AEC office. In June of 1949, Rickover visited Bettis for the first time.

About a year earlier, in April 1948, Admiral E. W. Mills of the Bureau of Ships had broached the subject of underwater nuclear propulsion at a symposium attended by high-ranking officials, including those with the Atomic Energy Commission. Backed by Captain Rickover, Mills had bluntly stated the need for a dedicated submarine project. "If I may be so bold as to venture an opinion," Mills stated in his speech, "I would guess that less than one percent of the work which will ultimately be required to design a submarine plant has now been accomplished . . . I sincerely hope that in the very near future, the Atomic Energy Commission in accordance with the recommendations of the various committees and of the Research and Development Board, will establish the development of a nuclear power plant for a submarine as a formal project at high priority."

Mills' public plea did not go unnoticed; a month later he received a letter from the AEC with an "ambiguous promise" that the project would be formalized and carried out. Rickover scoffed at the vague language, but Mills wrote again to the AEC in response and proposed that to successfully engineer a nuclear submarine in a timely manner, efforts would need to be coordinated with industrial organizations and laboratories simultaneously.

By that time, the reactor design that seemed most promising was the pressurized water type. "The decision was a logical choice for the pressurized water propulsion reactor," recalled Rickover. "It was a risk, but all development is a risk. Once the decision was made we did everything we could to reduce the uncertainty . . . several organizations helped us by running tests and performing analyses . . . As research was going on to ascertain the engineering properties of zirconium, Dr. Kroll was continuing his work to improve the processes used to manufacture zirconium at a low cost," Rickover wrote.

Argonne National Laboratory and Westinghouse Corporation were tasked with designing a land-based prototype that "would be a full-scale prototype, constructed on dry land, to demonstrate the feasibility of the concept, to 'work out the bugs' before it went to sea, and to serve as a training facility," noted Norman Polmar in *Rickover: Controversy and Genius.*

But where could the Atomic Energy Commission safely test an experimental reactor? It would need to be a remote location, far from prying eyes and even more important, a good deal away from any people, lest something go terribly wrong. In the first months of 1949, about 70 sites were assessed by the AEC. By March, all but one of those areas had been eliminated. A stunningly remote and exceptionally well-suited desert was about to be quietly transformed into a mecca of nuclear science.

Little Arco, Idaho was nothing more than a single main street and a small collection of houses nestled into a low, rolling desert ridge. The nearby Lost River Range of the Rocky Mountains were still brilliant with snow, while desert blooms were just starting to unfurl closer to Arco. About 800 people lived in the town that was very much in the middle of nowhere. For miles before and miles after, the scrubby Idaho land known as the Lost River Desert stretched from horizon to horizon, with tiny Arco being nothing but a blip on the map.

For readers of *The Post-Register* newspaper, a newly announced Atomic Energy Commission installation was front page news in the spring of 1949, and a fervent buzz remained quite some time after the initial announcement. The atomic facility would be located partly on land already owned by the government; a portion of the flat, desolate landscape was already being used as the Naval Proving Grounds for ordinance testing. At the time it was expected that the AEC "reactor testing station" would eventually encompass four hundred thousand acres and was compared to Hanford's plutonium facilities in the state of Washington.

The *Times News* in Twin Falls, Idaho, covered events as they unfolded. As with the Albany laboratory, a political tug-of-war ensued between the two states who vied for the facility (Idaho and Montana), but keen-eyed readers would have also read that the

Photo: Author's Collection
The area outside of Arco, Idaho, was stunningly beautiful—and far away from prying eyes— in 1949.

Photo: Author's Collection
As this March 1949 newswire shows, little Arco, Idaho, was expecting to benefit from the planned "Atomic Plant."
Unfortunately for Arco, Idaho Falls was soon chosen instead to host AEC headquarters.

government's new facility would be, in part, working on "an atomic engine for naval ships."

Over the next few days, residents of Arco and Idaho Falls—a much larger town of about 19,000 people, about an hours' drive across the desert—started to read what the "atomic unit" might mean for the Lost River Desert. The *Post-Register* noted that most Arco residents were "thrilled" at the idea and the biggest protestation was from fishermen who were worried about overcrowding at their favorite fishing holes.

The atomic plant was initially estimated to have a $500,000,000 budget ($5.4 billion in 2020 dollars) with the possibility of 6,000 jobs. Nearby Blackfoot and Idaho Falls were also expected to benefit from the installation, though beyond a vast increase in traffic, population, and jobs, nobody truly knew what to expect. Arco's initial jubilation over the project's announcement was quickly replaced with disappointment when, in May 1949, Idaho Falls was chosen instead as the project's headquarters.

As late spring turned to early summer in Albany, the beehive of construction activity that had surrounded the commercial zirconium plant faded as the facility was finished. The two-story brick building, resplendent with floor-to-roof windows, began zirconium production on June 8, 1949. Kroll's small pilot plant in Building 2 was phased out and the new plant—Building 26—began producing 500 pounds of the silvery metal per week, driving costs from $200 per pound to a mere $18 per pound.

Sponge that had been produced in the pilot plant was taken, crucible and all, to the sponge

Photo: Stephen T. Anderson Collection
Building 26, the Zirconium Pilot Plant, can be seen with the "Chlorination Shack" behind it.

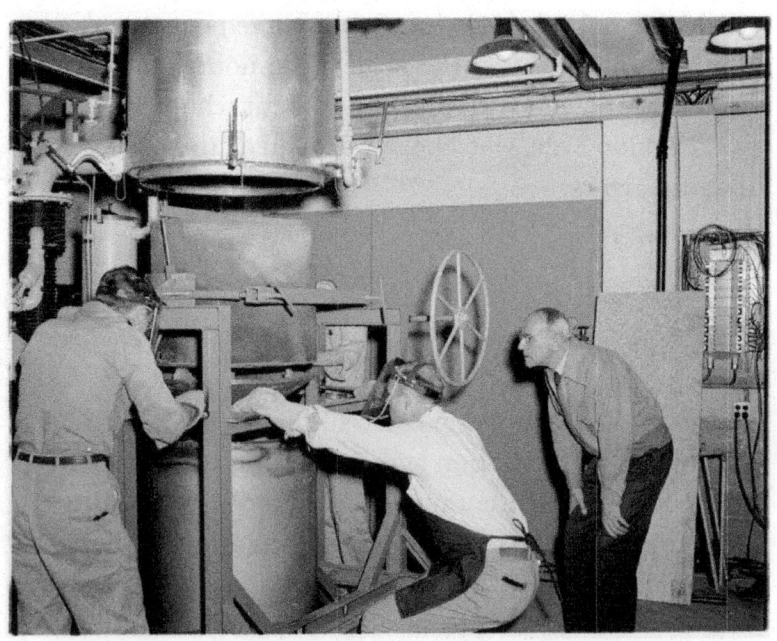

Photo: Stephen T. Anderson Collection
Dr. William Kroll looks on as workers adjust a furnace in Building 26, the Zirconium Pilot Plant.

handling department located in the basement of Building 2, where it was chiseled out of its pot and then cleaned and chipped into smaller sizes. Sometimes transporting the sponge was a difficult chore, particularly in inclement weather. "The winter of 1949 was a dinger," wrote melting chief Robert Beall, "we *sledded* the pots up through the snow."

All of the meticulous efforts of Kroll and his team were finally paying off; after spending several years analyzing variables in equipment, operating technique, time, and temperature, the process of producing large amounts of malleable zirconium had been achieved. The buildings and equipment at the Albany Bureau of Mines were now collectively valued at over one million dollars. About twenty staff were working full-time on "Operation Zirconium"—the catchy name given by the press to the project going on at the Bureau.

The nuclear submarine project initially had a faltering start, but because of Rickover's dogged persistence the project had gained intense momentum. On August 19, 1949, after recommendations were made at the Submarine Officers' Conference, a memorandum declared with daring confidence that a nuclear propulsion plant should "be ready for installation in a submarine by 1955." Russia's first nuclear test, just ten days later, underscored the need for haste. "Congressmen, surprised by and concerned over the first Soviet nuclear explosion . . . were receptive to Rickover's urging for a high-priority nuclear-submarine

Photo: Stephen T. Anderson Collection
Furnaces inside Building 26, the Zirconium Pilot Plant. Photo circa 1951.

Photo: Stephen T. Anderson Collection
1949 Northwest Electro-development Laboratory aerial photograph.

program," note Norman Polmar and Thomas Allen in *Rickover, Controversy and Genius*.

It is highly likely Captain Rickover made one of his first furtive Friday night flights to Albany in late summer 1949, just as the new pilot plant was churning out its first pounds of zirconium. Rickover himself recalled making "several hurried trips" to see the work being done at that facility to furnish zirconium for the first naval reactors.

"Usually Dr. Kroll, then a consultant to the Bureau of Mines, and several senior officials of the Bureau of Mines met me at the Portland Airport on Friday evenings. We would drive to Albany, inspect the equipment, and discuss the results of the production effort then underway. Dr. Kroll always gave me straightforward answers. He was a scientist. I am an engineer. Our common interest was zirconium. I think we both understood the problems the other faced."

Under the cover of darkness, the captain and the metallurgist walked along the thin road that headed south through campus. Heady summer nights in southwest Albany meant the ever-present sweet scent of dry grass, comfortable temperatures, and glittering stars, but it's unlikely that Kroll and Rickover would've noticed any of those things as they made their way to the two-story zirconium pilot plant.

"When Dr. Kroll and I met at Albany," Rickover later recalled, "we dealt with details. We had to. We understood each other because we based our discussion on principles—his were scientific, mine were engineering." As the two men conferred with each other that night on the next important steps in zirconium production, the clock was counting down. Could Rickover produce the world's first nuclear submarine in a mere five years?

Photo: Stephen T. Anderson Collection
The 1949 Bureau Christmas party. Note partygoers are using laboratory beakers to hold their drinks!

Photo: Stephen T. Anderson Collection
Revelers celebrate the end of a productive year at the laboratory. Here, physicist Robert Beall can be seen far left (in sweater and glasses) and librarian Eleanor Abshire is in the center of the photo (in a dark dress).

In March 1950, Bettis Atomic Power Laboratory put the first zirconium quantities onto paper: they figured 30,000 pounds of reactor-grade zirconium—that is, low hafnium or hafnium-free zirconium—would initially be needed for the Navy. In April, the Foote Mineral Company was contracted to produce 30,000 pounds of crystal bar by June 1951, but it turned out that the zirconium sponge produced by Foote was inconsistent and of poor quality and Bettis never received any of the contracted zirconium from Foote.

"We urgently needed zirconium for two reactors. The first was the Mark 1, the land-based prototype to be built in Idaho to demonstrate the feasibility of installing a compact pressurized water reactor in a submarine. The second was the Mark II," wrote Rickover, of the power plant for the actual submarine.

So the question of where to get the necessary quantities—and quality—of zirconium was still up in the air, even with the Albany Bureau's brand-new pilot plant churning out 500 pounds a week by 1950. Rickover recalled that Kroll's zirconium process was still being refined and not quite meeting the stringent standards needed for nuclear-grade material, though "the successful tests being done in Building 26 convinced the Navy that a larger plant with greater output would answer their needs," notes a history on Albany's Bureau.

Additionally, the question of quantity wasn't necessarily only about the two reactors being developed at the time, but an entire future fleet. An affordable, continuous source of reactor-grade zirconium was desperately needed. At this point there was a vehement disagreement between Rickover and the AEC regarding zirconium; Rickover had pressed the AEC to authorize Bettis to begin crystal bar production (which used Albany's sponge as a feed material). The AEC had initially refused and Rickover was livid.

"I had been assigned the job of developing a nuclear submarine," Rickover argued. "The schedule called for having the shop ready for operation by January 1955—less than five years away. Zirconium at this moment was crucial in the development of the reactor . . . the Commission was violating the principle that authority must match the responsibility."

Another visit was soon paid to the Albany Bureau by the U.S. Navy, although Rickover sent a team instead of appearing in person. Former Director Ray Wells recalled that the Navy group met with Albany department heads one afternoon regarding building a second zirconium pilot plant. Director Shelton was opposed to the addition, as he had been burned once before with a development plant, only to have the funding pulled. "The Navy and [Albany Research] Center people talked all afternoon," recalled one employee, "then someone from the Navy says, 'Gentlemen, I don't think you understand, the Navy, Admiral [*sic*, Captain] Rickover, wants you to start a plant on zirconium and they want it operating in 90 days."

"Hell, we've wasted three hours already," quipped facilities manager Glenn Kenagy, who then "dashed out and started up digging trees and the next day had the outlines for . . . the building."

In May 1950, a massive $325,000 budget ($3.5 million in 2020 dollars) had been approved for the construction of the bigger better zirconium plant at the Albany Bureau, to be built right next to the first. The original pilot plant had only been in operation for a year when the government requested more zirconium—and *fast,* due to a "hurry-up order," local news reported. The expansion would allow for the two pilot plants to collectively double the current output to produce a whopping one-thousand pounds of the "vital non-corrosive defensive metal" a week. Construction on the new plant began at the Albany Bureau just three days after the funds were approved.

In stark contrast to the ill-funded and slow construction of the first pilot plant, the second was built at a breakneck pace and with ample funding. General engineer Werner A. Phillips was drawing up plans just ahead of the actual construction. Thirty-six year-old Phillips had been a Bureau fixture since December 1945, when the World War II veteran had been hired in the engineering department at the Albany Bureau, where he worked alongside Kroll.

Phillips once remarked to coworkers that he was "considered most unlikely to succeed" in his youth, yet he applied himself diligently while attending the University of Detroit and took courses in advanced mechanical drafting. Later Phillips enlisted in the Marine Corps and saw action in Okinawa and Guadalcanal; while in the military Phillips studied civil engineering. He would eventually get experience in mapping, building construction, and tool design, which would speak to his work at the Bureau.

In his spare time, the slender young man toiled away at his drafting room at home to design local commercial buildings as well as around 300 homes, including his own. "Most of his engineering skill has been gained the hard way," noted a later Bureau publication, "by work, special study at home and by experience." The flood of construction happening at the laboratory provided Phillips the opportunity to shine.

Photo: August 1953 *Bureau Bugle*
Werner Phillips drew up quick plans for the zirconium production buildings on campus.

Photo: Stephen T. Anderson Collection
Building 28, the Zirconium Reduction Plant, was constructed in an enormous hurry to fulfill zirconium orders for the Atomic Energy Commission.

His role in designing and engineering the zirconium plants and other buildings on campus saved the government thousands of dollars. "I consider myself fortunate that I worked with Dr. Kroll when he was devising his process for the production of zirconium," wrote Phillips, "and have followed it through to the present production zirconium plant."

On the cool, partly cloudy morning of June 8, 1950, a large crane with a hanging bucket began scooping out shovelfuls of dirt to create the basement of the new plant. Concrete forms went up swiftly after that. Progress continued on at a furious pace and construction crews worked sixteen hours a day. Ninety men were hired to do the work, with the intention of keeping at least thirty men on payroll after the building was completed. The building would eventually be known as Building 28, but it was also known by other names: according to the local press the second plant was nicknamed "Topsy" by employees, apparently because it was built so quickly. In the press it was referred to as the zirconium production plant, to differentiate from the original 1949 pilot plant. But historically, Building 28 was most commonly called the zirconium reduction plant by employees.

As summer afternoons started to heat up, the site became a nexus of activity: construction workers perspired as they began installing steel girders for the new plant. Dozens of I-beams that were spread out along the ground made a good place for men to sit and eat lunch. Piles of lumber and plywood were scattered around the site. Concrete trucks poured slurry into basement forms as upright walls took shape. The first shipment of new instruments had just arrived and everything was in motion to be completed within two months' time. By June 29, blank instrument panels were installed inside the building and multiple cranes

Photo: Stephen T. Anderson Collection
Quick progress on Building 28, the Zirconium Reduction Plant, ensured the plant was finished in just 90 days.

Photo: Stephen T. Anderson Collection
Furnace installation in Building 28, the Zirconium Reduction Plant.

were working to lift wall panels into place. On July 11, a big photo of the new plant graced the pages of the local paper, which announced the expected completion date to be August 15.

By July 13 the zirconium reduction plant was beginning to look like a proper building. Walls were nearly up and roof trusses were installed under a glaring sun on the 84-degree day. One week later the roof was half finished, and those installing furnaces and doing instrumentation work inside were likely thankful that the building, with its open window frames, allowed a cool breeze to waft through the shady interior.

By mid-August, rows of gleaming new furnaces had been affixed to preconstructed footings. Masses of thick wiring snaked around the stout furnaces, which stood about waist-high to the average man on the ground floor of the plant. In the basement underneath, the bottom half of each furnace hung from the ceiling, with more wiring coming from each.

While the production plant was being finished with great earnestness, the employees in the original pilot plant were hustling to make as much zirconium as fast as possible. "Three shifts of about seven men a shift work 24 hours a day, seven days a week to turn out some 500 pounds of metal, nearly all of which is bought by the U.S. government for undisclosed defense use," the *Albany Democrat-Herald* reported. The media reported that sand from Coos Bay was still being utilized, but declassified documents from 1949 revealed that low-hafnium zirconium was being produced for the Navy using Brazilian ores, which contained less than 1% hafnium—a very desirable trait when producing nuclear-grade zirconium at that point.

The number of employees at the Bureau had swelled to over 100, which included scientists and technical staff, construction workers, fabrication, maintenance, and administrative staff. One such new hire was a brunette teen named Mae Jean Martin. At a statuesque 5' 7", Mae Jean was a local socialite and beauty who had been elected a Timber Carnival queen—but there were also brains behind the pretty pincurls. Miss Martin began attending the University of Oregon at age 16 and was a knockout student, aiming for a career in journalism.

By the time she transferred to Oregon State University in Corvallis, Mae Jean had a job at the local *Albany Democrat-Herald*, working as an assistant proofreader and stenographer. In August 1950, Mae Jean left her job at the newspaper for a secretarial position at the Albany Bureau, joining an ever-expanding female presence at the laboratory.[3] She would soon begin drawing comics for the *Bureau Bugle*, the Albany laboratory's employee newspaper—a skill that launched a career as a future staff artist for another newspaper.

As Mae Jean was learning the ropes from the rest of the secretarial staff, the new zirconium reduction plant was nearly finished. "Even now, equipment is being installed in the two-decked structure, while workers are putting in doors, and applying brick facing to the outside of the building," explained the *Albany Democrat-Herald*. It wouldn't be long before the reduction plant would be churning out precious, low-cost zirconium for the Navy.

Seven hundred miles to the east of Albany another type of construction had concurrently begun. As dry heat blazed in shimmering waves across the barren Idaho desert, the National Reactor Test Station was buzzing with activity as the building of the Mark I prototype reactor began. About the location where the Mark I was being built, Rickover employee Theodore Rockwell recalled that "the land prototype in Idaho offered an almost monastic ambiance where the extraordinary could be established, away from peer pressure of normal shipyard operations."

That cylindrical reactor would eventually be housed in a tall, cavernous building—and its counterpart, the actual propulsion for the nuclear-powered submarine, would be built simultaneously, as a new law declared: "Construction of the Mark I at the National Reactor Testing Station in Idaho began on almost the same day in August, 1950, that Public Law 674 was signed by the President of the United States. This law authorized the construction of the first nuclear-powered submarine," noted Commander Roddis in *The Nuclear Propulsion Plant of the USS Nautilus SSN-571.*

Another pivotal decision was made in August: the AEC relented and gave Captain Rickover the authority to obtain all the zirconium needed for the submarine project and beyond. This finally gave him the power necessary to move the project forward at lightning speed—something he'd desired from early in the project.

Back in Albany at the new zirconium reduction plant, rows of shiny equipment lined the main floor, and the two plants were turning out 900 pounds of zirconium per week. Three hundred of those pounds were coming from the new—but quite unfinished—plant. Despite thorough reporting about the hasty addition on campus, there was a definite air of mystery surrounding the project. A local news blurb pointedly noted that the Bureau had not revealed zirconium's role in national defense.

Photo: Stephen T. Anderson Collection
Reduction plant expansion to accommodate for more furnaces.

Photo: Stephen T. Anderson Collection
A completed Zirconium Pilot Plant, Building 26, and Zirconium Reduction Plant, Building 28.

By mid-September, construction was almost finished and Director Stephen Shelton anticipated that it would hit production capacity within two weeks. But just five days later, it was announced that another $100,000 had been allocated to the Albany Bureau to install five more furnaces, bringing the total to no less than fifteen furnaces. That addition was expected to be completed by the first of December and would allow the Bureau of Mines to produce an astounding 2,500 pounds a week. Even without the addition of more furnaces, 1,200 pounds of zirconium were being produced weekly for Rickover's propulsion project by the end of September. The new zirconium reduction plant had been built entirely in the span of only ninety days.

By November 1950, all hafnium separation was being performed at Oak Ridge's Y-12 facility, as it was the only place in the nation with the capabilities to tease problematic hafnium from its sister element, zirconium. Once that was done, the hafnium-free zirconium oxide was sent to Albany's Bureau to be processed into zirconium sponge. That sponge was sent to Foote Mineral Company and Bettis to be used as feed material to create high-purity crystal bar. Over twenty tons of crystal bar was produced by using tungsten-tipped, non-consumable electrode furnaces. Ingots four inches in diameter by a foot long were used to create the structural shapes for the Mark I. Additionally, the fuel elements for the reactor were composed of a zirconium alloyed with scant amounts of uranium.

But in Albany, all of this was hush-hush. Only Stephen Shelton and a handful of critical staff knew exactly why the government was hungry for ever-increasing amounts of zirconium sponge. It wouldn't be long before the cat was out of the bag, however.

CHAPTER NINE
CALLED "THE BUREAU OF MINES" BY THE MAN ON THE STREET
1950–1951

"Given the incomplete stage of technological development, the very tight schedule, and the uncertainty as to specification requirements, there existed no practical alternative but to use Government facilities to produce the zirconium for the Mark I reactor."

—Lawton Geiger, Atomic Energy Commission

There is no doubt that the exponential increase in activity in the southwest corner of Albany created a curious buzz, and many speculated about what was really going on in the pair of huge brick buildings resplendent with windows. At the end of 1950, a tell-all article written by the local paper gave the first accurate hint about *why* so much zirconium was being produced. The article's astute author had gotten wind of the April 1950 issue of *Science and Mechanics* magazine and quoted it in the header of his article: "When America's first atomic engine is completed in 1952, there's a good chance that a 'Cinderella' metal—zirconium—will be in it," the article began.

"One of the U.S. government's research agencies is interested in zirconium boride, which stands up in heat up to 6,000°F and which might be employed in the atomic power plant which the Navy and Westinghouse Electric Corp. are developing for ships. A land-based prototype of the engine, to be constructed at a cost of $25 million may be the first of a series which will drive submarines . . . in 1953."

For Albany residents who had been curious about the new activity at the bustling laboratory, the article was a bombshell revelation that explained the ever-increasing activity on the far end of town. Until now Director Shelton had only reported the metal was used for unnamed defense purposes.

By the end of 1950, more buildings—an electric smelter, an electrolytic zinc plant, and an additional warehouse—had been added beyond the two zirconium plants, creating a curious mishmash of brick collegiate architecture alongside industrial-style warehouses.

The submarine revelation in the local paper was accompanied by an all-encompassing review of the laboratory, which stressed that the zirconium project—part of the rare metals branch—wasn't the only focus. The astute reporter had also picked up on the fact that the Northwest Electro-development Laboratory was clearly no longer known by its clunky formal moniker. "Called the 'Bureau of Mines' by the man on the street," the article began, "this year Albany's station became headquarters for Region II. In this new capacity, the local project now includes the mining, metallurgical, fuels and explosives, health and safety, economics and statistics, and administrative divisions of Oregon, Washington, Idaho and Montana." The little laboratory that had struggled so much in the beginning had finally risen to become the lead facility across four Northwestern states.

A thorough overview of the site was revealed to the press, with detailed explanations of all the divisions at the Albany location. In the Mining Division, M. E. Volin had replaced S. H. Lorain as the division head, and in Albany there was a continued focus on finding new and unexplored ore deposits to benefit industry or for use as strategic materials for defense.

The Ferrous Metals Branch (ferrous metals contain iron and include alloy and carbon steel, cast and wrought iron) was housed in Building 2, the building that had been moved two times, and included ferro-alloy and direct smelting sections. In 1950 the focus was on researching "Northwest ores of iron and the ferroalloy metals, such as chromium, nickel, and vanadium," the article explained. Oregon's coastal chromium deposits had been well-studied, but nickel was another abundant regional material. A large industrial-style building, Building 25, was nearing completion on the east end of campus, specifically built for smelting research. Electric arc furnaces, a cupola (a cylindrical furnace for melting cast iron), and a blast furnace were all on the list for the new facility.

Another critical aspect of the Ferrous Metals Branch was to find where domestic supplies of strategic materials existed, in case of a wartime need where foreign ores could no longer be used. Additionally, Montana and Idaho's Phosphoria formations were under intense analysis for use as phosphate fertilizer, among other things. Former Deputy Director Howard Poppleton would later assert that these advances in fertilizer production were one of the Bureau's greatest contributions, beside zirconium work.

The Non-Ferrous Metals Branch (metals without iron, such as aluminum, zinc, and tin) included the mineral dressing department, plus hydro- and pyro-metallurgy, and were located in Building 23, the former Hauser Gymnasium during the Albany College days. The Mineral Dressing Division focused on how to make concentrated ores suitable as feed material for commercial smelters. At the time, zinc was another focus for this department, as domestic zinc reserves were becoming depleted. The new electrolytic zinc plant, called Building 17, started operations in 1950. Electrolysis was used to pull useable zinc from low-grade Pacific Northwest ores. The process developed by Albany's Bureau was estimated to save between $3 and $5 per ton of electrolytic zinc.

The Physical Metallurgy Branch dealt with metals, alloys, and fabrication, and studied different ways to work with them, such as heat treatment, rolling, or forging. This operation was housed in the combined smelter building (Building 25) and another connected building, Building 24. The Fabrication Section was responsible for creating alloys and then seeing if they could be worked into useable shapes (sheets or ingots) and then the metallographic section of the branch would further test those products.

The article continued to describe melting and forging in the Physical Metallurgy Branch, and how melting was done in an oxygen-free atmosphere within electric furnaces equipped with sensitive devices that monitor and control the temperature within. At the time, the largest furnace in Albany had an interior dimension of 3 feet high by 3.5 feet wide and 8 feet long. "This furnace operates at a bright red heat and uses as much electricity every day as the average home consumes in a year," the article noted.

The resulting metal was forged with a hammer that could smash solid metal with 800-pound blows, or be adjusted down to gentle taps. Or, the metal could be squeezed through a roller that was driven by a 50-horsepower motor. Hot ingots up to 10 inches in diameter could be pushed through the rolling mill and would come out the other end a scant 1/32 of an inch thick. When rods were needed, a swage would be used. Hot metal would be pushed through rotating dies that would strike the metal into a particular shape, as determined by the type of die used.

The Metallographic Department was in charge of testing the metals produced at the Albany Bureau. Samples were sent to the laboratory where a technician

Photo: Stephen T. Anderson Collection
Sheet rolling a strip of zirconium.

Photo: Stephen T. Anderson Collection
Ray Carpenter operates an electron microscope. Photo taken November 26, 1952.

Photo: Stephen T. Anderson Collection
Two employees work with the hydraulic press.

Photo: Stephen T. Anderson Collection
Aerial view of the southernmost end of campus, also known as the "Back Forty," before much of the Fir Oaks neighborhood was developed. Photo circa 1950-1951.

using an electron microscope—whose bulbous metal body looked very much like something out of a sci-fi flick—would look for weaknesses and determine the composition of the sample. Optical microscopes were also used in this department. A hardness tester would press a tiny diamond into the sample to determine hardness. Tensile strength was measured by literally pulling the samples apart, measuring how much force was required to do so. Shock resistance was tested by striking metal with a pendulum. Samples were also heated in a vacuum for heat treatments.

The Technical Services Branch, located in stately Building 1, included the petrographic, chemical, and physics laboratories and the mechanical section. Mechanical Services were located in the World War II–era machine shop: "A large and well-equipped shop is staffed by mechanics, machinists, welders, sheet metal workers, plumbers, pipe fitters, carpenters, mill rights, and electricians," the article said. The employees here were responsible both for keeping buildings on campus maintained and for building the bespoke machinery required for the brand-new processes performed on campus. As sunlight reflected off wood floors and the buzz of machinery created a deafening roar, "the construction staff designs and builds an amazing variety of special equipment required in metallurgical research."

Back in Building 1, the chemistry lab was one of the most advanced for its time, which was absolutely critical for making determinations about metals created at the Bureau. The Physics Section featured a spectrograph and an x-ray Diffraction Laboratory that was used to detect trace elements quickly and precisely.

In the Petrographic Laboratory, members of the public could bring in any type of rock (though not silver or gold) and petrographers at the Albany Bureau would analyze the specimen. By 1950, between 50 and 100 specimens were brought monthly to the laboratory to be analyzed. Uranium prospecting was of particular interest to seasoned miners, hobbyists, and even housewives, and the Albany Bureau was one of the few places on the West Coast to have a sample looked at. Any rock sample could be tested "by use of microscopes, spectroscopes, and thermal differential equipment."

As a testament to the quality of the laboratory and its staff, in six short years it went from being a tiny, understaffed affair with only a handful of projects to being a burgeoning operation with multiple departments and full-scale metallurgical capabilities.

By 1951, 335 people were employed at the Bureau of Mines and its rapid expansion continued at an unmatched pace, driven by Captain Rickover's relentless pursuit of zirconium for the Mark I (the ground-based nuclear prototype) and the Mark II (the actual reactor inside the nuclear submarine.) Theodore Rockwell, one of Rickover's close associates, noted the following:

> By the end of 1950 Captain Rickover had most of the organizational raw material he needed to carry out his program. The Navy had officially established an urgent need for a nuclear-powered submarine, and President Harry Truman had approved it, with a January 1955 sea date. The Atomic Energy Commission (AEC) had finally agreed to Rickover's plan to establish a group with responsibility and authority within

both agencies, and had agreed in principle to work with industry in carrying out the project. Westinghouse and General Electric had been brought in and the basic administrative procedures were in place. Rigorous training programs had been set up at Oak Ridge and MIT, as well as headquarters and within the laboratories in the program.

A good amount of technical decisions about the Mark I and II power plants had been solidified. Structural materials that touched the coolant (hot pressurized water) would be composed of stainless steel that was resistant to high temperatures. Shielding to keep submarine occupants safe would be made of water, lead, and steel. Acceptable levels of radiation exposure hadn't been firmly decided on, but whatever they would be, Rickover insisted levels would be conservatively low. In January 1951, the Naval Reactors Program started looking into using hafnium (zirconium's entwined sister element) as a possible control rod material, though Argonne was working on silver-cadmium rods at the time, and Rickover considered hafnium a secondary choice.

Despite the tremendous amount of progress, there were still unanswered questions about zirconium. Until this point, attempts at producing an ultra-pure metal that had excellent corrosion resistance in a nuclear environment had fallen short. Though the quality of the nuclear-grade zirconium continued getting better with improved processes, corrosion resistance was still an area of major concern. In fact, the Mark I was being constructed as scientists and engineers were still trying to nail down a way to make zirconium so it would be truly corrosion-resistant within a nuclear reactor. "While corrosion resistance improved tremendously over that displayed by the early product, long periods were still experienced when no material useful for Mark I production was manufactured," recalled Benjamin Lustman in *Technical Development of Zicronium for Nuclear Reactor Use.*

    The focus started shifting toward creating a zirconium alloy that might be less affected by corrosion than pure zirconium. For those working on the project, there were big questions and even bigger gambles. As Theodore Rockwell aptly put it, "There is no guarantee any of this will work out. There may not be any alloy that is strong enough, or corrosion resistant."

    Dr. Benjamin Lustman had begun working at Bettis Atomic Power Laboratory in 1949 and was the manager responsible for core materials development, and was intimately involved in the search for an appropriate zirconium alloy for nuclear purposes. The final zirconium product was being actively tested at Bettis against high temperatures and pressure—mimicking the hellish environment of a nuclear reactor—but samples fell woefully short most of the time.

    "The corrosion resistance of the material available at that time . . . ranged from unacceptable to disastrous," Lustman wrote. In fact, out of titanium, zirconium, and hafnium, it was ironic that only zirconium showed an "exaggerated sensitivity to hot water corrosion resistance with respect to purity and structure." In other words, pure zirconium wasn't going to cut it. Additionally, zirconium deemed corrosion-resistant as crystal bar still "teetered on a razor's edge of acceptability," resulting in further troubleshooting and investigations into how the zirconium was becoming contaminated. It wasn't long until there were grumblings that crystal bar zirconium wasn't going to work.

While alloy development was being discussed at Bettis, work at the Albany Bureau was moving along at a breathless pace. As bone-chilling February weather blew through Oregon, $90,000 was allocated for the construction of yet another building to support the zirconium production at the laboratory. Werner Phillips once again hastily drew up plans just ahead of construction. The new building would specifically be for chlorination and would be a significantly large building built just south of the machine shop. Chlorination was a vital step in the zirconium process and for the first pilot plant, a little building known as the "chlorination shack" was built behind Building 26. It was an appropriately named wood building with a steeply gabled roof and as production needs changed, so did the little shack. Former Bureau Director Frank E. Block recalled,

> It was rumored to have been originally the contractor's shack from the earlier renovations. And it was often in the way and was moved since it was portable. As our chlorinators grew larger and became more complex this building was enlarged, but not improved to any extent. It was like the proverbial glue factory. No one wanted much to do with it unless he had to. Spending a shift in there more than cleaned my sinuses. But eventually it was improved because it was then important to the zirconium operations.

Shelton was concerned about the new construction staying on schedule because of a lack of skilled workers knowledgeable in construction using a different type of building block, which was later

Photo: Stephen T. Anderson Collection
Construction workers battled snowy conditions while constructing Building 4, the Chlorination building.

Photo: Stephen T. Anderson Collection
Stephen Shelton (left) and Dr. William Kroll converse in front of Building 1.

referred to as "pumice block." The addition of the new building, to be called Building 4, brought the government's total investment to $440,000 ($4.5 million dollars today). By the end of February the new building's footings had been laid, mostly using local laborers.

While construction was moving along, a key relationship at the Bureau was about to implode. Dr. Kroll, the usually mild-mannered metallurgist, had now been consulting on the zirconium project for a full five years. Director Stephen Shelton had been there for just slightly less time. Both men, according to peers, were well-respected and kind-hearted gentlemen, though both were understandably headstrong when it came to their professions. Their disagreements may have been brewing since before the first zirconium pilot plant had been built, or perhaps friction began under the extreme pressure to produce a consistent, corrosion-resistant product for Rickover and the Naval Reactors Program.

At the time Kroll, was also embroiled in a drawn-out battle with the United States government over the titanium patent he had received in 1940. In December 1941, the Alien Property Custodian seized everything stateside owned by immigrants from Japan, Italy, and Germany. Though Kroll was from Luxembourg, his patent rights had been assigned to the German electric company Siemens before he fled Villa Leclerc. Because of this, his patent was impounded indefinitely. Kroll had been footing the legal bills to earn the rights to his royalties and had "grown increasingly perplexed and bitter" about the process. Perhaps this additional strain had pushed him to the breaking point.

Or even still, maybe Kroll's relationship with Shelton had deteriorated because of reports that Kroll refused to communicate with the few female scientists at the Bureau, creating issues within projects. Edith

Rupprecht was the only female physicist at the Bureau at the time of Kroll's departure and may have been one of the women stonewalled by the metallurgist. Whatever the reason, by June 1951, Kroll and Shelton had a heated disagreement over final equipment design for zirconium production. Shelton knew that they were running out of time; Rickover needed immediate answers and Kroll "had to get out of the way," recalled James Overby Shelton, Stephen Shelton's son. A fiery exchange of words followed.

"Some people make a living with their brain, but I don't know how *you* make *your* living!" Kroll reportedly exclaimed to Shelton during the heat of the argument. For Shelton, that was the final straw.

The timing couldn't have been worse. With the addition of two new buildings dedicated solely to Kroll's process of producing commercial quantities of zirconium, and with more on the way, this was an unimaginable time for Kroll to leave the Bureau. Yet Shelton stood firm and asked Kroll to resign. By the end of February, Kroll's office in the first zirconium pilot plant was empty. The scientist who had unlocked the mysteries of titanium and zirconium was gone.[4]

CHAPTER TEN

SEPARATION ANXIETY

March 1951–March 1952

"Seems that zirconium lets in radiation like a window lets in light."

—Henry Gilbert, Dec. 1951 <u>Bureau Bugle</u>

Kroll's departure seemed to have little to no effect on the rapid development of the Albany Bureau. By the end of March 1951, the 11,000-square-foot stark white chlorination building was nearly completed, marking a mere 30 days since the project began—despite severe weather that hampered the new construction and delayed its completion by a week. Workers teetered on scaffolding as inches of snow covered everything, including the blocks used to build the outer walls. Even with the construction nearly complete, operations couldn't begin right away, as interior equipment had also been delayed. Director Shelton hoped the new facility would be up and running within three weeks of its completion.

While the chlorination plant was being built in Albany, the Atomic Energy Commission was actively seeking commercial producers of zirconium and hafnium, requesting interest from corporations. But without firm production guidelines or material quantities, generating interest was extremely difficult. At the same time, another $350,000 was allocated for another major building project at the Bureau, but this time, Bechtel Corporation of San Francisco would be designing the building, with the usual Bureau crew doing the construction.

Ground was broken on April 17, 1951, and one week later foundations were poured. The local news never tired of reporting on the new structures. "The

Photos: Stephen T. Anderson Collection
Purification tower construction preparation as it looked April 17th, 1951.

Photos: Stephen T. Anderson Collection
Bechtel Corporation of San Francisco designed the Purification tower, with local workers handling construction.

new plant, fourth major addition to the zirconium project, with [sic] house a purification set-up for raw metal used almost exclusively in the defense effort. Engineering and contracting for the new plant is the Bechel [sic] corporation of San Francisco. The Albany Sand and Gravel company is doing the excavating."

The new plant would consist of three connected buildings: Building 29 would be a long, single-story brick building whose north end would attach to a second structure, Building 30. Just as with the other new construction, this project would move forward at lighting speed with completion expected by September 1. With this new addition, over $1,000,000 ($10 million in 2020 dollars) had been allocated to new construction at the Albany Bureau.

To neighbors of the site it probably felt like ongoing construction was now a permanent feature of daily life. Unless readers had caught the article in the local paper the year prior that had revealed possible atomic reactor uses for zirconium, the only thing the public really knew about the frantic construction was that it was for "defense purposes." Readers of the April 1951 volume of *Popular Science* magazine, however, had an easy-to-understand article all about the zirconium production going on in Albany. This article may have been the source of local gossip that speculated there was a nuclear reactor at the site.

"To extract the metal," the article explained, "the new Bureau of Mines process begins by heating zircon sand with graphite. Resulting carbides, treated with chlorine gas, yield separable chlorides of zirconium and silicon. In a reduction furnace, the purified zirconium chloride gives up its chlorine to molten magnesium. Spongy zirconium metal remains. It is freed of impurities in a distilling retort, and then melted down into solid ingots of up to 25 pounds each."

It then described how the secret to producing zirconium was using vacuums during production to protect the metal from regular air. Even the finished ingot was sealed in iron until it was ready to use.

A May 1951 restricted AEC document, *The Development of a Melting Method for Conversion of Zirconium Sponge to Corrosion Resistant Ingot,* revealed what was happening behind closed doors regarding the urgent need for more nuclear-quality zirconium: "The Atomic Energy Commission requires zirconium metal having the following specifications: 1. The metal must be free from hafnium. 2. It must be free from other impurities of undesirable neutron cross section." The document also alluded to a new purification facility to extract hafnium from zirconium: "At the present time development of metal meeting these specifications has progressed to the point where a process for removal of hafnium before further purification of zirconium oxide and for reduction of zirconium oxide to sponge zirconium metal is feasible on a production basis, and a plant may be set up to operate."

The aforementioned plant was Building 29 and Building 30 on the Albany campus. The paper continued to describe the woeful lack of corrosion resistance and how the AEC desired to eliminate the crystal bar step. "Since zirconium is badly needed, it has been necessary to resort to the costly iodide [crystal bar] process for treating sponge zirconium in order to get a zirconium of satisfactory corrosion resistance. It is highly desirable that the need for the iodide process be eliminated in the very near future." This could be achieved by special melting techniques to produce highly corrosion-resistant zirconium with the right nuclear properties—

Photos: Stephen T. Anderson Collection
The Purification tower, minus scaffolding, is nearly complete.

Photo: Stephen T. Anderson Collection
View from the Purification tower, looking south. Note homes in the Fir Oaks neighborhood, top of photo.

i.e., free of hafnium and other impurities that would affect zirconium's transparency to neutrons.

Three laboratories had been working tirelessly on melting techniques: MIT, Battelle Memorial Institute, and the Albany Bureau. Each facility had a different melting technique, and at the Bureau the type of zirconium produced was the kind using the "purified Y-12 oxide" that Kroll and Gilbert had discussed in late 1949. Details on the pros and cons were thoroughly discussed, including methods, impurities that resulted from the different methods, and consistency of the resulting product.

The conclusion was that no matter what type of melting method was used, the Atomic Energy Commission needed zirconium that was free of impurities, corrosion resistant, and—most important— consistent across all batches. "It would be expected on the basis of these considerations that the sponge zirconium produced [at the Bureau of Mines] from Y-12 oxide might be superior to standard Bureau of Mines sponge, since it contains less impurity . . . though there is certainly no basis on which to say that a satisfactory yield of corrosion resistant zirconium will be obtained without development of special melting practices," the AEC concluded.

While the AEC continued to tirelessly work on achieving a nuclear grade, corrosion-resistant zirconium product that could be produced consistently, construction at the Albany Bureau continued. As temperatures rose and cottonwood seeds drifted lazily across clear blue skies, the new building progressed steadily. Everything was running on schedule, with one set of brick walls already up on Building 29.

A curious sight now graced the construction area: instead of a matching brick façade to blend with the rest of the collegiate architecture, a thin, multi-story tower was beginning to rise above the neighborhood and it was getting taller with each passing week. The tower was ensconced in a lacy wood scaffolding and a tall crane was used to hoist building materials to workers high upon the tower, creating quite a spectacle for neighbors.

As the summer of 1951 blazed on, residents were curious about the strange tower that was climbing higher and higher at the Albany Bureau. With its only stated purposes being for "defense," whispers started circulating that perhaps it had something to do with producing parts for a nuclear bomb. Longtime Albany residents were a tight-knit group and as an influx of new employees moved to the area some residents were wary of the laboratory and its staff. With only about 10,000 residents, the area still had a small-town feel—and that's exactly how some wanted it to stay. Ever-increasing numbers of government employees and contractors were seen as a threat and some business owners started taking matters into their own hands. One business went so far as to refuse to sell their appliances to new Bureau employees, leaving new folks to find a local resident to secretly make the purchase for them.

The Atomic Energy Commission was having troubles of its own as well. In June 1951 they once again tried to entice private companies to jump headlong into commercial zirconium production, but the twenty-six companies who were invited to produce metal as pure and strong as possible (but without increasing hardness) didn't bite at the less-than-appealing offer. The Albany Bureau continued pumping out commercial quantities of zirconium for the Naval Reactors Program.

One step forward was when the NRP initiated fabrication of control rods made of hafnium—though the investigation was still considered a backup plan. The brilliant white tower nearing completion at the Albany Bureau would soon be known as the "purification plant," and its sole purpose would be to tease the miniscule amounts of hafnium out of zirconium through a delicate network of six-story Pyrex tubes. This elegant process would provide hafnium free, nuclear-grade zirconium, all while providing pure hafnium for other uses. But since the tower wasn't finished yet, Oak Ridge National Laboratory would continue to provide hafnium-rich concentrates for the NRP's control rod investigation.

While workers were bustling around the Bechtel construction, another secret project prompted more construction on the edge of campus in July 1951. Warm wind whipped across the tall grasses growing on the "back forty," a wide-open field unused by the Bureau. The furthest building from the campus entrance was a small pilot plant on the southwestern corner that had been built in 1949 for one of the earliest projects done in Albany, the magnesium reduction work inherited from Ford Motor Company. In July 1951 the long-standing magnesium work finally came to an end.

Hanford Atomic Works had a problem that only the Albany Bureau could solve: several million pounds of contaminated aluminum-silicon alloy and copper-tin alloy had accumulated in scrap storage cribs at the Hanford site, but they contained valuable materials that needed reclaiming. The enlarged building would be a plant "to recover the tin and copper from . . . the material that had been used for the cladding of the uranium in the early reactors [at Hanford]," noted former Deputy Director Howard Poppleton. The facility would be the only one of its kind in the country. Ground was broken in July and crews began adding onto the existing magnesium pilot plant.

Photo: Stephen T. Anderson Collection
The tin recover project focused on recovering tin and copper from contaminated cladding from Hanford Atomic Works.

Photo: Stephen T. Anderson Collection
"The Nonferrous Metals Branch is operating the only electrolytic tin refinery in the United States. The starting material is a mixture of dross and scrap containing about 25 percent copper and 75 percent tin. Based on this grade feed, the plant produces about 1,000 pounds of refined tin per day. The worker is shown charging a 50-kilowatt electric furnace with scrap. This is the first step in the process to remove impurities from the tin." –from
Bureau of Mines Field Operations Region II 1953

Other projects were quietly humming along in the background, not as well publicized as the very visible zirconium production work, but nonetheless critical. Ductile chromium, like the magnesium project, had been continually worked on at the Bureau since 1948. Creating high-temperature chromium alloys was not successful, but exploration into drawing chromium into fine wire and sample shapes for other research facilities was successful.

Another area of research that began in 1948 was double consumable electrode vacuum arc melting, which would become vital to the AEC's goal of eliminating the crystal bar step during nuclear-grade zirconium production. While the process had a long and complicated-sounding title, *double consumable electrode vacuum arc melting* simply explained exactly what was going on: "double" meant the zirconium was melted twice, once in a first-melt furnace, and then again in a remelt furnace. The electrode was used to attach the metal to be melted to the inside of the furnace. A consumable electrode meant the electrode composition was the same as the metal being melted, and as the arc of electricity melted the ingot, the electrodes would be consumed and intermixed with the ingot. However, as the electrode is melted by the heat of the electric arc, the distance is shortened so the arc maintains the same length. Of course, this process was done in a vacuum devoid of regular air to eliminate contamination of oxygen or nitrogen.

Photos: Stephen T. Anderson Collection
A double consumable electrode vacuum arc furnace.

Photos: Stephen T. Anderson Collection
Leland Yerkes, one of the key contributors to zirconium melting technology.

In 1951 the melting process was still being fine-tuned, but now it was proceeding without Kroll's valuable input. Thankfully, Kroll's closest associates were still at the Bureau and were contributing to the success of everything that happened after his departure. Robert Beall, Henry Gilbert, Leland Yerkes, and Floyd W. Wood were crucial employees working on this process. Beall, a physicist, was particularly pivotal in alloying and melting. "Beall's development of consumable electrode melting was one of the fundamental developments of the zirconium story," notes one history on the center.

Robert Beall, who went by Bob, was a 1941 graduate of the University of Washington and held a degree in physics. The thin young man with glasses and a pencil moustache had been hired at the Albany Bureau in November 1949. When Beall arrived, zirconium production had just begun in the 1949 zirconium plant, with zirconium experiments still occasionally being run in the north end of Building 2. Methods of analyzing the final product after experimenting with melting techniques were a necessary component of producing nuclear-grade zirconium and this genre of analysis became a strong point for the Albany Bureau. "Much of the success of the Bureau's zirconium program resulted from the strong analytical capabilities developed at the Albany center in support of the basic research and pilot plant operations. Comprehensive analytical schemes involving wet chemistry, gas analysis, and both optical and x-ray emission were developed for the analysis of zirconium containing ores, the pure metal, and zirconium alloys," noted a booklet highlighting the successful processes developed in Albany.

Photo: the Bureau Bugle
A method of forming zirconium crucibles was developed by the Physical Metallurgy branch called "deep drawing." Crucibles were used extensively in the Chemistry Laboratory.

Photo: Stephen T. Anderson Collection
Robert Beall was instrumental in developing zirconium melting technology.

Another important development was the creation of zirconium crucibles. Crucibles are vessels of differing sizes that are used in a laboratory setting to contain materials that need to be heated to extremely high temperatures. The Bureau had been working on a project involving peroxide fusion—a method of preparing samples for wet chemistry—and a more durable crucible was needed. In keeping with the spirit of fabricating whatever was needed on site, zirconium crucibles were formed at the Bureau and were found to have a life expectancy up to *twenty times* longer than traditional crucibles.

As summer 1951 reached its peak, the Atomic Energy Commission was still trying to romance corporations into contracts for commercial zirconium—and now hafnium—production. A meeting was held in Chicago, hosted by the AEC, with representatives visiting from around the country, but despite interest from all, nobody was willing to sign on the dotted line. "All the companies were interested in obtaining a Government contract, but none was willing to accept the risk of building a new plant and committing itself to a fixed-price contract," lamented Lawton Geiger of the AEC. There was simply too much uncertainty in this brand-new proposed market for two virtually unknown metals. Plus, the Mark I prototype had not begun operations yet, so there was no proof the project would ever actually succeed.

By the end of July, news about zirconium's possible nuclear uses had been touted in the media across the nation. While the first nuclear submarine project was (and still is) mostly classified[5], general non-specific information about its progress was slowly being released to the public. Newspapers and magazines published technically rich information about the many uses of zirconium and how the Navy had its eyes on zirconium for its nuclear properties—even though a proper corrosion-resistant alloy had not yet been developed. The Salem, Oregon *Capital Journal* even mentioned the next new project that was being worked on: the world's first nuclear aircraft engine[6], in addition to the Mark I naval reactor.

    The hafnium separation tower, or purification plant, was looking like a proper building by the time August rolled around: all windows were in, the roof was finished, and the scaffolding surrounding the tower was gone. In the same month, General Dynamic's Electric Boat Division in Groton, Connecticut was awarded the construction contract for the *Nautilus*. The pieces and parts of constructing the world's first nuclear submarine were coming together in rapid fashion. However, the Atomic Energy Commission was still seeking contracts to be awarded to two or more suppliers (as Rickover had demanded) for zirconium sponge. The quantity had been defined: 300,000 pounds for five years. When 35 firms would eventually place bids, no contract was awarded.

Another type of separation work had begun at the Albany Bureau: the solvent extraction and separation of tantalum and columbium, which is now called niobium. Tantalum is a lustrous blue-gray metal with high corrosion resistance and niobium is a light gray, crystalline transition metal that looks nearly identical to zirconium. For over a century, chemists had been puzzled about how to tease these two elements apart as their separation was "considered one of the most difficult in inorganic chemistry," asserted one technical report.

Just like with zirconium and hafnium, tantalum and niobium have similar chemical properties but different physical ones. And just like zirconium and hafnium, the two had to be freed completely from each other to be useful. In 1951, small-scale work was begun in Albany to develop a chemical separation method to produce impurity-free metals.

In the other separations project, equipment installation inside the white tower was performed by Bureau employees. Young Robert Govro was assigned to work on assembling the delicate glass Pyrex tubes that ran the entire height of its five stories. "When they got the building finished," Robert recalled, "they hired about maybe six or eight of us guys from parts of the plant who'd already been there. When we went in the building the first morning, there were big boxes of Pyrex glass tubing. They were 5" in diameter and 10-12' long, and those all had to be coupled together with stainless steel fittings to be made into the columns inside the tower."

"The first thing we did was assemble the glass tubes, and someone would go to the second floor and pull up a section, and when we got to the top, we had some things to manipulate the tubing to whatever position you wanted it. There were probably about eight of those columns in that tower."

Sometimes installation didn't go quite as planned; when one is working with stories-tall glass tubes, things can go very wrong. "Those big glass columns . . . a few of them got dropped and every two or three weeks you'd hear a great big crash and one of them dropped 30 or 40 feet . . . that was bad news

Photo: Department of Reclamation
The view up into the Purification tower.

Photo: Stephen T. Anderson
The light-filled Purification tower held hundreds of feet of Pyrex tubes held together with Teflon gaskets.

because they were expensive. The [Teflon] fittings you joined them together with—at that time, hardly anybody in the world knew anything about Teflon. Teflon is a very acid-resistant material. We had gaskets to fit these pipes together and a cast metal flange that was coated with a glass ceramic coating, a kind of dark red color, and they had places to put some bolts so you could clamp them together . . . we were right on the cutting edge of using Teflon in chemistry work. You'd put a piece of pipe up, then a gasket on, and you'd position the next pipe on top of it, and clamp the two things together, and work your way up the column."

With the Bureau's separations plant nearing completion, Rickover and the Naval Reactors Program were wondering if it would be wise to eliminate the crystal-bar step of zirconium production, even though crystal-bar zirconium was used in the Mark I prototype reactor. Glaring inconsistencies with the quality of crystal bar, plus its high cost caused "a growing dissatisfaction with the continued use of crystal-bar product," noted Benjamin Lustman, author of *The Metallurgy of Zirconium*.

Fall leaves swirled around campus as temperatures dropped and neighborhood children planned their Halloween costumes in October 1951. Tendrils of smoke rose from the tiny cottage-style homes across the street from Building 1 and as the days got shorter, employees at the Bureau were continued to work on making a better zirconium product. A gentleman by the name of Walter Hurford visited the Albany campus that month to meet with employees of the melting department to work out some problems they'd been having with zirconium ingots. Mr. Hurford was the head of melting development at the Westinghouse Atomic Power Division and his visit heralded the beginning of the Albany Bureau's experiments with melting.

That fall, two distinctly different methods of melting were tested. One approach was to fabricate a zirconium alloy into a bar shape and then consumably remelt it. Another way was to chop up zirconium sheet and then non-consumably arc remelt it. Both methods were successful, though the sheet method gave the best results.

The silvery-gray cylinders made at the Bureau were thoroughly analyzed and assigned quality grades: B1 (suitable for remelt as an electrode), B2 (suitable for remelt as chopped sheet) and the lowest-quality ingots were given a C grade and rejected. Using formed electrodes, an 8" first-melt ingot was rolled and forged to 2" by 2" bars, which were consumably remelted in an 8" crucible. This technique was coined the "828 process" by Bureau employees and it became the standard for creating a sound, homogeneous ingot; three tons of metal was melted this way. "The '828' process demonstrated that enough blending of the ingredients of the metal can be achieved by the forging and rolling and consumable remelting technique to result in the necessary improvement in homogeneity and soundness," reported one analysis.

When Hurford returned to Westinghouse he met with his superior, Robert Gordon. Gordon had been promoted to Manager of the Special Alloy Development Department, which was tasked with creating new alloys for defense products. They discussed what might happen if the intermediate step of bar fabrication was skipped. Gordon felt strongly that time and money could be saved if the fabrication step was eliminated.

Photo: Stephen T. Anderson Collection
An employee works with silvery zirconium ingots. Note the tall electrode (far right) is composed of several ingots welded together.

Westinghouse and the Bureau continued to collaborate to make strides toward an optimal way to produce a perfectly mixed, nuclear-grade zirconium, or zirconium alloy, ingot.

The last *Bureau Bugle* of the year included a fantastic description of the zirconium process at the end of 1951, as told by Henry Gilbert. Of course, not all employees on site were intimately familiar with the "big project" going on, so a layman's explanation was appreciated. "The pass-word *[sic]* in the production of ductile zirconium metal is 'make it pure," Gilbert began, "—get out the iron, get out the magnesium, get out everything. We're lucky there is even any zirconium left by the time we get through," he quipped.

But a significant problem that Kroll and Gilbert had encountered over the past few years was that during melting, the high-purity, crude zirconium metal would dissolve any kind of crucible they tried to use. Kroll, Gilbert, and their associates had discovered that a graphite crucible was the only thing that could contain molten zirconium—but it would also contaminate the zirconium with "two tenths of one percent graphite which is four to five times more than is desired.

"Why be so particular about two-tenths of a gnat's eyebrow?" Gilbert wrote, then explained that for the Atomic Energy Commission's purposes, anything else other than pure zirconium (at that point) was completely unacceptable. "Seems that zirconium lets in radiation like a window lets in light—if the zirconium is impure (like a dirty window), the radiation can't make the grade."

So the problem remained of how to melt zirconium without picking up any contamination from the operation itself. With the analogy of how a coffee pot isn't melted by the flames under it because it contains water, Gilbert explained that water was put on the outside of the crucible, and an electric arc was used to obtain the melting temperature of 3360°F. To reduce contamination, the arc welding rod was composed of zirconium (the "consumable" part of "consumable electrode arc welding".)

Chopped pieces of zirconium sponge ("which look like small gray lumps of bread," Gilbert noted) were poured into a die and then pressure was applied with a hydraulic press. When the die was opened it revealed a 20-inch long by 2-inch square ingot which would become the electrode for the melt.

An electrode that large needed a mind-boggling amount of power; Gilbert noted they coupled "twelve welding machines" to achieve the melt. "Thus with our little water cooled 'coffee pot' (slightly modified at a cost of 8 or 10 thousand dollars), four or five men, a machine shop and a dozen welding machines we can melt real good zirconium ingots, and if one can believe [melting chief] Mr. Beall he can't melt too much to suit our creditors," Gilbert joked.

———•◄——•———

To refine the zirconium production process by eliminating the crystal bar step, five separate companies were recruited to experiment with the melting and fabrication process. Zirconium sponge was provided, free of charge, to those companies. In the end the conclusion was this: "On the basis of experimental work done by the Bureau of Mines and Bettis, supplemented by the experience of the industrial firms, Bettis recommended and Naval Reactors approved the process of utilizing arc melting of consumable electrodes made of compacts of zirconium sponge with other alloy constituents in water-cooled copper crucibles. The initial ingots would then be used as the electrodes for remelting into larger ingots. The double melting was necessary to assure good homogeneity of the alloy."

In this case, the term *homogeneity* simply meant that as zirconium was melted and re-melted, the particles within would spread evenly throughout. Particles could be impurities or other metal types for alloying. Imagine biting into a cookie with a lump of baking soda that hasn't been mixed in. Just as with cookies, having a concentration of one ingredient that hasn't been thoroughly mixed resulted in a poor product.

Westinghouse Atomic Power Division had struggled with homogeneity with their crystal bar product and their zirconium-uranium fuel elements. Initially they used the accepted practice of rolling and forging into zirconium sheets. That sheet was then chopped up and melted—though with a non-consumable, tungsten-tipped electrode furnace. "Acceptable" levels of homogeneity were reached but the process was tedious, expensive, and—worst of all—introduced slight levels of contamination into the metal, which in turn made the metal more brittle. Those were three big strikes against that method.

At about the same time that skipping the crystal bar step was being discussed by Rickover and his associates, engineers and metallurgists were beginning to wonder if using highly pure zirconium wasn't the key to a corrosion-resistant product. "Those experienced in the art and science of corrosion worried that continued purification of the product was not necessarily the correct path," noted Lustman. Alloys were discussed and testing began on zirconium alloy samples, with the Bureau, Ames Laboratory in Iowa, and Battelle all working simultaneously on the issue.

With the nuclear submarine project now running full steam, it was fitting that on December 12, 1951 the Navy announced the name of the world's first nuclear-powered submarine: the *USS Nautilus*. "A better name for the world's first nuclear submarine would have been hard to find," noted authors Richard G. Hewlett and Francis Duncan in *Nuclear Navy*. With a nod to Jules Verne's fictitious submarine, the name had been assigned in October. "Choice of the name had been somewhat fortuitous, at least as far as Rickover knew," said the book. "The Navy practice was to place the names of newly decommissioned submarines at the bottom of a list and then reassign those from the top as new submarines were built. Somehow or other the match was made in the Navy bureaucracy, and on October 25, 1951, Secretary [of the Navy] Dan A. Kimball established the designation SSN for nuclear submarines and officially named the first ship the *Nautilus*."

1951 had been a momentous year of continual change and forward progress at the Albany Bureau, but the site's safety record had taken a hit. In the December issue of the employee newsletter the headline sternly admonished: "BUREAU OF MINES BLACK SHEEP? IT'S A FACT!! THAT'S HOW WE RATE IN THE NATIONAL SAFETY PROGAM OF THE BUREAU OF MINES." There had only been one publicized accident thus far; in January 1950, Robert Beall had just been hired by the Bureau as a chemical engineer. His wife and daughter still lived at their home in Seattle when Beall was working with a piece of magnesium that caught on fire. His neck and shoulders were burned and he was rushed to the local hospital, just blocks away.

As the year progressed, it's highly likely there were other small fires, explosions, and accidents that went unreported by the press, likely hushed by the Bureau because of the classified nature of the work.

By the end of 1951 over 300 employees graced the Albany Bureau and the events of the past year were celebrated on New Year's Eve with a bash befitting the burgeoning laboratory. Young secretary, new *Bureau Bugle* editor, and comic artist Mae Jean Martin drew Dogpatch-themed decorations that dotted the walls of the recreation room in Building 2; buxom Daisy Mae joined Li'l Abner and homely Sadie Hawkins. Streamers fluttered across the room and balloons dangled from the ceiling.

The evening began with a delicious dinner. Partygoers filed through the buffet line, spearing slices of baked ham or roast beef and adding sides of cheese and relish. Guests forked salad onto already-full plates, picked their refreshments, and made their way to small, festively decorated tables.

Employees packed the dance floor as the juke box belted out slow-dance hits like "Cold, Cold Heart" by Tony Bennett and "Too Young" by Nat King Cole. The old floor creaked as partners swayed to the sound of the hits of 1951. Everyone paused at midnight to don party hats, cheer, kiss, and make as much noise as possible as they heralded in the New Year. Dancing and merrymaking continued into the morning as possibilities of a new year dawned.

Because the Albany Bureau was now knee-deep in AEC contracts, all of 1952 would once again be shrouded in media silence—at least on the local level. Pressures to succeed had never run so high at the laboratory. Security was tightened so that visitors could no longer wander freely about campus; any non-employee was directed to check in on the second floor of Building 1. Room 205, the telephone room, was now also designated as the "registration room," where an identification badge would be issued. The visitor's name, employer, and profession would be visible on the badge, although the *Bureau Bugle* joked that "despite the tremendous number of requests from our unmarried personnel to include marital status, addresses, and telephone numbers on the visitor name plates, the idea had to be discarded due to the small size of the badges."

Now entering its eighth year, the Albany laboratory teemed with 350 employees, with three shifts working around the clock to churn out zirconium for the Navy. "You were tired all the time," employee Robert Govro quipped as he recalled the furious pace kept on campus.

The workdays may have been hectic, but social life and community involvement at the Bureau was at an all-time high that year. The recreation room on the second floor of Building 2 served as a public meeting space for dozens of groups—churches, scouts, even boat safety classes—gathered in the basement of the former orphanage. A large number of Bureau employees were highly involved in other civic groups and service organizations. Between the competitive card groups, sports teams, blood drives, the annual Easter egg hunt, and the employee summer picnic, the Bureau was becoming a true hub of the small town of Albany.

In the first half of 1952 four things needed to be worked out immediately for the Naval Reactors Program: first, finding out if a zirconium alloy would have the best corrosion resistance; second, figuring out what that alloy would consist of; and third, figuring out how to improve homogeneity in that alloy. The fourth was getting the Purification Plant—the thin white tower—up and running to produce nuclear-grade, hafnium-free zirconium for all of the above.

If the previous year's safety record had been appalling, 1952 proved to be even worse. E. Don Dilling had been hired in 1944 and was said to have "his hand in almost every project, and when trouble arose or a new gadget had to be made the cry 'Get Dilling' was always expected," noted one *Bureau Bugle* write-up. Dilling was the head of a local radiation monitoring team, composed totally of Albany Bureau employees, that had been organized in Albany for "determining radiation intensities following possible atomic explosions in the Linn county area." Dilling was working alone in the basement laboratory of Building 2 on a chilly, drizzly Tuesday in March. "It seems that on occasion, there appeared in a reduction retort an unidentified black material," Robert Beall later recalled. "When a large quantity appeared one day, Don Dilling took the bucket full to his small lab in Building 2 to examine."

Dilling had just finished testing the blackish residue when the vessel he was holding violently exploded. The force was so great that basement windows were blown out and the three-inch-thick stone workbench Dilling had been standing by was blasted in two. Laboratory equipment all around him was destroyed and a fire immediately ignited.

Nearby employees rushed to Dilling's aid, knocking down the fire with carbon dioxide extinguishers. Other employees called for an ambulance. Those who helped pull Dilling from the explosion could see he'd suffered deep cuts to his face and chest, and the hand that had been holding the vessel was grievously mangled.

Dilling was whisked to Albany General Hospital by ambulance, which was thankfully just a few blocks from the laboratory. He was rushed into surgery to repair the wounds, and some of his injuries were so severe that he needed reconstructive surgery. The next day the hospital reported that Dilling's condition was improved and no amputations had been necessary. He was eventually released and returned to work in the same department, though a month later his hand was still in a cast. Fellow employees thought he'd been lucky to survive, though he lived with his injuries for the rest of his life.

Less than two weeks later the situation repeated itself. On the morning of March 14, Loren S. Schultz, and assistant in the zirconium plant, was working near a chlorinator furnace when the lid rocketed off, hitting him in the face while superheated carbon monoxide gases burned his skin. Once again, nearby employees ran to help. Schultz was rushed to the hospital in an ambulance. He returned to his post in the chlorination department after two weeks of healing from burns to his face.

Laboratory Blast Injures Metallurgist

Photo: *Albany Democrat-Herald*
The shattered stone laboratory workbench that E. Don Dilling was working at can be seen at the top of the photo.

Photo: Stephen T. Anderson Collection
A worker uses a hopper to prepare and distribute ores.

There's no doubt that Director Shelton was under tremendous pressure from Bureau higher-ups to curb accidents. The Bureau of Mines had recently published a report, based on AEC-related work, on how to reduce hazards while working with zirconium, titanium, and thorium, among others. Not-so-gentle reminders were published in the *Bureau Bugle*, asserting that safety precautions were for everyone's own good and not to be taken lightly. Still, explosions and fires would continue to plague the lab.

Construction on the Purification tower was completed in early 1952 and security around the gleaming white tower was unusually restrictive. Lawton Geiger, from the Pittsburgh branch of the AEC, wrote to director Shelton regarding who was—and wasn't—allowed in the building. "The building in which the hafnium separation work will be performed should be treated as an administratively controlled, limited area into which only authorized persons will be allowed access," insisted Geiger. Employees that were associated with the project would be put on a list that was managed by the site's security officer and head librarian Eleanor Abshire. Everything operated on a need-to-know basis with AEC projects. It's almost certain Rickover or his Navy group had made several trips to Albany by now, first to confer with Kroll, then later to inspect the purification setup, which had been previously performed at the Y-12 facility at Oak Ridge.

With Buildings 29 and 30 completed, the zirconium process was now fully contained at the

Albany Bureau. This was certainly a momentous time for the local laboratory and Rickover, who had been dealing with processes scattered across the country. Now zirconium and hafnium would be prepared in one location, with one group of highly qualified people working together to create nuclear-grade zirconium sponge.

From start to finish, the zirconium product moved through buildings on campus for each individual step. The process began as beige-colored, low-hafnium zirconium oxide ore from Brazil (and other sources) arrived by trainload at the station and was trucked to the Operations Building. Inside the elegant structure with towering arched windows was an ore dressing area, located on the north mezzanine.

From here, the zirconium process officially began: debris and impurities would be removed and the concentration would be slowly stirred in a ten-foot tank that was three feet deep with water and a mix of chemicals. A skimmer would whisk off foam that formed at the top of the tank; solid impurities would filter out into a separate tank and the desired product, zirconium oxide sludge, would feed into another tank. Most of the chemicals used throughout the separation (also called purification) process were highly corrosive, so tanks, tubes, pumps, and fittings all had to be corrosion-resistant. Holding tanks and vessels were all lined with glass and fittings were made of Teflon.

From there, the improved ore—which now looked like goopy sludge—would go to the brand-new, five-story tower for a process called liquid-liquid extraction. Inside the tower diffuse sunlight gleamed off of the thin, sixty-foot tall glass columns that extended the height of the tower. The six-inch-wide Pyrex tubes were located against each wide, windowed wall, backlit by glass-block windows. A wide walkway allowed access to each wall of columns. The zirconium oxide sludge was fed into a tank and mixed with a proprietary solvent. On the other end of the columns, another aqueous solvent was fed simultaneously. As the two liquids moved through the columns, aerator plates at the bottom of the tubes sent glittering bubbles of oxygen up into the tubes to break up particulates.

As the zirconium sludge moved left to right, down the first tube and up through the next, it was broken up by the aqueous solution, and after snaking through hundreds of feet of tubes, the minute (but detrimental) amounts of hafnium were broken free from its sister element, leaving a purified zirconium oxide slurry to be collected at the other end of the tubing. On the opposite end, purified hafnium was collected.

After the hafnium had been completely separated from the zirconium hydroxide, the hydroxide was precipitated (separated from the solution) and moved onto a filter press. The filter press consisted of a series of 3' tall by 1.5' metal frames holding stretched nylon filter cloth. After being pressed several times, the zirconium hydroxide turned from a sloppy goo into damp, cakey sheets.

Inside the brand-new chlorination plant, the zirconium hydroxide cake would be fed into a rotary kiln for drying. The kiln was a 25' long tube angled toward the ground so that gravity would help move product as the tube slowly rotated. A gas heater at the low end of the kiln would completely dry the zirconium and then the zirconium powder would be collected. It would then feed into a calcining furnace where it would reduce down to a white, granular oxide. That granular material would be mixed with carbon and then pressed into briquets the size of a small egg.

From here the product would be moved on to chlorination. Inside 6' tall steel furnaces a large, cold coil called a condenser was attached to the top. Zirconium oxide was added to the bottom and heated. Chlorine gas would then be pumped into the bottom of the furnace and the zirconium would collect on the coils at the top of the furnace, resulting in a yellowish-gray zirconium tetrachloride powder.

Reduction of the crude zirconium tetrachloride was the next step, which took place in the new zirconium reduction plant. A row of sunken reduction furnaces handled processing the material; hydrogen was added to the zirconium tetrachloride and then sublimed (turned to vapor) to remove unwanted impurities. Then molten magnesium was added into a steel pot at the bottom of the reduction furnace. The air within the furnace was pumped out to create a vacuum, and replaced with helium. The magnesium would react with the tetrachloride to produce zirconium and magnesium chloride.

In the next step, the magnesium chloride and any leftover magnesium ore would be distilled out of the zirconium in another furnace. The zirconium was placed in a crucible at the bottom of the furnace and once again, regular air was removed from inside the furnace, creating a high vacuum. Helium was pumped back in. After some time in the super-hot furnace, pure zirconium sponge would remain in the bottom of the crucible. Any sponge that clung to the side of the crucible and had to be chipped out. This presented a fire hazard so the crucible was flooded with argon gas to reduce the chance of spontaneous ignition.

From here the sponge was taken to a dry room, which was located in a wing of the reduction plant. True to its name, the air in the dry room had little to no

Photo: Stephen T. Anderson Collection

"Zirconium tetrachloride production: before the oxide can be chlorinated it must be mixed with the proper amount of carbon, and then pressed into briquets for ease of handling. This machine presses the mixture of oxide and carbon into dense briquets about the size of a small egg." —Bureau of Mines Field Operations Region II 1953

Photo: Stephen T. Anderson Collection

"Crude zirconium chloride is volatilized in a hydrogen atmosphere and condensed on a water cooled coil to remove iron and other impurities. The furnace top and coil are transferred to another furnace where the chloride is reduced to metallic zirconium." —Bureau of Mines Field Operations Region II 1953

Photo: Stephen T. Anderson Collection
A worker carefully chips away zirconium off the sides of a pot.

Photo: Stephen T. Anderson Collection
An ingenious hopper system allowed zirconium plus alloy material to be poured into the top and then evenly distributed among thirty buckets.

humidity and anyone with exposed skin would quickly feel uncomfortably parched. Here the sponge was carefully chipped apart into smaller pieces by a hydraulic press fitted with a chisel point, then crushed in a cylindrical machine called a "gyratory crusher." The pieces were then stored in fifty-pound lots.

Next came creating that perfectly blended homogeneous zirconium ingot. At this point, zirconium alloys were being created and tested at the Albany Bureau, so it wasn't just pure zirconium that was being mixed and melted. In the zirconium plant, finely crushed zirconium sponge plus pea-sized chunks of alloy ingredients were poured together and mixed into the top of a large hopper. The mixed granules would be evenly distributed into thirty buckets at the bottom of the hopper, creating thirty individual portions ready to be pressed.

Using a hydraulic press that exerted 50 tons per square inch, the granules were formed into 2" square bars that were welded together to create electrodes. The electrodes were then slowly fed into one of the 30,000-amp, 20-volt arc furnaces to be melted. The electric arc—much like a tiny, continuous bolt of lightning—would melt the electrodes as they moved into the furnace, turning them into a pool of molten metal at the bottom of the six-inch, water-cooled crucible within the furnace. The end result was known as a first melt ingot.

The ingot would be buffed, cleaned, and the little dimple inside the end of the ingot (called a "shrink pipe") would be sawn off in the machine shop by a special hydraulic hack saw, specifically set aside to only cut zirconium. Two first melt ingots would then be joined together by arc welding them with zirconium wire for good electrical contact, then remelted. The

Photo: Stephen T. Anderson Collection

Here, a row of "bombs" are set up to test corrosion resistance. Without proper corrosion resistance, the alloys produced for the future nuclear submarine would be worthless. Rigorous testing and copious note-taken was key to producing the winning alloy.

Photo: Stephen T. Anderson Collection

Despite having multiple classified projects at any one time, the Bureau had a robust local public relations program that gave a solid overview of current projects. Here, a display at the Albany Timber Carnival shows multiple aspects of the laboratory's ongoing work.

result would be a second-melt ingot, which was purer and had better homogeneity than a first-melt ingot. Throughout the melting process there would be tests to analyze the quality and composition of the ingots.

Because the Bureau was testing different alloys for Rickover and the Naval Reactors Program, stainless steel "bombs" were used to test corrosion resistance, which at this time was the big issue plaguing the development of the nuclear submarine. The bombs were simply washing machine-sized boxes that could be filled with test liquid and the alloy in question, then sealed and heated to an extremely high temperature for a sustained amount of time. This test could simulate the intense conditions that zirconium alloys would face inside a nuclear reactor.

"The Submarine Thermal Reactor (STR) for the *Nautilus* had to be able to generate steam for a 60,000 HP output in a boiler the size of an ordinary bedroom," recalled Earl T. Hayes, the Bureau's technical liaison to the AEC. "That's all the room that could be had. The hotter you run a steam cycle the more efficient it becomes. As I remember the boiler operated at 550°F and 1200 PSI . . . consequently the Zr [zirconium] had to meet exacting standards to qualify. The Albany lab had at least a hundred stainless "bombs" holding specimens at 600°F and 1500 PSI for screening and testing purposes."

The Bureau and the other laboratories involved with Rickover's project were quickly closing in on solving some of the long-standing questions: which zirconium alloy would work best in a nuclear environment, and how could a high-quality, homogenous alloy be produced? Big changes to answer those questions would require courageous leadership, calculated risks, and just a little bit of luck. The year at hand would be one of the most intriguing time periods of the "golden age" of the Bureau of Mines in Albany.

CHAPTER ELEVEN
UNCOMMON MIRACLE METALS
March 1952–December 1952

"The metal [zirconium] is spectacular stuff—so unstable in powdered form that it may blow up violently just being transferred from one vessel to another. It burns fiercely, and water just spreads the blaze. Yet in the form of a solid plate, ingot or bar, zirconium can be forged at red heat without danger. It is one of the most inert metals known in resisting corrosion attack from most acids."
—Jack R. Ryan, New York Times, *April 19 1953*

"Zirconium, modern chemists agree, is a two-faced so-and-so; in one form, it is appropriately called the 'Cinderella metal,' but in another it seems cursed with the temperament of a crazed Missouri mule."
—Milton Silverman, Saturday Evening Post, *November 8, 1952*

In March 1952, Earl T. Hayes gave a public presentation on the "Little-Known Uses of Uncommon Metals," where he spoke of the creativity of man when it came to rare metals like lithium, beryllium, gallium, indium, selenium, titanium, germanium, and cerium. Such unheralded metals had been crafted into useful niches. For example, beryllium-tipped tools had been used at the Bureau to reduce sparking when workers had to chip away zirconium clinging to the insides of copper crucibles. Presentations like this were a way of keeping the local population in touch with the broad scope of work being performed at the Albany Bureau and beyond, without getting into specifics of more classified work being done on site.

The year 1952 was all about uncommon metals at the Albany Bureau—the unfamiliar metals zirconium and hafnium and their alloys were being developed for the Navy on the fly as necessity dictated. One set of new zirconium alloys was being tested at the Bureau in boxy "bombs" set up for measuring corrosion resistance. "Despite the adoption of crystal bar zirconium as the core structural material for the Mark I reactor, an effort was instituted by Naval Reactors to develop a corrosion-resistant alloy of zirconium which could use the Kroll-process sponge directly rather than after de Boer–process [crystal bar] refining," recalled Benjamin Lustman, author of *The Metallurgy of Zirconium*. "The continual improvement in quality and reproducibility of the sponge no doubt played a large part in this decision." With the Bureau's commercial scale-up and vastly improved equipment and instruments, the final zirconium product was looking better and better. But metallurgists were still working on an alloy "recipe" that would provide long-term corrosion resistance for the zirconium used in the actual *Nautilus* reactor.

Other sites involved in corrosion-resistance tests included Battelle Memorial Institute, Nuclear Metals, Inc., and Naval Reactors at Bettis Atomic Power Laboratory. Bettis's D. E. Thomas was charged with heading up a group called the Zirconium Alloy Corrosion Committee. Two goals of the committee were to identify elements that were detrimental to corrosion resistance, as well as find elements that could vastly improve corrosion resistance.

"Fortunately, Bettis already had underway an active program of corrosion tests," Rickover explained later. "These included the study of a number of zirconium-base alloys which contained other elements to obtain improved corrosion resistance. Included was one ingot in which a small amount of stainless steel had been accidentally added. The tests showed the beneficial effects of iron, nickel and chromium, which are contained in stainless steel. This discovery was a good example of serendipity. But in another sense, it was not really chance. A well-run project should be able to recognize and take advantage of the unexpected."

Metallurgists already had a bead on what other additions to zirconium might help: tin, tantalum, and niobium were three other elements under intense examination. Of the three, tin had the best nuclear properties and was most effective. At first, a 5% tin addition was tested, then slowly reduced to 2.5 weight percent. That amount was "a good compromise between corrosion resistance, strength, and fabricability," noted Lustman. The alloy was soon dubbed Zircaloy. Since multiple facilities were working on alloy composition, it isn't clear who first arrived at the proper alloy ratio. "I always thought I found the tin addition first but at the development speed who can tell—but it wasn't Bettis," Earl T. Hayes insisted.

While the work to develop the perfect alloy could be intense and all-consuming at times, there were lighthearted moments, too. Teases of spring were in the air as April rolled around and the Bureau hosted an Easter egg hunt on campus. Organized that year by Robert Govro's bride, Beverly, the Easter egg hunt would become a beloved tradition that was looked forward to by many children. One-hundred and fifty children attended 1952's hunt on a chilly Saturday morning. The eggs, provided by the parents, were divided and hidden in three different areas on the expansive campus for three age groups.

There were special prizes in certain eggs; Leland Yerkes's son Roger was lucky to find the coveted "golden egg," which he turned in for a dollar. The silver egg was discovered by Janice Neal, who received a large Easter basket as a prize. "I remember one year sitting down on the ground, frustrated because I hadn't found one of the golden eggs, [then I] realized I was sitting on it," Barbara Snow recalled in a childhood memory. "The Easter egg hunt and annual Christmas party were two events we looked forward to every year!"

Bees buzzed happily among the pink and white horse chestnut blossoms along Broadway Street as spring swept across the Willamette Valley. Something else was buzzing around town: the hotly debated topic of whether area businesses should switch to "fast time" (daylight savings time) or not. In May, Bureau employees were asked to vote on daytime work hours as well as whether or not the laboratory should shift to daylight savings time. "Bureau officials explained that because of standard time, the local lab is 'four hours away' in telephone conversation with Washington," noted a *Democrat-Herald* headline. Nearby towns were already making a move toward a time change, making business hours confusing. "The daylight time net drew closer around Albany today as three cities within the immediate vicinity prepared to take action on the question within the next week."

Ultimately, the majority of Bureau personnel voted to move to "fast time" before the City of Albany moved ahead with the decision. Laboratory hours switched to "fast time" on May 19 and daily hours shifted to 7 a.m. to 4 p.m. A humorous write-up in the *Bureau Bugle* shed some light on the decision: "The winning party, known as the Early Birds and represented by a rooster, soundly defeated the Barnyard Party, whose emblem was a lowly pig." The snippet reminded readers that round-the-clock shift workers would be unaffected by the time changes. Not long after, all of Albany moved to daylight savings time.

The AEC had been seeking out a non-government entity to produce a steady amount of zirconium for some time, and in May 1952 they finally attracted a corporation to do just that. When hearing of the AEC's search for a zirconium producer, two men from Cincinnati, Frederick A. Hauck and Malcolm B. Nicholls, contacted Carborundum Corporation of Niagara Falls, N.Y. Hauck's company, the Florida Ore Processing Co., was experienced in extracting rare earth metals from Florida sands.

Nicholls's company, Continental Minerals Processing Corp., was brought on as a consultant to Carborundum to provide research. In an agreement with the AEC, Carborundum signed up to produce 150,000 pounds of zirconium *and* hafnium sponge annually for five years after obtaining a $2,443,000 certificate of necessity to build a subsidiary plant on eighteen-and-a-half acres somewhere near Buffalo, New York. The goal was to produce the two metals for less than $15 per pound. The contract with Carborundum was the first successful agreement the AEC had landed, and it's likely Rickover gave a sigh of relief after papers were signed.

It is interesting to note Rickover's early confidence in hafnium; after all, tests were still being run to determine if it would work as a suitable material for control rods within the shipboard nuclear reactor. Cadmium rods were still being investigated and the decision to switch to a different material had not yet been made.

Meanwhile, at the Albany Bureau, hafnium was being produced after being separated from its sister element, zirconium. Robert Govro recalled that "when I worked in the separations department, the world's supply of hafnium was eight grams, about the size of a quarter." Once they got the plant up and running, a foot-long, 3" diameter ingot was produced, representing the world's largest—and most expensive—amount of hafnium. Employees would make their way to the purification building on their lunch hour to get their picture taken with the world's largest known quantity of hafnium. "When anyone had the opportunity, they'd go down and pick it up" with gloved hands, Govro recalls. The world's supply of hafnium had increased to 30 pounds, and that ingot was "very, very valuable."

A year prior, a small building on the south end of campus that housed the magnesium pilot plant was enlarged significantly to accommodate a much larger project simply called "tin recovery." The long, white building stretched along the southwestern border of campus and within the walls, a unique classified project had been quietly running since 1951.

To the workers in Building 17 the project seemed benign; the Bureau had begun receiving large quantities of scrap metal from an undisclosed source. Certain aspects of the operation were easily spoken of; it was casually explained to the press that the scrap being processed was about 25% copper and 75% tin. This metal would be fed into 50-kilowatt furnaces that lined the sides of the building. The scrap would melt inside the furnace and workers wearing heavy leather gloves and face shields would pour the molten metal into 300-pound anodes.

The next step would take place in a slotted steel tank that held 500 gallons of a caustic salt-and-sulfur electrolyte. Workers in heavy boots would stand atop grates on the top of the tank and, using a gantry crane, would lower the anodes through the slots and into the corrosive mix. The anodes would corrode and dissolve the tin, and a sludge of black impurities collected at the bottom of the tank.

As an electric current buzzed through the caustic electrolyte, the dissolved tin would leave the solution and cling to bare steel sheets called cathodes. Four days later the cathodes would be lifted out of the top slots by crane and moved to another area of the building, where a worker would use a reciprocating hammer to scrape the tin deposits cleanly from the steel cathodes. After those four days in the solution a total of 30 pounds of tin collected on each sheet.

Those slightly-crumpled sheets of metal that had been peeled from the cathode were stacked and placed into a wheelbarrow and then carted to a 15-kw furnace, where they were fed in one at a time. As soon as the tin melted, an aerator at the bottom of the furnace would send little bubbles up into the molten metal, which would collect tiny solid impurities and bring them to the surface which would then be skimmed off by a wooden paddle. The purified tin would then be poured into water-cooled molds. The result were silvery, foot-long 50-pound ingots. The mirror-like bars would be stacked and shipped back to the undisclosed supplier in 60,000-pound lots.

This classified process ran for one year and was the only electrolytic tin plant in the entire United

States. At its peak the plant was turning out 1,000 pounds of high-purity tin a day. Workers likely knew that the project was being performed because tin was a critical strategic material in short supply at the time, but details of the project weren't declassified until the year 2000.

There was a dark side to this otherwise innocuous-sounding recovery process: Director Shelton had been approached by Hanford Atomic Works in 1951 to see if the Albany Bureau could help them solve the problem of large piles of scrap that had been collecting at Hanford as a waste by-product of plutonium production. "The work was undertaken because both tin and uranium, critical materials in short supply at that time, were being accumulated in sizeable amounts as an unusable waste," the Bureau revealed in 1977.

Within that waste were materials that needed to be recovered—not just tin and copper, but uranium was well. The metal had been run through reactors before being sent to the Bureau, causing the metal to become highly contaminated in the process. There wasn't enough uranium in the scrap metal to justify "an elaborate refining process," asserted Hanford, but it was "desirable . . . that the uranium be refined to as high a concentration as possible consistent with good economics to minimize the reprocessing costs once it leaves Albany," one declassified document stated.

The recovery of copper was vital because Hanford was using significant amounts of virgin copper in their daily operations. Since the copper would eventually be alloyed it didn't need to be totally free of tin, but Hanford officials did want it to be virtually free of everything else. The process of recovering the materials was more complex than what had originally been publicly released in 1953; the dross (foreign matter that created a scum on the molten metal's surface) that remained after melting down the initial scrap contained high levels of uranium—6% when analyzed by Hanford. The tin anodes were also analyzed and were found to contain 0.2% uranium.

In January 1952, Hanford requested that the Albany station devote a "small amount of time" to investigate a way to recover several million pounds of uranium-contaminated aluminum-silicon alloy that had been collecting in scrap storage cribs, using a similar method as tin recovery. It was estimated that the alloy had about 1% tin and .17% uranium. From the scrap, Hanford wished to extract two products: pure aluminum, and the aluminum-silicon alloy.

In all, 200,000 pounds of crude copper-tin alloy scrap (70% tin, 25% copper, 1% aluminum, and .5% uranium) were fed into the plant, resulting in a grand total of 135,000 pounds of purified tin that was shipped back to Hanford for reuse. Hanford estimated that at the outset, there was 75,000 pounds of copper and 3,000 pounds of uranium contained in the material.

This operation resulted in contamination of the building and grounds that wasn't realized until decades later. In the late 1970s and early 1980s, the government began an extensive cleanup effort aimed at Manhattan Project–and Cold War–era facilities. Amounts of unusual radioactive material—primarily Ag-110m (a radioactive silver isotope), plutonium, and various non-natural uranium isotopes—were found in the Back Forty field, prompting those in charge at the time to look into the matter. After talking with past employees it was determined that the tin recovery project was the likely culprit.

Howard Poppleton, former Deputy Director of the Bureau, recalled that "the AEC assured us . . . this material had not been in the reactor. So the Bureau set up a small plant to recover the tin and copper electrolytically. And they did over one hundred thousand pounds. And we went on believing that none of that had been in the reactor."

Curiously, an article published by the *Eugene Guard* in the summer of 1952 would accidentally combine the zirconium process with the tin recovery process, revealing outright that the tin and copper waste was from Hanford and it was a contaminated by-product of plutonium production. The reporter nonchalantly mentioned a pen stocked with barrels full of uranium that was bound for Hanford. If there had been any question of what the project was truly about and who the client was, it was all laid bare in the article. Despite the environmental impact of the project, the actual process was hailed as an industrial success and was adapted to be used in a commercial setting.

Summer 1952 was possibly the most critical time for the *Nautilus* project and for operations at the Albany Bureau. The nuclear submarine project had now been secretly laboring along for about three years, with the cantankerous H. G. Rickover at the helm. On June 14 at General Dynamics Electric Boat Division in Groton, Connecticut, during an elaborate ceremony, the keel of the newly-named *USS Nautilus* was laid, signaling the beginning of the vessel's construction.

The keel-laying ceremony must have felt monumental for Rickover and all those instrumental in overcoming all the hurdles faced thus far in the creation of an entirely new type of underwater vessel. On that day in June, as President Harry S. Truman wrote his

Photo: Wikimedia Commons
President Harry S. Truman signs his name during the keel laying ceremony of the USS Nautilus.

Photo: Wikimedia Commons
Admiral Rickover inspects the USS Nautilus.

initials on the keel plate, the action symbolically gestured that the theoretical was indeed becoming tangible. After a speech lauding the role and impact of nuclear science thus far, a crane "picked up a huge bright yellow keel plate and laid it before the stands. President Truman walked down a few steps and chalked his initials on the surface. A welder stepped forward and burned the letters into the plate. The public could have had no better demonstration that the *Nautilus* was under construction."

In Albany, spring blossoms gave way to brilliant green foliage and cool drizzly nights turned to sultry summer evenings. Crickets made a cacophony across the Back Forty expanse and the scent of freshly unfurled cottonwood leaves wove throughout the southwestern neighborhood. On the evening of Saturday July 5, 1952, three high school boys were outside around midnight at the corner of Eleventh and Elm Street, when they glanced at the night sky. To their surprise, they all witnessed an unidentified flying object hovering directly above the Bureau of Mines—the first such sighting in Albany in almost two years, the local paper reported.

The boys reported that the saucer was 200–300 feet in diameter and as they stood there watching, it hovered silently about 3,500 feet over the "Bureau of Mines building," which may have been referring to Building 1, the Administration Building. Orange exhaust emitted from the craft as it descended toward the Bureau, then no exhaust could be seen as it hovered in midair. After hovering, the UFO "shot back into the sky," trailing bluish-red smoke as it headed westward. The three boys alerted the police about their sighting and were referred to the military to make a report about the incident. Technical sergeant Robert Scott of the Air Force recorded the sighting and notified the air base in Portland.

While a single UFO sighting might be a curiosity, two UFO sightings over two government facilities might be considered slightly alarming—especially if the sightings were on the same day, and over facilities doing highly-classified work for the Atomic Energy Commission. At 6 a.m. on the same morning, four veteran pilots, three of them World War II veterans, were flying a C-46 transport plane for Connor Airlines. They were cruising at 9,000 feet en route to Denver, with wispy clouds above them. Suddenly they all spotted something stunning: a white, almost transparent disk was hovering 10,000–15,000 feet above them, in the area above Hanford Atomic Works.

"We passed the object as it stood suspended in space," pilot Baldwin recalled. "Couldn't pick it up on radar." Like the Albany craft, the four men noticed vapor trails "like the tentacles of an octopus" emitting from the UFO. As they passed, it "stood still at first . . . then seemed to back away and change shape . . . becoming flat . . . gaining speed . . . and then disappearing," noted the official declassified report. Baldwin grabbed for a camera but was too late. The pilots actually reversed course and passed through the area again, but the craft was long gone. Like the three Albany youths, the four pilots made a report to the authorities.

"All of us have been flying a number of years and we've seen all kinds of clouds and formations, but none of us have ever seen anything like this before,"

Baldwin concluded. UFO sightings around Hanford and other sensitive sites persisted.

"These airborne oddities were taken very seriously," notes Australian researcher Paul Dean, who studies the history of the UFO topic from the government and military declassified documents angle. "Pilots, and in particular military airmen, were requested to be on the lookout for, and indeed report, any UFO activity near Hanford while flying," said Dean. "What's really weird is this: the same thing had been happening for two years in the skies above the Oak Ridge nuclear weapons facility in Tennessee. Even now, the majority of these strange events have never been solved despite significant investigation."

Of course, the Albany Bureau, Hanford, and Oak Ridge were all heavily involved in Atomic Energy Commission contracts. "The USAF [United States Air Force] and the old Atomic Energy Commission tech and security people were all in agreement. Something was really intruding into the airspace above the USA's most sensitive sites," notes Dean.

Whatever was seen over Albany didn't generate too much of a buzz among the population; even after it hit the paper after the weekend was over, and there were no further sightings locally. A big uranium find that month garnered far more state and local attention than the "flying saucer" sighting. A Portland man who mixed deer hunting with prospecting came across a possibly significant deposit of uranium, which the Albany Bureau asserted was the best sample they'd ever analyzed. News spread across the state about the find, though the hunter maintained a "tight-lipped silence" about the location of his find.

A. H. Roberson, chief of the Albany Technical Services branch, concluded that "If these samples are representative of a newly-discovered deposit of considerable tonnage, they should be of value in the extension of the domestic tonnage program." If the Portland man's find resulted in a producing mine, he'd earn the AEC's $10,000 finder's bonus, plus $3.50 a pound for the refined ore. After the initial announcement there was no further mention. Only two locations in Oregon became famous for uranium; the White King mine near Lakeview, which produced 115,000 tons of ore, and the nearby Lucky Lass mine, both of which began being mined in 1955.

As for Rickover's submarine project, continuous improvement on the zirconium process was the number one focus. Homogeneity had been an all-consuming issue that had required much study and experimentation. The introduction of magnetic stirring coils in the furnace had improved mixing capability so that no inconsistencies remained within alloyed ingots. "Since remelting costs money and takes time, the Bureau of Mines devoted considerable effort to measures designed to make satisfactory ingots with only one melting, such as improved methods of adding tin and magnetic coil stirring techniques. Nevertheless, fabrication and remelting continued to be necessary for a large number of ingots, either at the Bureau or their destination, until after July 28, 1952."

The game all changed when a new consumable-electrode arc furnace called the Model II arrived. Within a month, the new furnace was being used to create one ingot per day from an electrode that had been rolled and forged, dubbed the "828" process. The crucible diameter was slowly increased without any technical issues, until a ten-inch-diameter ingot was produced—a truly hefty piece of metal. By the end of July, the Bureau had created ingots with the Model II furnace by using the direct double-melting technique, but without the intermediate steps of forging and rolling.

The new ingots were homogenous and sound—perfectly mixed and suitable for nuclear use. This streamlined process became known as the "610" method. This new way of melting zirconium alloys was a win-win: direct remelting without intermediate fabrication wasted less alloy, reduced contamination, cost far less because the metal wasn't worked as much, and retained soundness. It was a leap forward in zirconium production.

Because of Rickover's engineering wisdom, all aspects of the project were worked on simultaneously, and decisions about major changes were often abrupt. But Rickover asserted that his fluid decisions were not on a whim, but based on the highly regarded suggestions of the scientists and engineers intimate with the project. One such decision was made in August 1952. "By the summer and fall of 1952, significant milestones were beginning to whiz past like telephone poles past a speeding car," Theodore Rockwell recalled of the time.

One summer evening at Bettis, a meeting was held with Westinghouse staff, Lawton Geiger, and Rickover. Harry Mandil, one of Rickover's advisors, brought up the point that crystal bar production would need to ramp up soon; Rickover had just been tasked with developing the first nuclear aircraft carrier. Rockwell remembers the following explosive exchange:

> "We can barely make the fuel elements for the Mark I prototype with the units we have, and we have to get started on the shipboard core before

long," Mandil stressed. "Can I bring you a specific approval in the next few days?"

This seemed like a reasonable and noncontroversial proposal, so no one was prepared for Rickover's response. "I want to use sponge metal."

There was a startled chorus of "What?! Are you serious? We can't do that!"

But the Captain was firm. "The crystal bar process was a very ingenious laboratory method for increasing the world's total supply of pure zirconium metal from less than an ounce to many pounds. But it's a tricky and expensive laboratory process. My God, can you really picture us making tons of crystal bar, to fuel hundreds of ships, by depositing metal, atom by atom, out of hot iodide vapor onto special electrodes? No, sponge metal is the way we'll have to produce zirconium sooner or later, so we might as well get started."

At the Bureau, jaws dropped at the idea of using sponge. "About this time, the reactor at the Idaho test site was yielding suitable data, Westinghouse was geared up to make crystal bar ($100/lb) for the operating submarine reactor," recalled Robert Beall. "Then Rickover dropped a blockbuster. The sea-going *Nautilus* reactor would be made from arc melted sponge ingots rather than crystal bar. Westinghouse was downcast. Shelton was ecstatic. I was horrified as we hardly had a process."

There was even more of an uproar at the Atomic Energy Commission. Lawton Geiger tried to diplomatically reason with Rickover. People from Bettis also reminded Rickover that fuel elements for the Mark I core were currently under production. They all asked the same thing— "Do we throw it all away?" But Rickover calmly explained that while he'd previously asserted that the "the Mark I equals Mark II"—as in, both the prototype and actual reactor core should be the same. Rickover then a scribed a new equation on a nearby blackboard that spelled "Mark Two does not equal Mark One." Rickover explained, "The first equation says we won't postpone tackling any shipboard problems just to get the prototype on line. But the second equation says we can always make an improvement in the second plant, if there's a better way to do something. If we need to. And we need to."

The meeting came to abrupt end when Rickover refused to argue with the naysayers any longer, saying he had a plane to catch. Further, he wanted his nuclear-grade zirconium sponge in three months' time. "And amid further cries of protest that three months was too short to prove anything," Rockwell wrote, "he left."

It was executive decisions like that—ones that at first glance seemed like tremendous gambles—that were actually calculated risks, driven by the perfect storm of working within the brand-new industry of nuclear power development, with unproven metals and within an astonishingly unforgiving time frame—one created by Captain Rickover himself. The captain's hair-raising gambles were one key element of the project's eventual success. "It is a tribute to the vision of Admiral Rickover and his staff that the latter course [Kroll-process sponge produced at the Bureau of Mines], initially dubious but eventually justified, was adopted and supported in the face of this beguiling alternative," Lustman wrote regarding the switch. However, a stockpile of 40,000 pounds of crystal bar zirconium was retained by Bettis and Foote—just enough for one more reactor—in case things with sponge didn't work out.

So with a word, the crystal bar provided by Foote Mineral Company was stricken from the process.

As high-powered decisions were being made by the Navy regarding zirconium production, the public finally got a small, slightly skewed glimpse into the purpose of the "tall, lovely tower" where "the visitor is not invited to look . . . over."

In August 1952 the *Eugene Guard* published a nearly full-page article on the facility. Reporter Dan Sellard acknowledged that "little is known to the public but vital in its contribution to the economy of the Northwest, the bureau is currently engaged in a dozen research tasks—all pointed toward making metals in the area contribute to the national welfare." But the article went on to confuse some of the projects being performed at the site; at one point, the author even erroneously combined the tin recovery project with zirconium production.

The author seemed surprised that there were no armed guards on site, despite the AEC-contracted work being done. "The Bureau seems to operate on the theory that its work is more down-to-earth than 'top secret' and after all, its research is in processing and not inventing." Previously, there had been lengthy discussion on whether armed guards and barbed wire fences were necessary for the site, though ultimately they were decided against. Such security measures, it was decided, would likely draw more attention and speculation about the top-secret work being done on campus.

"Lest the impression be left that such things as plutonium and uranium are just kicked around for anyone to take, let it be said that there are 'classified' sections of the plant," where visitors are not allowed, and the author stressed there were no atom bombs "lying around." Cameras were allowed, but a guide shadowed the photographer at all times so no unapproved pictures were taken.

What *wasn't* secret was the excitement for the Bureau's annual employee picnic, which in 1952 was held at Avery Park in Corvallis instead of on campus. Temperatures had been on the cooler side with morning clouds that threatened rain, but that didn't stop six-hundred employees, spouses, and their children from crowding the park to celebrate. Folks casually dressed in checkered shirts and slacks gathered around picnic tables crammed with "spud flakes," casseroles, salads, pickles, condiments, buttered rolls, ice cream, cakes, and "oodles of baked ham" so good that the *Bureau Bugle* quipped "that committee either knows how to cook or has a cook who knows how."

The morning clouds burned off and a hot August sun baked the baseball field as players took to the diamond. Team Zirconium was pitted against the Physical Metals branch (dubbed the "Mets,") which resulted in a fine competition. Player D. C. McKerahan had a spectacular home run that sent the softball flying into the middle of an adjacent diamond. "The pop was flowing like water," as chilled refreshments were passed out to keep players cool. After 10 innings the Mets blasted past the Zirconium team, with a final score of 14 to 11. Other games coaxed competition between employees, with Robert Govro sprinting past all others to win the sack race, and librarian Eleanor Abshire and her partner winning the three-legged race. Horseshoes and an egg toss also provided entertainment for the adults, while the kids participated in their own age

Photo: Stephen T. Anderson Collection

Avery Park in Corvallis, Oregon, was the perfect location for a Bureau-wide picnic, with plenty of room for hundreds of attendees. Photo circa 1950.

Photo: Stephen T. Anderson Collection

Rows of employees, their spouses and children, line long picnic benches during this 1950 Bureau picnic at Avery Park. The annual picnic was one of the most anticipated social events of the year.

divisions for sack- and three-legged races. Many who attended stayed late into the day and it was deemed "by far the finest picnic we have had to date."

The washing-machine-like "bombs" at the Bureau and at Bettis had been constantly running corrosion tests on zirconium alloys, particularly the one dubbed Zircaloy. This alloy had initially been the most promising for corrosion resistance within a nuclear environment, but as testing continued it became evident that Zircaloy wasn't as ideal as initially hoped. "Unfortunately," wrote Benjamin Lustman, "as happens so frequently in advanced research and development programs, this euphoric state of affairs soon came to an end." Long-term corrosion studies revealed the corrosion rate increased at a certain point and stayed constant thereafter, and even worse, past a certain point the new alloy behaved no better than the non-alloyed metal.

"An immediate halt was called to the further processing of core product containing Zircaloy-1 [what the alloy would soon become known as] and an urgent search instituted for a fallback position," Lustman explained. But all was not lost; copious note-taking during corrosion tests provided a base of knowledge from which to continue a search for a better alloy.

Lustman recalled that a melter at Bettis had been working on alloys when he (either accidentally or on purpose) added some stainless steel to the mix. "It was widely suspected that the error was less than ingenuous, the melter reasoning that, since stainless steel was widely known to be highly corrosion resistant, its addition to Zircaloy-1 could only be beneficial.

Whatever the motives, the resultant material did have outstanding corrosion resistance."

The *Nautilus* reactor was already under construction when Zircaloy-1 was found to be inadequate, so Rickover made another daring decision on August 28, 1952: after conferring with scientists from Bettis and metallurgists from the Bureau, he chose to authorize the production of Zircaloy-2, which consisted of 1.5% tin, 0.12% iron, 0.10% chromium, and 0.05% nickel. "I selected it for the *Nautilus* reactor before an ingot had ever been melted, fabricated, or tested for corrosion," Rickover wrote.

The implications of this single decision were staggering, but Rickover stressed that his fluid pivot to Zircaloy-2 was born from "careful consideration" and the wisdom of those who were directly involved in producing the alloys, not administrators or managers. The minds, hands, and hearts of the metallurgists and scientists involved with zirconium were Rickover's guiding light through a period of time when a single wrong choice could doom the entire project.

Just as Rickover was meeting with Bettis scientists about making the switch to a new alloy, workers were reporting to their stations in the electrolytic tin plant in Building 17 at 8 a.m. on August 28 to find flames licking up around some of the electrolytic cells. Workers took immediate action to extinguish the blaze and the fire department was summoned. As soon as it was safe to reenter, damage was assessed and it was found that seven of twenty-four electrolytic cells were affected by the morning's flare-up. "Damage was confined to the wooden electrode supports and to the paper sheath on the fiber glass insulation" surrounding the cells. Though the actual origin couldn't be pinpointed, it was assumed a short circuit in a cell heater was the culprit. Luckily nobody was hurt in the incident and the fire was minor enough that production was resumed when the damaged equipment was replaced. But the Bureau's safety record had taken yet another hit.

Fall 1952 brought many changes for the Albany laboratory, including a shakeup in personnel. One of the greatest contributions of the Bureau of Mines in Albany was the people produced by the laboratory and the enormous skill set those professionals held. Even in the early days, accomplished employees were sought out by other companies and institutes worldwide to share their wealth of knowledge. The first big wave of contributors left in September.

"BUREAU LOSES KEY MEN" shouted the *Bureau Bugle* that fall. Carborundum Corporation in Niagara Falls, New York had lured away the Rare Metals branch chief, William W. Stephens, as the company was working hard to establish its zirconium plant. Stephens was slated to head up the entire operation for Carborundum, a position worthy of his accomplishments: when Stephens had been hired into the Rare Metals branch there were only ten people working on the zirconium project; by the time he left, Stephens oversaw more than one hundred and fifty workers. Chemical engineer Ralph Nielsen also spent a year at Carborundum to assist with operations.

E. Don Dilling, the employee who had suffered tremendous injuries from the explosion in Building 2 earlier that year, took over Stephens's position as Chief of the Rare Metals Branch, which was reorganized into four sections. Chemical Processes would be headed up by James H. McClain and be in charge of direct chlorination and chemical purification/separation in the big white tower. The Metallurgical Plant Section would reduce zirconium chloride to sponge as well as reducing hafnium to sponge after the separation step and would be overseen by H. P. Holmes. Robert Beall would lead the Metals Section, which would be tasked with melting zirconium and zirconium-alloy ingots for the AEC. And lastly, one of Kroll's closest associates, Henry Gilbert, was moved into the Research and Development Section to help "develop improvements on the present processes and delve into new process for old metals and new processes for new metals," noted the *Bureau Bugle*. These experiments would be performed on a small scale with intent to adapt for future large-scale work.

Stephens wasn't the only employee to be drawn away by another entity; H. Gordon Poole, the former Chief of the Nonferrous Metals Branch, had accepted a temporary position in Colombia, South America, as Foreign Minerals Division consultant. After that job ended, he intended to return stateside to accept a job as Associate Professor of Metallurgy at Case Institute.

The Ferrous Metals branch was also facing a tremendous loss, as twelve-year Bureau veteran Robert Rasmussen accepted a position with Quebec Metallurgical Industries Ltd in Ottawa. Rasmussen's wealth of knowledge was lauded by his fellow workers for his impact on the local metallurgical economy: "The processes, research, and patents developed under Robert's direction and supervision have already resulted in the establishment of two large metallurgical plants in the Northwest and may very well become the foundation upon which are built several more major Northwest metallurgical industries," noted a former Ferrous Metals employee Phil Dettmer. "Robert has a particular knack of inspiring one to do his best; due, perhaps, to the fact that he himself is always driving for the best performance."

Rasmussen shared some details about his future post, as reported in the *Bugle*: " 'My new position will be in the development of reduction processes, principally electric smelting, and in the application of the processes in production plants.' " He also added without hesitation, " 'I regret leaving the many good friends that I have in Albany. The Ferrous Metals Branch is a mighty fine group, staffed with capable and enthusiastic people. I have enjoyed the electric smelting research immensely.' "

Although key staff were changing places, a historic moment occurred in September: the Albany Bureau began providing zirconium sponge, 90% of which was melted into zirconium-alloy ingots intended for the actual *Nautilus* reactor. The Bureau of Mines station in Boulder City, Nevada took the blended sponge and compacted it, then sent it back to Albany to be melted into 100-pound ingots. Up to five of these first-melt ingots were welded together to form a huge electrode, which was melted into a massive 300-400-pound ingot.

Things were finally syncing up for nuclear-grade zirconium alloy production in Albany: the crystal bar step had been eliminated, saving loads of time and expense. The "828" process had been replaced with the "610" process, leaving out a time-consuming intermediate step of forging and rolling, and magnetic stirrers were implemented to help improve homogeneity. And Zircaloy-1 had been stricken from production in favor of the tin, iron, chromium, nickel and zirconium alloy dubbed Zircaloy-2. Hafnium, the most uncommon of all metals being produced commercially in Albany, was being considered as a possible control rod material. The zirconium production facilities in Albany were running full-speed, 24–hours a day. And despite a loss of vital employees, the Albany Bureau was still staffed with first-rate metallurgists. Everything was humming along beautifully . . . until one fateful night in October, when everything went to hell.

The dark autumn sky could be seen outside the two-story, floor-to-ceiling windows of the Zirconium reduction plant on the evening of Wednesday, October 22, 1952. The two-year-old building had been pressed into continual round-the-clock usage since about September 1950 to fulfill the Atomic Energy Commission's insatiable need for zirconium. A spacious 50-foot addition had recently been constructed on the east end of the building for additional furnaces so even more zirconium could be produced for the AEC.

    The evening started out like any other, with fifteen shift workers busily tending to the rows of furnaces, checking and double-checking instruments and making sure everything was on schedule as the Albany Bureau produced zirconium alloy for the *Nautilus* reactor. The subtle clank of overhead cranes lifting furnace lids and the hum of electrical equipment filled the air. But at 7:20 p.m., a ventilation pipe from a sandblasting machine sent tiny particles of zirconium and magnesium upward, where they burst into flame. As soon as they realized that there was a fire in the rafters, the fifteen men on duty scrambled to fight the fire with nearby extinguishers. But it didn't take long for the workers to realize they were in real danger: flames were greedily eating away at the wooden roof while spreading down the walls at the same time. Electrical panels, conduits, and the wall interiors were being consumed faster than the men could quell the flames with fire extinguishers.

Waves of searing heat moved through the building as pieces of the roof began falling down. Workers fled the building. Campus was evacuated entirely, including the panicked ladies playing bridge in the recreation room in Building 2. An alarm sounded at the Albany Fire Department and firemen made the oft-traveled route to the Bureau, only to arrive as flames spewed from every broken window. Workers continued to fight the fire alongside the firemen as a hellish orange glow tainted the night sky. Bureau employees who'd heard the alarm at the station responded as well, speeding to campus to help save the building. Four fire trucks came wailing to the site while the Bureau's own emergency truck responded with additional equipment and lighting.

Neighbors from the Fir Oaks addition ran out of their homes at the sound of falling timbers and the obstinate roar of the out-of-control blaze that flared up twice the height of the building. Columns of smoke plumed out between individual bricks on the outer wall as the interior structure became weakened and burned away.

People flocked to Liberty Street on the east and Broadway Street on the west to watch in horror as the million-dollar building burned for nearly two hours. Hundreds of cars clogged side streets as gawking townspeople watched firemen try to quench the inferno and keep it from spreading to the other buildings—and the rest of the neighborhood. State police, Linn County deputies, and nearly all reserve police from Albany were on hand to keep the throng of onlookers far enough away from the scene because there was a very

Photos: Stephen T. Anderson Collection
The Bureau's largest fire to date broke out on the night of Wednesday, October 22, 1952. The Zirconium Reduction Plant (Building 28) suffered extensive damage, but an aggressive cleanup and rebuild ensured zirconium would still be available for the Atomic Energy Commission.

Photos: Stephen T. Anderson Collection
The aftermath of the Oct. 22, 1952 fire.

real concern that the building would explode.

Firefighters were informed that a treacherous enemy lurked beneath their feet as they battled the fire: in one corner of the basement were hydrogen tanks and large quantities of magnesium. If the fire reached those tanks a devastating explosion would erupt. A crew of firefighters were stationed at the stairwell leading down to the tanks, battling the fire away from the entrance. Another immediate concern was protecting several hundred thousand dollars' worth of zirconium sponge in unsealed buckets that were earmarked for the AEC. Those containers were being stored in the northwest corner of the building and a second crew of firefighters safeguarded the stockpile so it wouldn't burn. "If any one of those three [hydrogen, magnesium, or stored zirconium] caught fire, the other two would probably have burned also," recalled Robert Beall in his written recollection.[7]

By about 9:30 p.m. the zirconium plant was a smoking, blackened shell. Hundreds of windows had been shattered and their metal frames had been bent and warped by the heat. Fragments of glass formed a glittering halo around the building, reflecting spotlights and siren lights. Ladders were propped up against blown-out windows. Tired firefighters and all the employees who'd stayed to help wandered the scene, sooty and with the acrid taste of smoke in their throats, assessing the damage and clearing debris.

Assistant Regional Director Mark Wright was at the scene that Wednesday night instead of Stephen Shelton, who was in Norris, Tennessee on official business—which likely meant he was conferring with Oak Ridge officials about zirconium operations. Wright was able to inform Shelton of the situation but the

Photos: Stephen T. Anderson Collection
Albany Fire Chief Don Hayne (in white hat) discusses the fire with Bureau personnel.

Photos: Stephen T. Anderson Collection
Bureau personnel assess the extent of the damage done to charred control panels in Building 28.

Bureau's brand-new phone system had been crippled by the fire, and incoming calls could not be received. Employees immediately scrambled to make repairs so lines would be up and running the next day.

As the night went on, fire trucks left and the second shift of overnight workers arrived. Undeterred employees picked right up where the others had left off and started clearing fallen timbers from furnaces. Glass was swept up. Melted and burned electrical parts were inventoried and slated for replacement. Barrels were arranged around entrances and planks put up to block passers-by from wandering in. But around midnight another fire flared up in a pile of debris and the fire department was called again. One truck responded and quickly extinguished the flames. Amazingly, no personnel or firefighters were injured throughout the night.

  A truck remained on site through the next morning and personnel kept a wary eye in case anything else should reignite. News of the disaster spread quickly through the state and most major newspapers made a mention. As a fresh crew of workers arrived Thursday morning the damaged roof and upper walls were already being torn away in preparation for rebuilding. Any equipment that was salvageable—which was thankfully more than had initially been thought—was being cleaned off and prepped for repair. Charred roof beams were lifted off furnaces and disposed of. Workers clad in coveralls and hats picked up debris inside, navigating a floor clotted with clumps of ashen remnants. The final damage estimate was between $150,000 to $200,000 dollars ($1.5–$2 million in 2020 dollars.)

  Without missing a beat, efforts were made to get the plant operational as soon as possible. "Repairs are being made as soon as the building is cleared enough to allow workmen to proceed," noted the *Bureau Bugle*. "A new roof is planned with part of the present one already removed. The brick sidings have been torn down where the wooden backing was burned away and part of the steel superstructure will have to be replaced." On a hopeful note, the *Bugle* concluded, "As repairs proceed it appears that the damage is not as bad as was first believed." A full day after the fire, a worker who was helping clean the plant came across a thermos jug. Despite being completely scorched, the coffee inside was still warm.

The local media took note that the November 8, 1952 issue of *The Saturday Evening Post* featured a tell-all about the classified goings-on at the Albany laboratory. "Apparently the silence concerning the uses of zirconium have been broken," the *Odds 'N Ends* column of the *Albany Democrat-Herald* announced. "Zirconium plant in Albany was the same one which burned recently in that $150,000-$200,000 fire. Too bad the *Post* missed this feature: the plant may be out of operation for several months," the paper quipped.

———•—•———

Ironically, a public open house had been scheduled for November 21, and although cleanup and reconstruction were happening at the damaged zirconium plant, the public was welcomed onto campus for guided tours. "So many have expressed a desire to observe work being done at the local laboratory that it was decided to host an open house for the public," Director Shelton told the local paper. The campus would be open from noon to 7:30 p.m. that day.

The event was regulated by the same committee responsible for social activities and get-togethers, the

Bureau of Mines Associates, and any visitors needed to register in Building 1 before departing with their designated tour guide. Gone were the days when visitors could freely wander around from building to building. The areas available for viewing were the electrolytic tin plant, electric smelting, ore dressing, melting and fabricating. The tall white tower, Purification plant, and zirconium plants were strictly off-limits, per AEC security regulations.

The laboratory was flooded with more than 700 visitors during the open house event, proving that the public was increasingly curious about the Bureau of Mines' operations. Tour groups swelled to up to 30 people per group, spending an hour and a half with their guide. Some attractions were similar to previous tours, with visitors getting to see the impressive collection of geologic samples that glowed under ultraviolet light and hearing a Geiger counter chatter when waved over pitchblende ore. The tin recovery plant was a big hit during the open house, with visitors amazed that 150,000 pounds of refined tin had been produced.

Although the zirconium plants weren't available for viewing, the chlorination building was open and a fresh zirconium ingot was on display. "I can't pretend to understand it," one guest said of the laboratory's operations, "but I do appreciate something of the magnitude and importance of the work," reported the local paper. It was also noted that workers were hustling overtime to get the zirconium plant fixed in thirty days' time.

The *Saturday Evening Post* article that came out on November 8—the one the *Albany Democrat-Herald* mentioned—was an incredibly detailed account about zirconium, from its difficult beginning as a fiery, temperamental metal through its patient taming by

Foote Mineral Company through their crystal bar method of production. It extended into Kroll's involvement with the Bureau, though just like the earlier *Eugene Guard* article, the *Post*'s description of Albany's laboratory wasn't very accurate. Despite that, the piece took a topic that could be technically off-limits and breathed life into zirconium production with colorful anecdotes about the early years of development.

"When AEC scientists bumped into the remarkable new applications of the temperamental metal, and decided to buy it in ton quantities, American industry could produce it at the rate of only a couple of pounds a week and the price of about $500 a pound. Today it is coming out of strange, costly, hush-hush plants at the rate of hundreds of pounds a day, and at a cost of approximately fifteen dollars a pound," the *Post* wrote in "The Wonder Metal That Blows its Top."

At the time of publication, word had not gotten out that Rickover had chosen sponge metal over crystal bar; some details remained classified at that point. Layer by layer the media was peeling away the secrecy surrounding zirconium production and by now enough information had been offered publicly that a well-read, attentive reader could easily piece together Albany's contribution to the nuclear submarine project. "To many observers, the future of the fiery metal is bright. The age of zirconium has begun," the *Post* concluded.

But there was one metal that still hadn't been addressed much in the press: mysterious hafnium. The world's largest quantities of the silvery metal were being produced in the white tower at the Albany Bureau and the Navy was taking note. At the end of 1952 Rickover and his crew were becoming more and more wary of the current control rod material.

Argonne's test on silver-cadmium control rods for the Mark I showed their performance was completely unsatisfactory.

In a meeting held at Bettis in December, people from Naval Reactors and Argonne came together to discuss what had happened. The control rods were composed of a silver-cadmium alloy core surrounded by stainless steel. Test rods had been pulled out of high-temperature, high-pressure autoclaves the morning of the meeting so attendees could view results. These tests were designed specifically to simulate what years of exposure to a nuclear environment would do to specific materials. But what happened to the silver-cadmium rods during those "accelerated corrosion tests" wasn't pretty.

"The fears of those working on the control system were realized," noted author Benjamin Lustman. "Close examination of the rods revealed locations where the stainless-steel sheath appeared to be slightly raised and pulled away from the silver-cadmium core. This would of course be disastrous, since further ballooning of the sheath could cause binding of the control rod and endanger safe and controllable reactor operation."

Control rods were a critical component of reactor design: their sole function was to regulate the reaction within the reactor. Rods would be raised (to allow reactions to accelerate) or lowered (to slow reactions). By their nature, control rods needed to absorb neutrons in order to work properly. Whatever material the control rods were made of, they needed to be the exact opposite of nuclear-grade zirconium, which was virtually invisible to neutrons.

Rickover didn't waste any time conducting a "test" of his own. During the meeting he took a hammer and smashed a test rod. The stainless-steel sheath split cleanly away from the core—a clearly unacceptable result that indicated possible failure during use. Rickover immediately announced hafnium would be the replacement material for control rods.

Rickover's chief physicist, Dr. Alvin Radkowsky, had been eyeing hafnium as an ideal control rod material for some time. But physicists at Argonne National Laboratory were worried that hafnium wouldn't absorb neutrons as well as silver-cadmium had. Only rigorous testing would prove whether the switch would work.

Just as with the other midstream changes, opting to use hafnium was a serious risk that could result in delays for the *Nautilus* program. The facilities that produced crystal bar zirconium were soon put to use creating hafnium crystal bar instead. "The experience on reduction, purification, and fabrication accumulated with crystal-bar zirconium was directly applicable to hafnium," said Benjamin Lustman. Tests were begun to evaluate hafnium's effectiveness as a control rod material.

In an interesting twist, the Foote Mineral Company contract to provide a secondary source of zirconium fell through at the end of 1952—but for the first time ever, the Atomic Energy Commission suddenly had private companies soliciting offers to enter into commercial zirconium and hafnium production. The coming year would be the ultimate litmus test to prove whether all the innovations, blunders, and sudden adjustments surrounding zirconium and its sister element hafnium would pay off. Out in the desolate Idaho desert, the STR (Submarine Thermal Reactor) Mark I prototype reactor was nearly complete.

CHAPTER TWELVE

SUBMARINE IN THE DESERT

January 1953–December 1953

"In the middle of last century, out in southern Idaho, amid the sagebrush and the steppes, the Navy kept a secret site. In that place—dry and arid, far from the sea and very much unlike it—scientists and engineers simulated a nuclear-powered submarine."

—Robinson Meyer, The Atlantic, *Oct. 8, 2014*

Darkness had just fallen on the night of February 24, 1953. Residents of the area surrounding the Albany Bureau of Mines were just returning home from work. In the Fir Oaks addition—one of the most well-to-do areas in Albany—neighbors had become accustomed to the "excitement" that came with living near an experimental laboratory, including fires, explosions, and the parade of emergency personnel that followed. So when a tremendous explosion rocked the neighborhood that night, it's likely many folks came streaming from their homes to see what had happened at the Bureau.

But the calm and quiet that followed was unusual. Nothing appeared to be on fire or otherwise destroyed; no firetrucks or ambulances came zooming to the site. Neighbors returned to their homes, wondering what they'd just heard. The next night the local paper gave a partial explanation. "Explosion of a 'bomb' at the Northwest Electro-development Laboratory here at 5 o'clock last night was done deliberately and under controlled conditions," the *Albany Democrat-Herald* explained. "Consequently . . .

Photos: Stephen T. Anderson Collection
1953 aerial view of the Albany Bureau of Mines campus, looking east.

Photo: Will Davis Collection, American Nuclear Society
Exterior of the Submarine Thermal Reactor (STR) Facility outside of Arco, Idaho.

no one was injured and little damage was done to the shed in which it was set off." The blurb also noted that the blast was part of a classified experiment aimed at uniting metals.

While there were many operations at the Bureau in 1953 that remained classified, a trickle of secrets about zirconium and the *Nautilus* project was being released by the Atomic Energy Commission. Since the beginning of the year, Westinghouse had been revealing some critical details regarding the power plant for the *Nautilus*. "The first atomic power plant has resulted in hundreds of additions to engineering know-how," noted an article in the *Corvallis Gazette-Times*. Local readers would've appreciated the reference to the several thousand pounds of zirconium per month that were being used by Westinghouse for three power plants, including one for an aircraft carrier. In remarkable detail for the time, the article outlined current concerns that engineers were dealing with regarding the Mark I prototype, one being properly controlling the enormous power output, the likes of which had never been dealt with before.

Representatives from the Albany Bureau were also making major contributions to collective knowledge about never-before perfected melting methods, derived from meticulous work performed on zirconium. In a powerful triple-whammy of Albany metallurgical prowess, Bureau employees presented their findings to an audience at the American Society for Metals at the Western Metal Congress in Los Angeles.

Chemical engineer Henry Gilbert and physicist Robert Beall discussed their revolutionary paper (prepared with former employee W. W. Stephens,) "Process of Consumable-Electrode Arc Melting of Zirconium," and Regional Director Stephen Shelton and E. Don Dilling gave a speech on Albany's method of manufacturing zirconium. Finally, metallurgists Dr. Earl T. Hayes and A. H. Roberson and mechanical engineer O. G. Paasche presented their paper, "The Zirconium-Nickel Phase Diagram." By now, Albany's influence in the metallurgical world was undeniable.

There were other nationally-anticipated developments regarding zirconium at the beginning of 1953: in Akron, New York, the Carborundum Metals Corporation was working to finish their highly anticipated $2,500,000 zirconium plant. The 5-year contract with the AEC stipulated that Carborundum would deliver 150,000 pounds of zirconium and hafnium sponge a year. Meanwhile, repairs on the zirconium reduction plant had been made after the disastrous fire and Bureau was still providing zirconium to the AEC, all while working on new aspects of hafnium production. "With the aid of tremendous efforts on the part of Don Dilling , Glen Kenagy, Martin Farlee , and many others, the plant was put back into operation without too much delay," Robert Beall wrote.

The biggest question on everyone's mind, whether at the Nuclear Reactors Group, out in the desert at the Mark I prototype facility, or at the Bureau, was whether or not the six years of intense planning, experimenting, innovation, and adjustments would result in a functioning nuclear reactor. "As Operation of Mark I was about to begin in late 1952, there remained many unanswered questions, and there was not always assurance that satisfactory solutions would ever be found. Even Rickover, returning for a visit to Mark I at this time, said, 'If the *Nautilus* makes two knots on nuclear propulsion she will be a success,' " noted Commander E. E. Kintner of the U.S. Navy, in his recollection, *Admiral Rickover's Gamble*.

"The year 1953 was extremely busy for all persons working on development and manufacture of the reactor cores for the Mark I and Mark II power plants. As soon as the Mark I core was shipped to Arco, Idaho for the initial nuclear power run, all facilities and personnel at Bettis worked around the clock as needed to meet the schedule for the *Nautilus*," wrote Westinghouse's Dr. Robert Gordon.

By March 1953, everyone's anticipation regarding the upcoming Mark I testing was reaching a fever pitch. Almost four years exactly after the first announcement of the establishment of a new atomic site, the National Reactor Testing Station, located in the remote eastern Idaho desert, was complete—and completely abuzz with activity.

Down a long road that gracefully snaked away from U.S. Highway 26, past guard shacks, security checks, and away from the public's prying eyes, was the cavernous warehouse-type structure where the Mark I was awaiting power-up. Two-thirds of a ribbed simulated submarine hull stuck out of a "sea tank," a round water-filled tank that surrounded the core within the hull. Gangplanks along the upper stories of the building allowed personnel to see straight down onto the prototype reactor.

Those involved with the Mark I knew there was a plethora of things that could go awry once the reactor was initiated. Being able to safely harness and control the tremendous amounts of concentrated energy generated by an atomic reactor was paramount. Of course, the reactor would have to be functioning first to see if energy could be controlled. There was even talk of starting the Mark I from a remote location a mile away, but that plan was eventually scrapped.

Engineers wondered if the radiation shielding would be adequate within the Mark I; instead of

Photo: Will Davis Collection, American Nuclear Society
"Inside the land-locked hull, first atomic submarine engine was generating power when this picture was taken."
—From "They Harnessed the Atom" promotional brochure

Photo: Public Domain/ OSTI.GOV/opennet
This photo, taken during the construction of the National Reactor Testing Station, Submarine Thermal Reactor (STR) facility, shows how incredibly desolate and isolated the area is.

traditional heavyweight shielding, the prototype had small, light components and there were serious doubts it would be able to protect future operators within the *Nautilus*. To make matters worse, since the *Nautilus* hull was already under construction, the weight of the heat shielding had to be absolutely precise. If calculations were off, the submarine wouldn't be able to dive safely.

    The Mark I also needed to demonstrate proper heat transfer. The core would generate tremendous amounts of heat while in operation, and it was designed to remove heat from the fuel elements and move it to where the heat could be converted into useful power. Overheating would destroy elements and dangerous amounts of radiation would be released. As the reactor ran at increasingly higher power, this heat transfer process could become more perilous.

    The engineers also had a problem with something aptly called "CRUD," or "Chalk River Unidentified Deposit." At the end of 1952, Rickover had surreptitiously sent fuel element samples to be tested in the Chalk River reactor in Canada. Results had been nothing short of disappointing; a layer of rusty "crud" had formed on fuel elements that had been irradiated. "The Chalk River results seemed to indicate that the STR reactor core, already a questionable heat transfer quality, might clog up entirely and overheat like the radiator of the family automobile," explained Kintner in *Admiral Rickover's Gamble*.

    Additionally, the moving parts within the reactor were lubricated by hot, radioactive water. There were doubts that all the parts within the reactor could withstand long-term exposure. Lastly, there was a very real fear that the life of the core simply wouldn't last. "If its power life was days or weeks, it would be acceptable for combat use. If it would provide continuous power for only a matter of hours, it would be no better than the electric storage battery used by conventional submarines. When Mark I began operating, it was feared that its core life was only a few hours and that much additional development would be necessary before the *Nautilus* could operate long enough to be useful in combat," reasoned Kintner.

Before the test scheduled for March 30, Rickover made another trip to Idaho with AEC Commissioner Thomas E. Murray. Meticulous testing on all aspects of the Mark I had been performed "until they were as nearly perfect as they could be made," noted Kintner. Rickover watched these start-up preparations with rapt attention, eager to see if the quarter-of-a-billion-dollar venture would be a success or utter failure.

It was a stunningly clear, cold night in the eastern Idaho desert on the night of March 30, 1953. Piercing stars blanketed the indigo sky. The monolithic rectangle that was the National Reactor Testing Station glowed a cool blue in the light of a full moon. Personnel involved with the first test of Mark I hustled to the building, their breath visible in the 26-degree air.

There were undoubtedly some very nervous people present as the clock ticked past 11:00 p.m. that night. If Rickover was concerned that the project wouldn't work, it's unlikely he let it show. Realistically, there were so many things that could go wrong with this brand-new technology that it was hard to imagine *anything* could go right—but as the Mark I achieved criticality at 11:17 that night, the incredible happened: It worked. And it worked *well.*

For two hours the Mark I operated at several thousand horsepower, which was only a fraction of its full capacity. "That first operation was amazingly successful," remembered Kintner. "Six years of study, organization, planning, conniving, fighting for funds, building laboratories, manipulating people, developing new materials and devices had paid off. The first day of Mark I had surprised its most optimistic proponents."

Despite the initial test, the Mark I wasn't considered a proven success—yet. The reactor continued to be tested as it stayed in the low-level power range for almost two months as data was collected from its operation. Everyone involved was eager to bring the Mark I to full power to test its operating capabilities.

We don't know if Bureau employees were aware of the success of the first test, but there seemed to be a pervasive party atmosphere that spring. Gatherings were held in the recreation room of Building 2 for couples' engagements, and retiring and exiting employees, usually on a Friday afternoon.

Librarian Eleanor Abshire had always loved a good dance, so when she got the idea for a "Hobo Party," others agreed it was a smashing idea. A remote location near Corvallis was chosen and directions were posted in the *Bureau Bugle*. One Saturday night in April employees and their guests drove along a pothole-riddled dirt lane to Colorado Lake Resort ("don't drive too far or you will end up in the lake," warned the *Bugle* invite.) Guests were instructed to dress in their best hobo garb and bring their own "pot luck midnight lunch" to the lakeside pavilion.

Bureau employees and their guests were not disappointed by the early spring outdoor party, which proved to be a bit chilly, though two roaring firepits provided warmth for all who gathered around. Firelight reflected off the slender lake as music from the jukebox filled the wooden pavilion where guests in patched rags danced to lively beats. A five-man band was assembled from Bureau employees, complete with bass, saxophone, electric guitar, clarinet, and piano. The pianist was late upon arriving, as his wife had just given birth in Corvallis.

During the night, extra funds were collected for clarinetist Art Henderson, whose clarinet had been stolen from his car after he'd performed at a previous event. After the hobo dance, a check was presented to Art to buy a new clarinet. The gesture was so touching that Art was nearly in tears upon receiving the donation. As for expressing his appreciation, Art said "It is hard for me to put it into words . . . To a musician, his musical instrument is like a left arm." He didn't realize how many friends he had at the Bureau and was blown away by their kindness. That kind of community-minded giving and family-like closeness wasn't unusual for Bureau employees of the era.

Sandwiches were brought by ladies in attendance, and men brought potato salad, pickles, olives, chips, and appetizers. Hot coffee warmed those by the fire and soda cooled off those who were a tad too warm from dancing. A costume contest was held and prizes were handed out for best (or worst?) dressed. "The official Bureau hobo is Dick Robertson, Physical Metallurgy Branch, whose whiskers and patches fooled nobody . . . Female honors went to Mrs. Gloria Worth, a guest of Jim and Lil Crom. Her sloppy, faded shirt, and way-too-large pants were a sight for sore eyes," announced the next edition of the *Bugle*.

The much-awaited Easter egg hunt was held on a warm April Saturday. About 100 youngsters searched high and low for eggs that had been donated by parents in the week before; ten cents plus four eggs for each child planning to attend were to be brought to the

Bureau in advance. Children were divided into four age groups, with prizes for each group. The grass was left uncut so eggs would be tougher to find, even if hidden in plain sight, but when the mower finally did come around, it created a bit of a mess, as a dozen undiscovered eggs were still left on the ground.

Another hit activity at the Bureau that spring was the newly-formed Dance Club. On Friday evenings in the second-floor recreation room in Building 2, employees and their guests were treated to an instructional session taught by a professional teacher before attendees paired off, dancing their newly learned moves to jukebox hits from Glenn Miller and Tommy Dorsey. For April 1953's dance session, thirty people packed the dance floor for foxtrot, rhumba, the breaks, Latin dancing, and "a teaser of tango." Cookies and coffee were served between dances, provided by the Bureau Associates.

In the Idaho desert, the Mark I testing was gaining serious momentum. As days lengthened and the desert landscape warmed up in late spring's glow, Rickover and AEC commissioner Thomas E. Murray traveled back out to the desert outside Arco, Idaho, to witness the first full-power run of the prototype reactor. As the two men looked on, operators coaxed the reactor to its maximum potential. Author Rockwell remembered it was a momentous occasion:

> "Murray . . . understood and backed Rickover's struggles to arrive at this crucial day, and the Captain wanted him to have the honor of opening the throttle valve and allowing steam

generated by the reactor to enter the turbine for the first time. When this had been done, and it was clear that the power plant was operating smoothly and steadily, Rickover and Murray climbed up out of the hull and walked down the wooden stairway to the floor of the building. From there they walked back to where they could gaze in silence at the shaft of the power plant turning slowly under the power of nuclear fission. It was an emotional moment; the atom had at last been made to produce a useful quantity of power."

Kintner recalled that "there were many happy people in the Idaho desert the night of May 31, 1953. The happiest was Captain Rickover, who had had the vision, constantly forced the program against opposition, and provided the technical judgment to steer it through areas far beyond those previously known." Testing continued twenty-four hours a day, seven days a week, with incremental increases in power. Everyone involved knew the dangers of each increase, but such tests were absolutely necessary to prove the reactor's reliability.

To everyone's great relief, the Mark I proved to be a "calm and stable machine, even when treated roughly, as its inexperienced operators often treated it, showed no tendency to become an atomic bomb. There was no indication of any dangerous overheating in the reactor fuel elements." Additionally, the radiation shielding proved even more effective than expected, allowing less than half of the initially calculated amount of radiation through. At this point, estimated reactor life was looking excellent.

There was one problem that was perplexing operators, however: numerous unexpected shutdowns were occurring because of overly sensitive safety circuits. While the safety sensors were meant to be sensitive, they were so touchy that it was becoming detrimental to operation. Something as minimal as footsteps walking past the reactor compartment could trigger a "scram," effectively shutting down the reactor every time. ("SCRAM" was an acronym for Safety Control Rod Axe Man, allegedly named after the poor fellow whose job it was to hold the axe at the rope holding a control rod at the first nuclear pile in Chicago.) As time passed and operators analyzed the issues plus safety data, they learned to circumvent unnecessary scrams so the Mark I could operate smoothly.

Being able to run the reactor at full power for a limited time and getting excellent data was a success in itself, but Rickover knew that wasn't enough. On June 25 the Mark I reached full design power without failures of any sort. The reactor ran for forty-eight hours and at that point the engineers were satisfied with data they'd gathered, but Rickover was not. He figured cumulative problems would only become apparent if the reactor was pushed to full operating conditions for an extended period of time—just as if it were truly at sea. Hearing that the engineers were going to shut down the reactor, Rickover moved to intervene.

"He had visualized that if the forty-eight-hour run turned out well, they should continue on a simulated cruise across the Atlantic. He reasoned that such a dramatic feat, if successful, would end the doubts in the Navy that nuclear power was a feasible means of propelling ships. It would give the project the momentum and breathing space needed to carry on the development without constant harassment until the *Nautilus* could get to sea," Kintner wrote. But it was difficult to convince anyone present that going past forty-eight hours at full power was a good idea. In fact, once Rickover announced he wanted nothing less than a transatlantic run, Kintner absolved himself of any responsibility should something disastrous happen to the $30-million prototype reactor.

Rickover agreed to assume full responsibility if things went awry and a simulated course to Fastnet, Ireland was charted in the control room. Forty-eight hours into the run everything was looking fine, but as soon as engine-hours hit almost sixty hours, problems arose. There was a buildup of carbon dust, instruments started to act up, a main coolant pump began making a worrisome noise, and at sixty-five hours, a main condenser tube failed. Once again senior project employees pleaded with Rickover to shut down the test, but the Captain stood his ground.

"Rickover's reply was firm and calm," Theodore Rockwell remembered. "This plant is a warship, not a floating laboratory or test-bed. This run will show people that this thing is real. It's not a toy. If I let you shut down the plant, it will be weeks before we're back on the line again. No, I'm not going to let you talk me out of this. It's too important, dammit! That's non-negotiable, so let's drop it."

So the Mark I continued operations, with each shift making quick adjustments and repairs to keep it virtually chugging across the Atlantic. After ninety-six hours of continual operation at full speed, the reactor "reached" its destination. "Now there could be no mistaking that nuclear power had been effectively harnessed to do real work on a practical scale," Rockwell wrote. When the reactor was evaluated after the run it was found that besides small tweaks and improvements, there were no significant problems or damage. The success of Rickover's run paved the way for the rest of the project to proceed on schedule and with a newfound confidence.

"To those of us who had participated in the STR [Submarine Thermal Reactor] project, who knew how many chances were taken, how far previous engineering knowledge had been extrapolated, the fact that all the unknowns had turned out in our favor was a humbling experience. Rickover, paraphrasing Pasteur, put it this way: 'We must have had a horseshoe around our necks. But then Nature seems to want to work for those who work hardest for themselves,' " remembered Kintner.

For those in the know back at the Bureau there must have been a sense of profound elation (and a collective sigh of relief) as the good news about Mark I's transatlantic run reached Albany. Even though there was reason for celebration, zirconium work never slowed at the Albany Bureau; on the contrary, AEC contracts and zirconium, hafnium, and Zircaloy 2 experimentation continued. In the summer of 1953 an extensive—though strictly confidential—Zirconium Progress Report was written up at the Albany Bureau for Lawton Geiger at the Atomic Energy Commission.

The report covered a zirconium and hafnium production contract plus a Bureau of Ships order. Zircaloy 2 melting activities performed during the summer were also discussed. In the period covering July 1–August 1, the reduction plant completed 151

Photo: Stephen T. Anderson Collection
A 1952 photo of the petrographic laboratory at the Bureau.

Photo: Stephen T. Anderson Collection
Pete Romans using a Baird spectrograph. Photo circa 1952.

runs, which produced an astounding 21,300 pounds of zirconium, with the average batch weighing about 162 pounds. By comparison, only 721 pounds of hafnium were produced, with each batch weighing about 224 pounds. In the metals section 8,282 pounds of Zircaloy 2 was alloyed in a months' time.

The Nonferrous Metals Branch reported that progress on unalloyed zirconium was promising; corrosion tests showed increasing resistance to corrosion in high temperature environments. The report also mentioned an investigation into creating a zirconium-iron alloy. Studies to improve consumable electrode arc melting were initiated, and experimental work on recovering Zircaloy 2 scrap had begun.

A. H. Roberson of the Technical Services Branch discussed sourcing high-hafnium zirconium sand from a number of different places. In a sharp contrast with the early days of nuclear-grade zirconium production, when low-hafnium source material was desired, the AEC was now looking at zircon sands that would provide the biggest bang for the buck when it came to hafnium content. Sands from Australia, North Carolina, and Sri Lanka were analyzed by Albany's Petrographic Laboratory.

The Atomic Energy Commission knew that continued work on zirconium, hafnium, and all the other components of nuclear-grade materials was essential because the *Nautilus* was no longer the only goal; now that the Mark I had proven its worth in initial tests there were big plans for the Nuclear Navy to expand—as well as some other secret plans that were in the works.

"I have an important announcement to make. It's not public yet, so keep your yaps shut," said Rickover to his senior associates in July 1953. He briefed the group about plans to create the first civilian nuclear power plant, and let them in on a little secret—instead of the plant being created by private industry, the government would take the lead. Rickover admitted there were some angry "companies and scientists" who felt the job should've been kept in the public sector, but a nuclear aircraft carrier project had just been scuttled, which opened up an opportunity for Rickover's crew, and the captain wasn't going to let the opportunity pass him by. He instructed his group to forget about the carrier project and focus solely on commercial power production. "If we never get to build an aircraft carrier reactor, so be it. But by God, this will be the best damn civilian power station humanly possible," Rickover insisted.

Because the *Nautilus* reactor—the Mark II—was still in production, and because the leap to commercial power was in the works, it was only natural that zirconium, hafnium, and Zircaloy 2 testing would continue at the Albany Bureau, and under Rickover's watchful eye.

Top brass came calling in the summer of 1953; on July 9 newly-appointed Assistant Secretary of the Interior Felix Wormser visited the Albany Bureau to become more familiar with laboratory operations. Wormser was a veteran of World Wars I and II and had an extensive background in mining and metallurgy, with memberships in the American Institute of Mining and Metal Engineers and the Society of American Military Engineers, and was a co-author of *Marketing of Metals and Minerals*. Wormser and his wife were the guests of honor at a dinner hosted by the Bureau Associates. The soiree was held at the luxurious Benton Hotel in Corvallis—Dr. Kroll's former residence and the most likely place to spot a celebrity in the Willamette Valley.

As summer wound to a close, the Albany Bureau gained twenty-eight new employees but only lost a few to retirement, transfers, or military service. Carborundum Metals was slowly drawing away Bureau employees as operations at their plant were ramping up. The Bureau's Ralph Nielsen toured the new zirconium plant while on vacation with his wife Viola, and the *Bureau Bugle* noted that former Albany employees William Stephens, Cal Morrison and George Sartory were working on completing Carborundum's new facility. The knowledge gained at the Albany Bureau—and all those locally involved—were affecting zirconium production on a national level.

In August the *New York Times* announced that the General Electric Company was planning to build a 71,000-square-foot laboratory in Schenechtady, with completion expected around 1955. The new facility would contain similar equipment to the Albany Bureau: an arc furnace, rolling mill, and other specialty equipment for studying zirconium, molybdenum, and other high-temperature metals and their alloys. "Apparatus for melting and casting metals under various atmospheres by means of induction melting, arc melting and other foundry techniques will be able to handle every known metal," the article assured.

Toward the end of 1953 radio and print journalists were given an unprecedented glimpse at the up-and-coming *Nautilus*. During a rare singular instance, the reporters were invited to tour the nearly finished submarine as it sat in the Groton, Connecticut shipyard, though the most interesting part of the ship—the part that housed zirconium and uranium components—was shrouded in canvas curtains. Some of the journalists scoffed at the amount of secrecy ("surrounded by a fog of 'security' so thick it could be cut by a knife—and most of it both pointless and fairly ridiculous," quipped one.)

Undue concealment aside, the journalists were still able to give readers an excellent visual description of the incredible craft. The Navy claimed the *Nautilus* was only halfway to completion but the keen-eyed press suspected this was a conservative estimate, as the steam-generating propulsion system was the only major component that hadn't been installed yet. Heat generated from fission of uranium within the nuclear core would turn water to steam which would power turbines, which in turn would generate energy to drive the craft's propellers.

While not unusually large, the *Nautilus* was noticeably wider than other submarines, to accommodate for the novel propulsion system. "There is, of course, the mysterious compartment atmidships *[sic]* which will house the mass of zirconium metal and uranium rods that constitute the atomic fire-box," noted one article. Another difference was that the *Nautilus* was a single-hulled ship, though that hull was thicker than normal to accommodate for deeper dives. Exactly how thick was anyone's guess, as reporters weren't allowed that bit of classified intel. Cruising speed was also hush-hush, though previous disclosures had hinted at submerged speeds over 20 knots (about 23 miles per hour) versus 15 knots in a traditional submarine, at short intervals. Her closed-cycle system didn't require air to operate and she didn't expel any vapors. The *Nautilus* was expected to only surface when entering or leaving a harbor. She was to go farther, faster, and deeper than any submersible craft before her.

Previous submarines had been limited to a single deck; the nearly city block long *Nautilus* not only had three decks but featured actual steel stairs instead of ladders. By comparison the interior was considered spacious and more livable for people aboard, who would be spending more time submerged than any crew before them. There would even be a six-hundred book library, a photography darkroom, and the mess hall could convert in minutes to a fifty-seat movie theater. Most luxurious of all, the Nautilus had enough beds for all her crew, negating the need for "hot bunking," the practice of multiple sailors assigned to the same bunk, each with their own assigned sleeping time. Aside from the unprecedented luxuries, the press was sure to stress that safety was paramount and lead shielding would keep those aboard safe from radiation.

The Navy disclosed that the *Nautilus* was being built faster than any other submarine before her, and Chief of Naval Operations Admiral Robert B. Carney noted he was going to strongly recommend building more atomic submarines once the two currently being built were finished. Surprised reporters would have then noticed a second submarine hull. In the slip next to the *Nautilus* was her sister ship, the *Seawolf.* Construction on the second submarine was ongoing, though not as far along as the *Nautilus*, as a slightly different propulsion system was being worked on.

Locally, Bureau metallurgist E. T. Hayes revealed Albany's direct involvement in the *Nautilus*'s development to a lively crowd in December. Hayes addressed a local Kiwanis Club at the Hotel Albany to reveal that the Albany Bureau was producing zirconium exclusively for the Navy's nuclear submarine cores. He clarified that while the zirconium wasn't involved in creating the nuclear reaction, it was literally the only metal that could sheath the handful of nuclear fuel (uranium-235) without affecting the reaction. The crowd was so enthused about the topic that Hayes was questioned by the audience for a full half-hour after his speech ended.

As 1953 drew to a close there was no question about the classified work being performed on the former college campus. The Albany laboratory had experienced breathtaking amounts of growth in the previous two years and now locals didn't have to wonder why; the exact application of zirconium had finally been revealed. Within the gleaming white industrial buildings and matching brick-and-window zirconium plants, two perfect materials were being produced for the world's first nuclear submarine.

CHAPTER THIRTEEN

BRIGHT DREAMS AND NIGHTMARES

January 1954–December 1954

> *"We made zirconium for use in the* Nautilus
> *It took the work of all of us*
> *We were making zirc' in '51*
> *and produced the metal, ton after ton*
> *When the* Nautilus *launched, we all gave a shout*
> *We did our part without a doubt.*
>
> Nautilus *launched January 21, 1954"*
> —*"Zirconium," by Robert Govro*

> *"By 1954 the Bureau of Mines had made its contribution to the zirconium process, and the attention of the research group was directed to other problems."*
> —*Robert Beall, in "Cold-Mold Arc Melting and Casting"*

The mood in Groton, Connecticut was electric on the morning of Thursday, January 21. A thick blanket of cold gray fog blanketed the Thames River, where 12,000 people were eagerly waiting for the *Nautilus* to slip into the sea. Dignitaries from Washington D.C., including the First Lady, had arrived at the Electric Boat Company shipyard on a special nine-car train.

In an eloquent speech, the Chief of Naval Operations, Admiral Robert B. Carney extolled the $55,000,000 submarine's future role in peace or war. "*Nautilus* is a symbol of man's dreaming, his bright dreams, certainly, and if man is not wise, nightmares, too," he remarked. Carney went on to praise all those involved with her creation but only named (now) Rear Admiral Rickover in his thanks.

Photo: Wikimedia Commons/Public Domain
First Lady Mamie Eisenhower nearly missed striking the USS Nautilus with a bottle of champagne as the submarine speedily slipped out of its launching cradle.

Photo: Wikimedia Commons/Public Domain
Commander Eugene Wilkinson (left), Commanding Officer of Nautilus, greets Rear Admiral Arleigh A. Burke, (right), as he steps onboard the USS Nautilus.

Rickover was seated in the front row of the launch platform but did not have a part in the ceremony. Those who worked with him noted that the slight, abrasive Rear Admiral was—for once—properly dressed in his Navy uniform, instead of his preferred civilian attire. Later, Rickover stood behind First Lady Mamie Eisenhower as she was poised to shatter a bottle of domestic champagne on the ship's bow.

At exactly 10:57 a.m., after speeches and prayers, onlookers watched as two men wielding a heavy timber struck blows to the launching cradle. The weakened beam split in two, suddenly releasing the massive submarine. Mrs. Eisenhower, looking somewhat surprised, nearly missed striking the ship as the flag-draped *Nautilus* speedily rolled away. Crew members and dignitaries stood atop the ship as she rolled along; some clung for dear life to the top railing while others stood casually as they rode the swiftly gliding craft into the dark waters of the Thames. At that exact moment, the heavy fog split and the newly christened submarine was bathed in brilliant sun, as if a heavenly spotlight were beaming down. The huge crowd erupted in jubilant cheers and tugboats sidled up to the craft to guide her to the docks.

Locally, the *Greater Oregon* newspaper happily announced that if it weren't for the zirconium produced at the Albany plant, nuclear propulsion wouldn't have been possible. "The launching of the *Nautilus* marked a new day in history, since for the first time an engine can operate a 2800-ton, 300-foot long submarine and keep the ship submerged all the way across the ocean. That such an engine is possible is due to the zirconium, produced at the Albany plant, the only place in the world where this metal is made in commercial quantities." The same article announced that other peaceful uses were underway; a commercial power plant was already in the works.

By all accounts January 1954 should have been a month of exuberant jubilation at the Albany Bureau. The local press had been touting the site's significant involvement in the creation of the *Nautilus* for an entire month prior, and the launch date of January 21 was widely publicized. Because of his pivotal role in zirconium development after Kroll's departure from the Bureau, Henry Gilbert and his wife had been invited to attend the auspicious event in Groton, Connecticut.

But instead, the monthly *Bureau Bugle* started out with an unusually dull—and almost worried—tone at the start of 1954. Instead of having their own write-up on the biggest project ever undertaken at the site, there was nothing. No accolades for the departments involved, no mention that one of their own had been invited to the ceremony, no recalling the fervent pace at which three shifts a day, twenty-four hours a day, churned out the "Cinderella" metal called zirconium. The witty banter and lighthearted tongue-in-cheek prose the *Bugle* was famous for was replaced with dry reminders that the laboratory would be needing to tighten its belt in every department to save money in the coming year. There wasn't a single mention of the stunning accomplishments surrounding zirconium, hafnium, and the *Nautilus*.

Henry Gilbert and his wife had been invited to attend the auspicious *Nautilus* launch, but the chemical engineer had just returned from a trip to Japan where he and Dr. Kroll had been invited by the newly created Japanese Titanium Society. While on the trip to Japan, Gilbert fell quite ill and upon his return to the States he ended up waylaid for weeks with an unnamed ailment. He returned to work mid-spring for a week, only to end up back at home per his doctor's orders. His prognosis remained unclear and the *Bugle* reported his physician still didn't have a name for Gilbert's condition.

For the first time since the laboratory's inception, there was open uneasiness among employees about health concerns. In her retirement note to fellow coworkers, the Bureau's on-site nurse, Joanne Cody, R.N., joked about breathing the last whiffs of zirconium dust and chlorination fumes before her departure. The grim reality at the Albany site was that groundbreaking scientific discovery had dangers beyond the spontaneous fires and explosions; particulates generated by metallurgy in general were suspected of causing lung issues.

Concern was so great that in mid-1954, internal medical specialist Dr. Charles Reed of Corvallis headed up an investigation, largely funded out of his own pocket. "Since no data is available on the affect *[sic]* of zirconium fumes on the respiratory system, Dr. Reed has asked for permission to perform this experiment at the station." noted the *Bureau Bugle*. The doctor placed seven guinea pigs in cages in several zirconium production areas around campus to try and determine if workers were exposed to detrimental amounts of particulates in those spaces. Leland Yerkes was charged with care and feeding of the animals, who received a diet of rabbit pellets, lettuce, and water. Staff working in the vicinity of the guinea pigs were warned against slipping them soda and candy bars, and for the love of all things, to not pick them up by the tails! "If the pigs must die it should be by natural causes," mused the *Bugle*. After six months, the animals would be euthanized and analyzed.

Adding to the collective worries at the Bureau were even larger issues looming in the near future, punctuated by site inspections performed by significant guests. At the end of January 1954, Lawton Geiger, the Pittsburgh AEC liaison, and two other AEC representatives visited Albany for an inspection of the campus, with discussions likely centering around big operational changes in the near future.

Though it was known that Albany would not be commercially producing zirconium and hafnium in the long run, the new Carborundum facility had just begun producing zirconium, so Albany would continue to provide the Navy with zirconium—at least for the time being. Hafnium would continue to be produced in Albany indefinitely, as it was the pivotal material for control rods, the hafnium/zirconium separation process being the Albany Bureau's own "secret sauce." After the stop in Albany, Geiger and company continued on to the desolate Idaho desert to inspect the Mark I facility.

The day after Geiger's visit a much larger group of visitors arrived on campus. The group of ten—which was practically a who's who of mining and metallurgy professionals—included Dr. Curtis Wilson, Dean of the School of Mines and Metallurgy at Rolla, Missouri. Curtis was a personal friend of Director Shelton, and his team were the guests of honor at a dinner held at the Hotel Albany. In a speech there were tones of concern about the Cold War. "This is an American age, but since World War II America has been weakening and the Soviet Union has been gaining strength through expansion. It is the people rather than the resources of a nation that make it strong. The worth of anything depends on the uses to which it is put, so it is up to us all to work hand in hand to make this country a better country."

For the next two days Curtis's group served as a Department of Interior survey team, to inspect and review the Albany Bureau. At the time of their inspection, the laboratory boasted 450 employees with an annual payroll exceeding a million dollars. The survey team met with division chiefs at the Bureau, reviewing their departments and projects.

Local visitors also flooded the lab in the first quarter of the year, including a group of 60 farmers from Linn and Benton counties. The group was treated to an in-depth tour of the Bureau campus, visiting every area of the laboratory except for one: the mysterious, off-limits white tower where hafnium was produced. Again, hints of Cold War secrecy wove into local perception. "Here Russia knows what is done but doesn't know how it's done," noted the *Greater Oregon* newspaper. "It is under good guard and if the Russians find out they will have to do it the hard way instead of learning our secrets."

Perhaps such awareness of the Soviet threat was heightened by the large number of Bureau staff who volunteered their time sitting atop Albany's city hall as part of the Ground Observer Corp (GOC), signal name "6 Coca." Members of 6 Coca would scan the skies for hours, watching for possible enemy aircraft. Human eyes were necessary because radar was ineffective at spotting aircraft under 5,000 feet. "One call from a civilian plane spotter could sound the alarm that would give our interceptor pilots in Continental Air Defense Command more time to challenge the invaders in the sky before they reached their targets," explained Lt.

Col. Albert B. Sporer, during a GOC anniversary meeting. Almost thirty laboratory employees had signed up to be a part of recurring 2-hour weekly shifts during the first year of "Operation Skywatch," with Bureau personnel office employee Elaine Eman filling the GOC secretary post (and her mother, the Chief Observer of the Corp).

During the lunch hour at the Bureau, a film on a 1952 H-bomb explosion was shown and employees were encouraged to take an active part in Civil Defense activities. It was recommended that households maintain a five-day supply of food. Little hints of ever-increasing vigilance were peppered throughout the year in the *Bureau Bugle*s. As if fears of nuclear attack weren't enough, rapidly shifting national priorities and budget concerns would continue to add immense pressure to the Bureau laboratory in Albany.

Even with good public relations programs and a (mostly) open interface with the public, glaring misconceptions about the laboratory were growing. One local article wrote off the Albany Bureau as "more of a factory than a laboratory-experiment facility, which was its original purpose." That statement couldn't have been further from the truth; groundbreaking research had always been running in the background, always overshadowed by the zirconium/hafnium work, but never lacking in respectable results.

The fact that the lab was seen by locals as a "factory" was disheartening, but the next dispute against the Albany Bureau was downright insulting: eleven years to the month since the establishment of the Bureau of Mines' Northwest Electro-development

Laboratory, Representative Ben Jensen of Iowa questioned why the site was placed in Oregon at all, and he called for the station to be moved closer to mining operations in Idaho or Montana. In March of 1954, the representative insisted it wasn't too late to move the lab, and he questioned the Bureau Director J. J. Forbes and the Director of the Minerals Division Paul Zinner if there was any good reason the lab was all the way over near the Pacific Ocean. Of course, those who had fought for the laboratory to be established in Albany were familiar with the reasons, and locals were instantly offended and rightfully worried.

"Our hackles rose the other day when testimony of a House Appropriations Subcommittee on the Bureau of Mines' budget was made public," responded an editorial in the *Albany Democrat-Herald*. The writer postulated that Jensen was confused and only meant to move the regional office, but closed with the sentiment that "Oregon should serve notice that it doesn't intend to let anyone take away this little publicized but extremely valuable federal facility."

News of the representative's challenge spread like a pond ripple, causing unease and concern, likely amplified by similar past challenges that had continued viciously for years after the Bureau's establishment in Albany. Much to everyone's relief, the idea was quelled fairly quickly, with Bureau Director Forbes declaring that it would be "difficult to conceive how such action [moving the laboratory] would improve the service to the industry."

Just as that matter was settled, another issue came up, this one equally stressful. A 1.5 million-dollar budget cut was ordered for fiscal year 1955, which could mean severe reductions in all departments—possibly even station closures. With the Cold War in mind, the Bureau of Mines shot back that such a drastic cut would curb research on defense materials, which the Albany Bureau was actively involved. Assistant Interior Secretary for Mining Felix Wormser had previously visited the Albany campus and was also strongly against the cuts. "These reductions are not consistent with the recommendations of every national policy group which has studied the minerals and fuels situation. These groups have recommended more aggressive effort in research," he insisted.

  Innovative employees at the Albany Bureau had already been incredibly successful at devising ways to save significant amounts of taxpayers' money through inventions and suggestions. Noble Hyde had worked in the white Purification tower since its construction days and was innately familiar with the process of separating hafnium from zirconium. Hyde noticed flaws in the system that controlled the interface between liquids that flowed throughout the multistoried glass Pyrex tubes; not only were two men required to make 'liquid level' adjustments, but the tubes where those adjustments were made often degraded very quickly. Because of the caustic liquids within, the tubes had to be replaced every three months. Even so, sometimes the tubes would crack and fail before the three-month mark, causing chemicals to drip and ooze on employees working below.

  Hyde invented a glass tube-within-a-tube that functioned as a gravity controller within the extraction columns and eliminated the need for rubber tubing altogether, creating a far safer work environment. Additionally, the glass tubes were permanently installed with no replacement necessary. One man could adjust the liquid levels with two fingers, greatly increasing efficiency. Overall it was estimated that Hyde's creation saved the Bureau an estimated $16,000 a year. For his efforts, he received a $300 prize and a letter of commendation from the Director of the Bureau of Mines, J. J. Forbes.

Another $300 prize was given to electrometallurgical plant operator D. C. Robinson. Robinson made a simple suggestion that greatly streamlined how graded zirconium sponge was handled. At the Albany Bureau there were three grades of zirconium: A, B, and C. Grades A and B went through one round of distillation and then were made into ingots. But C grade sponge had too many impurities and required another round of distillation. Each grade was sampled and analyzed before a distillation run, and about twelve samples needed to be gathered before a run was started. But Robinson suggested combining all the samples and only running one analysis so that only three samples were taken; one each for grades A, B, and C (after its second distillation.) Each sample cost about $12.50 to analyze, and it was estimated Robinson's much more efficient method saved the laboratory between $16,000 and $20,000—not to mention drastically improved efficiency. Scores of other employees received smaller prizes for suggestions on how to make the Albany Bureau a safer, more efficient, penny-pinching facility.

A money-saving experiment done the previous year by chemical engineer Ralph Nielsen and physical science aid Robert Govro was so successful that it made its way into a Report of Investigations. Nielsen, a young Navy veteran just like Govro, had been initially hired in 1950 after responding to a bulletin board posting for a civil service position. The day after graduating from Oregon State College, Nielsen began his summer job at the Bureau and eventually moved into a research position.

The duo's experiment substituted technical-grade sulfuric acid for a more expensive chemical called ammonium phthalate during the zirconium precipitation stage. It took Nielsen and Govro a bit of time to figure out the zirconium-sulphate ratio, but once that was solved, the process transitioned smoothly. By July 1954, the new process had been implemented, requiring only a few new pieces of equipment to handle the change. At the current rate of zirconium production, their sulfuric acid substitution saved the Bureau $4,300 per *month*.

    Another financial woe loomed on the horizon, although this new quandary wasn't exactly a surprise. In July 1954, Secretary of the Interior McKay urged the government to halt producing commercial quantities of titanium, zirconium, and helium (which the government controlled the entire domestic supply of.) There had always been the expectation that the process of manufacturing commercial zirconium would eventually be handed over to the private sector, but the swiftness of McKay's demand must have been surprising. After all, Carborundum had just barely begun production and the Navy still had a second nuclear submarine in the works (the *Seawolf*), and Rickover had just received the civilian power reactor project. Albany was assured that zirconium production would continue until private industry could sufficiently handle demand, but once the Bureau's zirconium plant shut down it could mean hundreds of hardworking people would be out of work.

A cool breeze ruffled through bright green tree leaves in late June 1954. A group of 125 people gathered around Director Shelton and Frank Stellmacher in a spot just to the north of Building 1 on a chilly Friday afternoon. Both men wielded shovels and were digging a deep hole; a young dogwood tree lay nearby, its roots bound in burlap. The tree was being planted in honor of 77-year old Stellmacher, who was retiring from the Bureau after eleven years of service to the site. Stellmacher was not only the oldest employee at that point, but longest employed person at the laboratory.

Stellmacher, who had lived on the property as a boy, had served as landscaper, maintenance man, and was the much-loved supervisor of the groundskeeping crew at the Bureau. Known for his green thumb, Stellmacher had once visited a friend's home, and upon seeing that the friend's wife had trimmed her rose bushes, Stellmacher took armloads of the cuttings, saying, "I can make them grow," his friend Mark Weatherford recalled in a touching tribute. "And he did make them grow and beautified that landscaped area."

By summer of 1954, Stellmacher was becoming a little hard of hearing but was notably spry, especially considering his age. On the day of his retirement, all those celebrating his career met in the recreation room in Building 2 and shared coffee and cake while Stellmacher was presented with a Commendable Service Award, and Honor Award Certificate, and a bronze medal with a miniature lapel button, plus a lifetime pass to the National Parks. The president of the Bureau of Mines Associates gave him a gold wrist watch, and the crew of janitors and gardeners presented him with a hand-tooled billfold. The groundskeeper was loved and admired by his Bureau family. "The men who have worked under him all have sincere feelings of respect toward him," said employee Ken Higbie.

"Perhaps his last great service to the community was making beautiful the grounds that surround the Bureau of Mines buildings on the campus of the old Albany college," offered Weatherford. It was clear that the patriarch of the Bureau grounds would be sorely missed upon his retirement.

Just days after Frank Stellmacher retired a bombshell was dropped: on a national scale, the Bureau of Mines was to be entirely reorganized. Among the big changes, the mining division (including health, safety, and coal mining inspection) would be separated from research divisions. Strengthening statistical data and analysis work was emphasized. With the reorganization, research on certain metals would be consolidated to cut down on duplicated work. Production activities (like zirconium in Albany and titanium at the Boulder City, Nevada station) were to cease. And the machine shop that had been left over from World War II days (where all the bespoke equipment for the laboratory had been expertly crafted) was on the chopping block too. Contractors were to be hired and machine shops would be discontinued, with maybe one or two shops remaining per region.

As if the reorganization wasn't enough, in late July it was announced that Albany would no longer serve as the head of Region 2. Also, the regions would be redrawn from nine geographic sections down to four. The new Region 1 would include Alaska, Oregon, Washington, California, Idaho, and Nevada, with Reno being the headquarters. It was stressed that the new changes weren't a reflection on the quality of work being done across Bureau stations; instead, the changes smacked of deep budget cuts and a reevaluation of what Bureau stations were now focusing on. The committee that had previously toured all Bureau facilities was trying to increase efficiency and eliminate nonessential activities at the Bureau, even though Albany and other stations were deeply involved in defense materials.

The loss of Albany as regional headquarters, the eventual shutdown of the zirconium plant, and the possibility of losing the machine shop technical crew would be a devastating blow to the laboratory, possibly reducing the number of employees by half—or more. In August alone, seven men were let go from the mechanical services department; likely anticipating the requirement to bring on contractors instead of using dedicated onsite employees. One estimate guessed that 300 of its 450 staff could be out of jobs by the first of the year.

Henry Gilbert had been intermittently ill and lost weeks of work at a time, bedridden at home on doctor's orders. Yet, Gilbert and fellow Bureau employee John Borg left in August 1954 to join the Harvey Aluminum Company in Torrance, California. As a going-away gift, Gilbert's fellow employees presented him with a tie clasp in the shape of the *Nautilus*, with a brilliant zircon stone set in the location of the reactor.

Both men were highly desirable candidates to help the company develop a rare metals program, though after a few months, 35-year-old Gilbert wrote to the Bureau that work was slow going and proceeding at half the speed of what was accomplished in Albany. From Gilbert's letter it sounded like he and Borg thought they'd be returning to Oregon soon and both bemoaned the cold, foggy weather, "and the smog is deadly," Gilbert remarked. Fumes and smoke from nearby oil refineries must have been wreaking havoc with Henry Gilbert's lungs, as he was suffering from berylliosis (then known as beryllium poisoning). The previously unnamed ailment which had plagued him during his trip to Japan at the beginning of the year now had a diagnosis, and the reality was grim.

At some point during Gilbert's employment with the Bureau he had performed experiments with alloying beryllium—a lightweight, steel-gray metal. Standards for beryllium exposure in the workplace had only been established in the late 1940s as nuclear weapon production increased. When Gilbert and others worked closely with beryllium, particulates that were breathed in would become lodged in the lungs, causing acute inflammation. Once beryllium particles enter the body, they never come out.

Symptoms of beryllium poisoning could come on quickly, causing debilitating coughing, difficulty breathing, and fatigue. With industrial smog as bad as what Henry Gilbert described, living in California was likely a nightmare for him. As Gilbert's disease progressed, the entrapped beryllium particles caused worsening pulmonary deterioration. Though his letter to the Bureau hinted that he'd hoped to return to Oregon, Gilbert and his family remained in California. He would eventually succumb to berylliosis thirteen years later at the age of 48.

It was at about this time that the guinea pigs at the Albany Bureau began to die off. By September 1954, two animals had already been found dead in their cages after about only two months. A poem in the *Bureau Bugle* memorialized their short lives:

> What have you got against this pig
> To lock me up in such a rig?
> And make me breath *[sic]* this dust until
> My chance for life is almost nil.
> I cannot understand or see
> Why you should take my life from me,
> And though I grind my teeth in rage
> I'm still locked up inside this cage.
> You crack bum jokes and laugh and scoff

While us poor pigs are dying off.
My pulse is weak, my heart beats slow
I know that I'm about to go.
I cannot see nor can I hear;
I feel the hand of death is near.
And so I give this life of mine
That you may live a longer time.
   —Anonymous.

The verses may have been in jest but the overall mood at the Bureau was not. Employees were scrambling to find out whether unemployment would be offered in case of mass layoffs, while others were quietly slipping away to the private sector to find work. Those who had worked anywhere near zirconium were suddenly wondering if years of dust exposure would impact their health—just like the caged guinea pigs. If there was ever a time that the Albany Bureau needed some good news, it was in the fall of 1954.

There was a bright spot of celebration in August 1954 during the annual public open house: the millionth pound of zirconium was produced while a crowd of excited onlookers watched. Nine years prior, zirconium tailings had been collected from a chromium separations plant near Coquille, Oregon, by Dr. Kroll. Ceaseless zirconium experiments had followed, with Kroll leading the charge, but always surrounded by a group of peers who continued the work. "It is the first time in history that a project has progressed from the test tube stage to the millionth pound stage in all the same laboratories. The men who work with this project should be very proud to be taking such an important part in their country's defense program," noted the *Bureau Bugle*. "Much blood, sweat, and tears (barked knuckles, the boss' sweat, and the chlorinator operators' tears) went into the early attempts," the article continued. "The bosses said they awoke many times at night in a cold sweat thinking of possible dangers, inherent in any new chemical process, that would cause failure." The ultimate goal had finally been achieved: for a metal that once cost $200 a pound, the pound produced on August 17 came with a price tag of $15—the ultimate proof that Albany had succeeded in making zirconium a commercially attainable material.

E. Don Dilling was "Master of Ceremonies" for the occasion as he went to each building to explain each step of production—with the exception of the process within the mysterious white Purification tower, due to its classified status. Five hundred members of the public from all around the country filed through the plant between 1:00 and 8:00 p.m. that day. In addition to the millionth pound of zirconium, a massive 430-pound ingot was on display, poised to be shipped off to its next destination.

Although zirconium production was scheduled to be handed off to the private sector as soon as Carborundum could produce enough sponge, the Atomic Energy Commission was still investing in Oregon's zirconium-related work. A $11,200 research contract was awarded to the University of Oregon for an unclassified zirconium study on corrosion. A $7,750 contract with Oregon State College was initiated for a study on radioactive materials. And E. T. Hayes continued to work as a liaison with Superior Tubing—the company that formed the zirconium cladding and welded control rods for the *Nautilus*. On November 9, 1954, Hayes attended the first meeting on zirconium testing with Superior Tube and General Electric. A declassified document covering the meeting's topics showed that corrosion tests on Zircaloy 2 were continuing at the Bureau. In an interesting full-circle moment, Hayes mentioned that R. S. Dean—the former Bureau of Mines assistant director who secured Dr. Kroll for the Albany Bureau—was now a consulting metallurgist in Maryland with expert knowledge in zirconium plating. During the meeting Hayes suggested Dean would have good ideas on using zirconium-plated uranium for future nuclear uses.

The Office of Defense Mobilization was in contract negotiations with the Albany Bureau to partner with the Boulder City Bureau station for a two-year titanium contract. The Boulder City site had plenty of knowledge to offer; they had been working on perfecting commercial titanium production since 1948. Despite that, titanium was still an expensive metal to produce, and the Bureau was working on changing that in the hopes that it would become a common, widely used structural material.

The defense contract with Albany was aiming to find an economical way to tease titanium from U.S.-sourced ores. At that time, Australia was the only provider of a titanium-bearing ore called rutile. Beach sands from Oregon and Washington state contained ilmenite, from which titanium could be extracted—but not in commercial quantities. This new titanium exploration had the potential to replace zirconium production in Albany.

The Boulder City, Nevada, Bureau of Mines site had been working on alloying and fabricating titanium since 1948, based on Dr. Kroll's patented process. By 1954, two-thousand pounds of titanium had been produced by private companies with government contracts and that quantity was expected to double; the military was beginning to view the lightweight metal as a valuable structural material. If titanium could be produced cheaply, "perhaps, titanium will become almost as familiar to us as aluminum is today," noted Frank Block's *Bugle* writeup.

A year prior, the Albany Bureau also responded to a request from the Army, through Watertown Arsenal in Massachusetts, to research methods of casting titanium. A memo signed by security officer Eleanor Abshire in April 1954 noted that Ordinance Project No. TB4-15, officially titled "Development of a Titanium Casting Furnace," was to be considered "Administrative Confidential," which meant the reports could be viewed by Watertown Arsenal and Bureau employees and had no correlation to the regular security classification "Confidential." Despite that, reports about the project were to be omitted from regular Bureau monthly progress reports.

The arsenal had been toying with using titanium as a base for an 81-millimeter mortar. The benefit to having ordinance that included titanium was reduced weight, which meant fewer men on an ordinance crew. If titanium casting could be perfected there would be limitless opportunities for the creation of lightweight parts, tools, ammunition, and more. The specific goal for this particular project was to make formed titanium castings over 40 pounds without introducing "deleterious contamination." Just as zirconium had a bad habit of picking up minute amounts of impurities, titanium's mechanical attributes were also negatively affected by small amounts of contaminants. "*Time* magazine reported that scientists had nicknamed titanium 'the streetwalker' because of its propensity to pick up anything," noted Kathleen L. Housley in *Black Sand: The History of Titanium*.

Photo: Stephen T. Anderson Collection
It is very likely that the world's first fully titanium bicycle frame was constructed at the Albany Bureau of Mines in the early 1950's, most likely during their foray into titanium work.

Photo: Stephen T. Anderson Collection
Two unknown employees pose with the titanium bicycle frame constructed in the Machine Shop (Building 5).

The Report of Investigation that covered the project spelled out the deceptive simplicity of the problem: for any attempt at casting metal, three things had to be accomplished. First, metal had to be heated to its liquid state. Second, it needed to be transferred to a mold, where third, the metal would need to stay contained while it cooled until it hardened. "The solution is, of course, never as simple as the statement," the report quipped, as titanium in its liquid state reacted with all high-temperature materials and tended to alloy with most metals. Just the act of trying to contain molten titanium—without it picking up impurities—was near impossible. Consumable-electrode arc melting was the breakthrough in creating pure ingots, but did not further the cast-shaping process.

Henry Gilbert and John Borg had been two main researchers on the project but after their mid-1954 departure from Albany, Robert Beall, Floyd Wood, and others continued experiments on creating castings that eventually became the basis for "space-age" structural metals. Early trials exploring different melting and pouring methods had small failures, but later experiments combining the Albany Bureau's methods of vacuum arc remelting, combined with a skull casting furnace[7] with a non-consumable electrode, led to successes in titanium casting—as well as a U.S. Patent.

———•◆•———

A maintenance man dipped his paintbrush into a can of white paint. Square by square, he painted over every glass pane in the southwestern corner of the machine shop. He didn't know why all the light needed to be blocked out, nor would he ever find out. By now he understood that some things that went on at the Bureau were on a "need to know" basis, and he didn't need to know. All that maintenance man really needed to know was what job needed to be done, and when it had to be finished.

But those with the proper security clearance at the Bureau were aware that a high-priority and highly classified thorium melting project had just been sponsored by the Atomic Energy Commission. And because of that, extra security measures were being taken to ensure that prying eyes wouldn't be able to view what was going on inside sensitive areas; the corner of the machine shop was one of those areas.

Thorium is a metal that is naturally slightly radioactive and three times more abundant in nature than uranium. While thorium couldn't be used directly as nuclear fuel, it could instead be decayed until it created fuel-worthy uranium-233, a process called "breeding." At the time, thorium was being considered as the next uranium, possibly even surpassing uranium as a future primary source of nuclear fuel for thermal reactors. It is highly likely that the project at the Bureau had something to do with the development of breeder reactors.

The Atomic Act of 1954 brought about changes at the AEC; one significant shift was from a focus on nuclear weaponry to peaceful uses of nuclear science, including medical research and civilian nuclear power generation. While the overall scope of the AEC was unchanged, there was new emphasis on peacetime nuclear applications. Investigations into the many forms of civilian nuclear power meant new projects for government laboratories.

The advent of breeder reactors in the early 1950s meant that any thorium needed for them had to be purer than ever before, which would present quite the challenge for the Albany Bureau. "[Melting] techniques once acceptable became intolerable," wrote Robert Beall. "Metal once considered highly satisfactory for an alloying ingredient was not at all suitable for forging and rolling to strict dimensional and soundness specification."

Because of the AEC's urgent need for high-purity thorium ingots in early 1955, Beall supervised forty Bureau employees who had been divided into four separate crews. Unfortunately, their experience was not with melting thorium and the challenge for the group would be to successfully meet the AEC's stringent specifications—under a tight timeline.

The Thorium Melting Group, as they became known, had a massive task ahead of them; thorium was a fickle metal to deal with. No refractory material had been devised that could withstand thorium's challenging temperament: heated, thorium would react with air and attract oxygen and nitrogen. There was no crucible in existence that molten thorium couldn't dissolve. Additionally, just like with zirconium, fine particles of thorium were pyrophoric and ready to burst into flame as soon as the furnace was opened. If thorium shavings were stored underwater for safety, hydrogen would be produced. If water levels weren't maintained, the whole container could spontaneously combust, "especially if the containers are stored under summer sun," noted Beall, though there was one instance of thorium igniting in cold weather. Taming the beastly molten metal would be an enormous task for the Bureau's melting group.

In an interesting twist, it turned out that the consumable-electrode arc furnace that had been developed at the Albany Bureau was a perfect fit for melting thorium. A copper crucible, intensely cooled on the outside by water, was found to be suitable for melting "derbies" of thorium, so named because the cylindrical hunk of metal resembled the top part of the popular men's hat.

Health and safety concerns inherent with working on radioactive metals had to be addressed; specifically, vapors would condense and fumes had to be properly captured so employees wouldn't be harmed. Through condensation, the daughter products of thorium (radium being one) would also become concentrated and embedded in the furnace itself and on the exterior wall of the ingot. Workers would protect themselves from radioactive fumes and particulates by having the furnace blown out by a flow of air connected to the room's exhaust system. After several remelts, thorium derbies were made into ingots about 8" in diameter and 3' long.

As with most classified projects at the Bureau, employees were on a "need-to-know" basis, only understanding their own tasks and not privy to the end goal. "All positions working with thorium or any combination with thorium (titanium-thorium, thorium-V, thorium-tantalum, zirconium-thorium, zirconium-hafnium-thorium-V) were classified Sensitive and required a 'Q' or 'L' clearance," noted Bobbie Ferguson and Christine Pfaff in *Albany Research Center, A History and Evaluation.* "Section Chiefs and some secretaries required the same clearance." (Additionally, the areas of higher sensitivity had to be secured before projects were started.) One of these high-sensitivity areas was referred to as the "Owl Room."

At some point during the Bureau's foray into working with radioactive materials, a melting laboratory for rare metals (thorium, zirconium, hafnium, and niobium) had been located in Building 31, the northeast wing of the L-shaped Purification plant. But eventually the cavernous west end of Building 4

Photo: Stephen T. Anderson Collection
Only a handful of photos exist of the "Owl Room," the area in Building 4 where thorium work was performed.

Photo: Stephen T. Anderson Collection
It is likely that special, classified thorium alloys were made for the Atomic Energy Commission in the "Owl Room."

(the chlorination building) was partitioned off for classified work, most likely having to do with secret alloys containing thorium, uranium, and beryllium. This space became known as the "Owl Room," reportedly because an owl made its home in the shadowy upper rafters.

Before cleared personnel could enter the Owl Room they had to don special suits and booties, though it is not known if these safeguards were in place during the earliest years. The huge room contained a main floor space with a mezzanine, furnaces, and banks of electrical controls and equipment for machining radioactive materials. The Owl Room remained a relevant work area into the 1970s, when its function expanded to machining, grinding, pickling, vacuum pumping and polishing poisonous or radioactive materials.

Robert Govro and his father, Clyde, both worked on aspects of the thorium melting project. "My job . . . was to go over to the melting department with a hand truck and take the ingots to another building and do a hardness test on them," Robert recalled. He would perform a nondestructive hardness test by taking the ingot and placing it in a hydraulic press. A ball bearing would be at the bottom of the ram, and the ram would be lowered with an exact, measured amount of pressure. Robert would make an indentation every four inches down the length of the ingot. After making the small pressings, an optical reader would precisely measure the diameter of the indentations. The size of the indentation would directly correlate to the hardness of that area of the ingot.

Robert's father Clyde worked in the machine shop, where a portion of that building had also been partitioned off strictly for working on classified projects. Workers, wearing their clearance and identification badges, donned protective clothing and respirators before entering the restricted section. Lathes and other machinery for shaping were located in this area. Here, the thorium ingots were machined to fulfill specifications set by the AEC for this particular project. Close to being finished, the product would be checked again, then sent to the next department. "Once the metal was . . . found to be acceptable, they would be shipped," Robert recalled. Workers at the time guessed the material was being shipped to Hanford.

The Bureau's effort to melt thorium derbies was wildly successful. In less than six months' time, "the Bureau of Mines assembled, adapted, and built the necessary equipment for electrode fabrication and ingot melting of thorium. They developed techniques and succeeded in maintaining a high rate of ingot production," said the *Bureau Bugle* of the accomplishment. "Their enthusiasm, cooperation, and teamwork were major factors in the success of the program," the article concluded. In the end, an "unprecedented" amount of high-quality thorium was produced by the thorium melting group. Robert Beall later confirmed that thorium (and uranium) projects performed in the 1940s and 1950s involved alloying shapes destined for use as nuclear reactor fuel. For this particular project, it's highly likely the thorium produced at the Bureau went on to breeder reactor experiments.

In addition to the melting success, the Albany Bureau was able to use this thorium research to set industrial standards for radiation safety. "Cooperative work for the Atomic Energy Commission has been carried out with thorium metal, and as a result the concerned laboratories of the [Albany Research] Center have accumulated experience on the hazards associated with this metal," noted a 1960 document on the subject.

Photo: *Bureau Bugle*
The Thorium Melting Group received top honors for their work. Those involved were (in no particular order): Fred Abshire, Bobbie M. Wyninegar, Willis A. Aschoff, Frank Caputo Jr., Glenn J. Dryden, Jimmie D. Gillham, Donald C. Goody, Noel D. Graber, George S. Westerman, Franklie R. Wagy, Roy E. Uhlenberg, Loren S. Schultz, Delmar L. Racette, Leslie M. Pierce, Richard L. Morris, Cecil E. Moreland, LaVern L. Lown, Marshall C. Leeson, Leonard W. Kuske, Clyde M. Kerns, Noble F. Hyde, Mernin A. Howe, Maxwell C. Houmann, John C. Hanna, Clyde W. Govro, Jack R. Beardsley, Charlie W. Yancey, Lambert Woudenberg, Floyd W. Wood, Bernice D. Wirowek, Alba H. Roberson, Anderson G. Pike, Harold J. Parsons, Custer S. Knurowski, Ralph M. Harman, John C. Beckner, Leon E. Aldrich, Robert P. Adams, Robert A. Beall

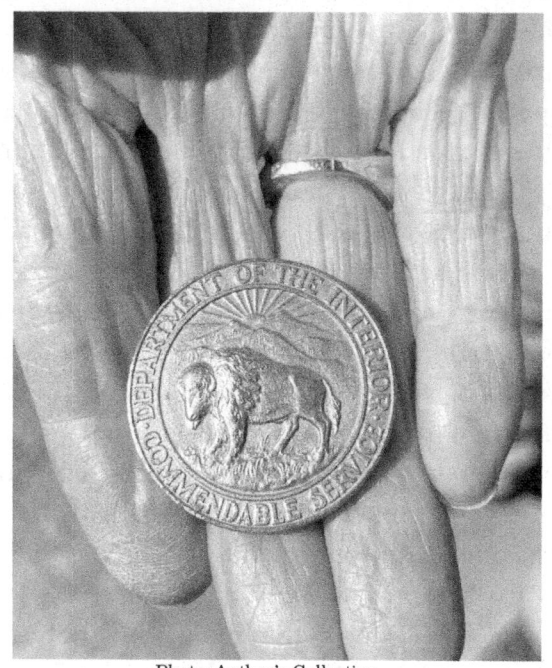

Photo: Author's Collection
Medal of Commendable Service presented to Clyde W. Govro for his work performed in melting thorium for the Atomic Energy Commission.

329

Another ongoing project at the Albany laboratory was ductile chromium, which was in its sixth year by 1954. Around 1950, a U.S. Air Force research and development contract regarding high-temperature materials and their applications helped urge along experiments. By 1954, a tidy sum of $152,000 had been spent on figuring out how to make chromium malleable, which was a "hard nut to crack," noted H. Andrew Johansen in the *Bureau Bugle*. Just as with zirconium, the presence of certain impurities—oxygen, in this case—caused chromium to be brittle and unworkable. The metal acted more like glass at room temperature, making it absolutely useless for making shapes. Up until two years prior, the Albany Bureau had been the only place working on the brittle, frustrating metal.

Then, in 1952, a curious thing happened—at nearly the same time, researchers in Australia and at the Albany Bureau stumbled upon the answer to the malleable chromium quandary. To create a metal that was workable, high-purity chromium was handled using special techniques, then an amount of surface metal was scraped away. "Such a simple solution after so many years of work!" Johansen remarked, though he added that more work was needed. Like other metals worked on at the Bureau, chromium was highly susceptible to drawing impurities from its environment, threatening contamination. After the purification process was perfected, the Bureau began producing finely drawn chromium wire for medical research. Drawing wire was a precision operation; high-purity chromium was submerged in a hot lead bath, then drawn through tungsten carbide dies.

Dr. William G. Meyers, a pioneer of nuclear science and medicine at Ohio State University knew that the Albany laboratory was the only facility in the world that could make malleable chromium. Chromium wire, drawn down to 0.031" thick at the Bureau, was irradiated at Oak Ridge to produce radioactive chromium-51. The half-life of radioactive chromium was exactly 28 days—the perfect amount of time for the type of cancer research Meyers was performing. Previously he had tried using radioactive gold but its half-life was too short; then tantalum, whose 111-day half-life was far too long for his purposes.

From 1955 to 1958 the Albany Bureau supplied Oak Ridge with different thicknesses of wire; that wire would be exposed to neutrons in one of their reactors. The irradiated chromium-51 wire was then sent to Meyers and others, including radiation therapy expert Dr. Melvin Griem in Chicago.

Dr. Griem worked at the University of Chicago–Argonne Cancer Research Hospital; as part of the Human Radiation Experiment series, he used small aluminum tubes to carefully insert between 3 and 60 of the thin, irradiated wires into his patients' cancerous tissues. The wire sent off localized gamma radiation for exactly 28 days; after the radiation period was over, the wires needed no removal. Sometimes patients required several rounds of implantation. There were encouraging results from initial treatments, and this form of treatment (now called brachytherapy) is still used for certain types of cancer, though not with irradiated chromium.

A noteworthy project that ended in 1954 was the research on the separation of tantalum and columbium (now called niobium), taken on by the Bureau to utilize the low- grade ores. Similar to the relationship between zirconium and hafnium, tantalum and niobium are chemically similar, but physically quite different and need to be teased apart if they are to be used. The problem of separating these two metals had vexed

Photo: Stephen T. Anderson Collection
An employee works on an array of equipment designed for tantalum-columbium separation.

Photo: Steven T. Anderson Collection
Gene Asai was a key contributor to high-purity chromium production.

chemists for over a century and had only been done in small batches through a slow and difficult process. Bureau scientists needed to see if a liquid-liquid technique (like with zirconium and hafnium) could be successful so separation could be performed on a much larger scale.

The first small-scale experiments were done in test tubes. Over 200 combinations of solvents and acids were meticulously tested and analyzed to see if they could be separated effectively. Two promising systems were further tested; in the end, one particular system (acid–methyl isobutyl ketone) made it possible to isolate the metals by themselves through liquid-liquid extraction on an industrial scale with over 99% purity. Once again, the Albany Bureau had tackled a difficult separations problem with overwhelming success. After four years of research, the findings were presented at the American Chemical Society Conference in New York.

Both from low-grade ores, tantalum and niobium became big players in years to come. Tantalum is used extensively in electronics as an insulating layer and as an alloy for high-strength, high-heat applications like rocket nozzles, turbine blades, and nose cones for supersonic aircraft. Niobium was discovered to be a valuable addition to stainless steel; niobium alloys are extensively used in the aviation industry for propeller blades and jet engines. One particular alloy called C-103—a niobium-hafnium-titanium combination—is used in the aerospace industry; rocket nozzles for the Apollo spacecraft were composed of this alloy.

One last significant development in 1954 centered around molybdenum (muh·**lib**·duh·nuhm.) The element with the tongue-twister name had gained a reputation for being difficult. Much like chromium,

Photo: Stephen T. Anderson Collection

These three men played leading roles the historic productions of the world's first casting of molybdenum, a heat-resistant metal, at the Albany Bureau. Robert A. Beall (left) melting project coordinator, holds a cylinder casting. E. D. Calvert (center) was the molybdenum casting project leader, and S. L. Ausmus, (right) was in charge of the casting furnace.

Photo: Stephen T. Anderson Collection

Doug Brown uses the new quantometer to analyze a zirconium ingot in the Spectrographic Lab, August 8, 1953.

molybdenum had a habit of becoming brittle with the smallest amount of contaminants, the guilty party usually being oxygen. "The production of uniformly ductile molybdenum is rendered very difficult as a result of this oxygen embrittlement," lamented Tom Campbell in the December 1954 *Bureau Bugle*.

As a refractory metal, silvery-white molybdenum had a super-high melting point of about 4800 °F. It had been classified as a strategic material since World War II and was strictly controlled by the government, though because of its difficult nature, it had not been produced in large quantities. Molybdenum had been previously produced by a laborious powder metallurgy process, but "considerable research" was being done at the Albany Bureau to find ways to easily and cheaply produce malleable molybdenum. Utilizing calcium to reduce the metal meant using reduction "bombs," which Campbell admitted sometimes turned into *actual* bombs—which wasn't supposed to happen at all. "As many of my readers know, this type of research had a tendency to get a little noisy at times," Campbell joked. Future Bureau research on molybdenum would lead to other breakthroughs for the metal; molybdenum alloys are used where a high-temperature, ultra-hard material is needed.

The last quarter of the year saw some changes in the analytical department. The Atomic Act of 1954 not only emphasized peaceful nuclear uses but also called for "effective dissemination of both scientific and industrial information." That meant a heightened effort to centralize data would be paramount. At the Bureau, a brand-new analytical division, the Mineral Industry Division, was established on the north end of Building 2. It was said that billows of sweet-smelling pipe smoke wafted through the hallways when men from the division were hard at work, compiling statistics and crunching numbers.

Another boost to the Bureau's analytical capabilities happened when the Physics Department had received a brand-new quantometer the year prior. The $47,000 machine had been custom built to detect what kind of impurities were in zirconium metal or oxide, and the quantity of each impurity. Before the quantometer arrived, a lab assistant would spend ten hours or more to determine ten impure elements in a sample using chemical methods. But with the new machine, analytical processes that once took ten hours would now take only five minutes! The machine was a type of direct-reading Baird spectrograph, which would read the colors (or spectra) given off when a metal sample was heated to a high temperature. The spectra were focused onto a photo plate that would be processed. The resulting image would show the range of impurities inherent in the sample.

Even though the quantometer was a wildly expensive machine (almost a half million-dollar expense in 2020 dollars), it provided a tremendous savings in both time and money. The machine was such a boon to the Bureau that D. M. Mortimore of the Physics Laboratory traveled to Pittsburgh to present a paper on how the quantometer could be applied to suss out impurities in zirconium.

Although 1954 had been a tough and uncertain year, the Albany Bureau was still deeply involved in experiments designed to make troublesome metals available for commercial use for the first time. Groundbreaking work persisted despite rumors of layoffs, severe budget cuts, and the loss of key personnel. On November 5, another milestone was reached in Albany, though this one much less publicized: the millionth pound of purified, low-hafnium zirconium oxide was produced. Cupcakes and coffee marked the occasion and a group photo of the grinning production crew graced the accompanying *Bureau Bugle* article. June 1, 1952 had marked the first day when crude zirconium tetrachloride began running through the plant, resulting in 6,000 pounds of zirconium sponge per week. By the spring of 1954, the amount had been increased to 10,000 pounds.

But there was also a hint of sadness about the million-dollar, gleaming white tower that stood tall above the rural neighborhood. "This beautiful building full of the very finest equipment . . . is scheduled to close its door late in January 1955," wrote James McClain, head of the department. "However, because of its nature, utility, and flexibility, it is well suited for other rare earth investigations and may open its doors someday to a new process," McClain noted hopefully.

More good news buoyed employees in November; after months of silence from the higher-ups at the Bureau it was finally decided that Albany would remain the regional headquarters. Moreover, Stephen Shelton would be the director for Region 1, with longtime Chemical Laboratory employee Mark Wright as the Assistant Regional Director in the Administration department.

"Oh, how glad we are that the tension has been lifted and reorganization plans finally are settled," said the *Bureau Bugle* editor Doris Wells. Indeed, it seemed that there was a collective sigh of relief through all departments at the Albany Bureau that winter. Admiral Rickover had even recently visited the site and was greatly impressed with the accomplishments of the laboratory.

On New Year's Eve 1954, a nervous crew sat aboard the *Nautilus*. Tension filled the air as all hands prepared to run the submarine through her first "fast cruise" simulation—a run that would test all of the ship's systems just as if she weren't docked. Theodore Rockwell was on board and was in charge of plotting criticality in order to measure exactly how many inches control rods needed to be withdrawn in order for the onboard reactor to reach criticality. Rockwell figured that so much calculating, testing, and tweaking had already been done to perfect every element of the reactor . . . yet he also wondered *why do criticality tests always have to be done at night?*

The test was slow and meticulous but as control rods were lifted, a concerning trend was noticed: power levels were remaining the same, hovering at the same point on the graph. Physicists on board did all they could to assuring all was fine, though some crew members wondered if the gleaming new reactor core would even be able to reach criticality. Finally, minutes before midnight, full power was achieved, paving the way for true sea trials to begin.

Rickover was aboard during the January 17th sea trial. At 11 a.m., the mooring ropes were loosed and the submarine moved toward open waters under electric propulsion. Suddenly, a terrible screeching noise howled out from the ship's engine room. At this point, turning back was no longer an option; to Rickover's ire, a crowd had shown up for the (unannounced) departure and turning back would be a public relations nightmare. Besides, the electric propulsion didn't have the power to fight against the outgoing current.

Photo: Steven T. Anderson Collection
The diving station on the USS Nautilus.

Photo: *Bureau Bugle*
Joe Thom, an accountant at the Bureau, was an avid writer for the Bureau Bugle and his positivity shone through his editorials. Thom had become deaf and learned lip-reading to communicate. "Joe has proven that handicaps are only tests of one's adaptability, rather than insurmountable obstacles, and his handling of his job and his 'never say die' spirit and pleasant personality have made him liked and admired by all of his associates," noted coworker A. H. Roberson.

The crew decided to maneuver to a spot in the harbor that couldn't be seen by the throng of onlookers to assess the situation. To everyone's complete relief, the terrible wailing sound turned out to be only a loose screw. With that taken care of, the *Nautilus* headed to sea—and met with brutal 12-foot waves. While on the surface, the submarine rolled a full 27 degrees as sailors heaved with seasickness. Some got minor injuries when they were thrown into bulkheads inside. The outer superstructure was losing pieces, teak decking was being torn apart, and the ship lost her running lights to the monstrous waves. The first dive couldn't come soon enough.

Diesel submarines needed precise timing when diving to make sure the air intakes were closed before submerging, but the *Nautilus* needed no such timing—she could dive and surface at will. As the ship dove deeper, compression on the hull was continually monitored. Precise gauges attached to the main shafts measured the amount of horsepower being generated. As the crew asked for more speed, the *Nautilus* responded with stunning grace. As the throttle was opened, more steam was allowed to reach the turbine, causing the propeller to turn faster. This action pulled steam away from the reactor, causing the reactor to cool down. Cooler water in the reactor would effectively slow down neutrons within the core. Since slow neutrons create more fission, the reactor power would naturally increase, meaning the control rods themselves didn't need much manipulation. "The crew had never seen any other propulsion system so user-friendly," recalled Rockwell.

Many more test runs followed for the *Nautilus*, including an 84-hour trip to Puerto Rico. The new ship performed well, though some issues flared up that were typical for a brand-new submarine: the drinking water turned salty, the ship's hull sprang a few leaks, oil dribbled in places it shouldn't have, and two small fires had to be put out. But for her skipper Captain Eugene P. Wilkinson—who had experience on five other new submarines previously—the *Nautilus*'s performance was stellar by comparison. She was formally delivered to the Navy on April 22, 1955, a tribute to Rickover's vision, leadership, and his gamble on zirconium.

CHAPTER FOURTEEN

THE HUSTLERS

April 1955–March 1956

"The current closing of the zirconium-hafnium production facilities heralds the beginning of a new chapter in the history of this station."

—Joe Thom, June 1955 Bureau Bugle

As glossy green cottonwood leaves unfurled around the neighborhood, signaling a new season, crews of workers began preparing the zirconium reduction plant for closure by taking apart all the furnaces. The three buildings associated with zirconium production—the chlorination building, the reduction plant, and the pilot plant—were all slated to be closed by July 1, 1955, just a few months in the future. What had been a hot, bustling nexus of activity on the Bureau campus was winding down to a whimper.

The sting of losing 65 employees (most of whom had transferred elsewhere) was scarcely lessened by the fact that the closure had been planned from the start. "For more than five years, the big deal here has been zirconium research and production. The closing comes as no surprise, however," Joe Thom wrote in the *Bureau Bugle*. Zirconium production for the *Nautilus* had been carried out on a temporary basis by the government, with the clear expectation that private industry would take over the technology (and hopefully the facilities as well) when the time was right.

Photo: Wikimedia Commons/Public Domain
Admiral Rickover descends into the circular nuclear reactor shell at the Shippingport Power Facility.

Photo: Wikimedia Commons/Public Domain
The development of Lockheed's U-2 high altitude reconnaissance plane birthed a new titanium alloy called Ti-6Al-4V.

The year prior, a group of government analysts had declared that 1955 would be a season of belt-tightening for the Bureau of Mines, and that any production facilities would be shuttered—the sooner, the better. Production of titanium at Boulder City, zirconium in Albany, and helium in Texas would cease.

While Albany leadership was considering what to do about employment losses, the Atomic Energy Commission was actively seeking a private firm to take over the now-idle buildings. Negotiations in the spring of 1955 included discussions with the Wah Chang Corporation of New York state. Wah Chang, founded by mining engineer Dr. K. C. Li in 1916, was an international company that specialized in tungsten ore and concentrate trading. Due to Li's belief that the metals industry held great potential to benefit the world, the name he gave to his corporation translated to "great development." The AEC still needed zirconium—*lots* of it—and the quicker the Albany plant could be reestablished, the better. Not only were more nuclear submarines planned, but Rickover's civilian power plant project was still moving forward. Groundbreaking for the Shippingport civilian reactor had taken place in September 1954, and Rickover had called for uranium oxide fuel elements clad in zirconium-alloy tubes.

At the same time that the AEC was seeking private corporations to run the Bureau's plant, few people were trying to secure the Bureau's future. A handful of dedicated employees at the lab donated vacation time, stayed to work late, and traveled to "confer with scientists of government and private industry with respect to work being done or to be done here. Those of us who go home every night to a home-cooked dinner and an evening of family or community life owe much to the hustlers who have to spend so much extra time at the plant or away from home," mused Joe Thom in the *Bureau Bugle*, regarding the zirconium plant closure.

Perhaps the biggest hustler at the laboratory at that time was Steven Shelton, who was actively thinking of ways to utilize the tremendous pool of Bureau talent that was now on the brink of disbanding, though Shelton's concern was with kick-starting a new local industry. The Bureau director wondered if a titanium plant might be just what the area needed, as commercially available titanium (the subject of Dr. Kroll's first patents) was increasingly in demand by the U.S. government.

One reason the government needed titanium was because of the development of the U-2, a top-secret aircraft designed by Lockheed's Skunk Works. In 1953, President Eisenhower had given the go-ahead for a new type of spy plane—one that would soar above the earth so high it would be virtually undetectable. The elegant, glider-like reconnaissance plane with pin-straight wings was designed to fly at astonishing altitudes, topping out at 70,000 feet to avoid detection. At that oxygen-robbing altitude, the aircraft would need to be as light as possible. In 1954, Lockheed won the contract for the development of the new reconnaissance plane, and in eight months, a new prototype was ready to fly.

The development of the U-2 and other aircraft necessitated the creation of a new titanium alloy, Ti-6Al-4V, which was used in the U-2's Pratt & Whitney J57 turbojet engine. During the U-2's development, U.S. intelligence erroneously suggested that the USSR's air fleet severely outnumbered that of the United States. More planes equaled the need for more titanium, and the push for acquiring the lightweight, silvery-gray metal intensified.

Director Shelton recognized the market was ripe. At an Albany Chamber of Commerce luncheon he introduced the idea of a titanium plant to the group. Shelton piqued the curiosity of mayor Charles K. McCormack, who followed Shelton back to his office at the Bureau to gather more information.

"What the hell is a titanium plant?" McCormack asked Shelton that afternoon. Shelton pitched his idea to the mayor. McCormack was so enchanted with the idea that he began a financing campaign by selling shares for a dollar, with the goal of raising half a million dollars for the proposed facility. Plans got off to a lightning-fast start in April 1955; clear expectations were already being announced for costs and production goals in order to successfully sell stock in the company. There were high hopes that production could begin in the fall of that year. In the press, a name was soon associated with the planned company: Oregon Metallurgical, or Oremet for short. While the new venture was gathering steam in Albany, a discovery of another sort was causing people flock to a remote area of Oregon, three hundred miles away.

Winds howled and silvery-gray rain came down in sheets. The sudden summer storm drenched the town of Lakeview, Oregon, blotting out views of the high desert. The tiny hamlet that hugged the base of the rolling Warner Mountains was known for its lumber output, sourced from the mountains and nearby Fremont National Forest. Two thousand people called the remote outpost home, but in mid-July 1955 the area experienced a swell of gun-toting, Geiger counter–wielding prospectors—plus two petrographers from the

Albany Bureau, who had landed just ahead of the storm.

Oregon had experienced a few false alarms when it came to uranium prospecting. In 1952 a Portland man thought he'd struck it rich and papers broadcasted his possible find, though the location was kept secret. This wasn't the case when John Roush, Erma and Donald Tracy, and W. H. Lehman collectively announced their tremendous find and local papers picked up the story.

Earlier in 1955, Lehman had been tending to his sheep in an area near Augur Creek when he'd collected some rocks stippled with telltale yellow-green crusting that indicated the presence of uranium. He passed the rocks to Lakeview-area rancher John Roush, who was no stranger to uranium prospecting. Roush had submitted several ore samples to the state prior to his 1955 find and had stumbled upon thorium-bearing quartz, but no commercial uranium. Roush and Donald Tracy were able to confirm the shepherd had indeed stumbled upon uranium, and Lehman was able to direct Tracy where to dig. Using a bulldozer to scrape away surface soil, more potential uranium-bearing ore was found on an outcropping. A partnership was formed between the group and one month before news hit the papers, the White King claims were established.

After Roush and several others staked 16 claims in the area, a San Francisco–based assayer evaluated the ore as having 1.37% uranium—far greater than the minimum .1% required by the AEC, and when news hit the papers, Roush was awaiting confirmation from the Albany Bureau. If the percentage panned out, his find would be Oregon's richest uranium find ever.

Word spread as fast as the wind that whipped through the southeastern Oregon desert, and the location—clearly spelled out in papers far and wide—brought around 500 grizzled ranchers and prospectors

Photo: Author's Collection

About 20 tons of uranium ore were collected in the Roush barnyard. "Among swarm of visitors who came to see samples are Don Peters, district ranger of Fremont forest, where find was made; son, Don Jr., 13. John Roush shows samples." From an unknown news clipping dated July 17, 1955.

Photo: U.S. Department of Energy

Thorium "derbies," so named because they resembled the top portion of derby hats.

"armed with shotguns or wearing six-guns strapped to their waists" from Nevada, California, Washington, other parts of Oregon, and even one man from Ohio. Local hardware stores reported their supplies of 4-by-4 posts were dwindling, as those were used to stake claims. Eager and optimistic prospectors also stocked up on dynamite while in town.

A week after the initial announcement it was confirmed that Roush's claim averaged .66% uranium; still a respectable strike that deserved attention from the AEC. Two field agents traveled to the Oregon desert to inspect the claim. Back in Albany, Bureau petrographer Hal Hess explained that Roush's discovery could be scientifically significant because, of the 100 or so known types of uranium, the sample out of Lakeview was unique: "The uranium-bearing rock so far found in Oregon is a new type which has an arsenic association," Hess said during a Kiwanis luncheon. When the ore was sold at the west's only buying center in Salt Lake City, the uranium haul would be worth $100–$200 per ton.

On July 22 a state geologist confirmed that the White King site was scientifically significant because the ore was found in volcanic rocks not previously known to be radioactive. "The uranium was reported to be in the form of a yellow-green film deposited in fractures in rocks, a crystalline material found in rock openings, or in the form of altered volcanic rocks," noted one article. The next day another mine, just a mile from the White King strike, was assayed by the Albany Bureau at an average of .68% uranium. The two sites produced commercial amounts of ore until 1965 and were Oregon's only successful uranium mines. Their discovery fueled "A-metal" fever ("A" for "Atomic") in the southeastern corner of the state and kept Bureau petrographers quite busy; in 1955 Hess and his crew processed about 700 uranium samples a month.

Other areas of research didn't slow down at the Albany Bureau, either. Ray Wells and S. H. Lorain, two former Albany employees now stationed in Alaska, had a problem they knew their former coworkers could solve. "Iron ore supplies in the Midwest are dwindling and a new supply from Alaska received in Albany for testing may become the forerunner of new industries in Oregon," noted the *Greater Oregon* newspaper. The low-grade ore had been processed in Alaska to produce 60% iron concentrate, which was then shipped to Albany. After further reducing the iron ore to achieve a 92.6% iron content, Albany metallurgists needed to extract a small but problematic amount of titanium within the iron.

Uranium and thorium work through the Atomic Energy Commission continued at a steady pace. "We quit melting sponge for zirc, got into thorium and others for AEC," recalled former employee Glenn Kenagy, in a Department of Reclamation history of the site. "Melting stayed same or bigger, lasted through possibly ten years. Started just before the shut down of zirc, so in 1954." Documents from the spring of 1955 reveal that—just as a few years prior—the new thorium melting project was highly classified and required meticulous security. Anyone handling or transporting thorium or other materials for the AEC required "Q" level security clearance, which is a designation issued to civilians by the government for those in contact with atomic or nuclear materials. "Q" level was on par with a Department of Defense "Top Secret" clearance, and during the 1950s, dozens of employees at the Albany Bureau required clearance. For Robert Beall's thorium production melting project in March 1955, even the forklift driver needed "Q" clearance.

Photo: Stephen T. Anderson Collection

A 1953 view of the machine shop (Building 5). Note the gas pump at the left-hand corner of the building.

Photo: Stephen T. Anderson Collection

Physical Metallurgy building (Building 33), was also known as the "Mole Hole" because it was sunken beneath ground level. Photo taken January 9, 1953.

It's no surprise that a tremendous amount of scrutiny was applied to metals handled during classified projects. Great care was taken to keep prying eyes off sensitive materials. For Beall's project, that meant keeping thorium ingots covered during transport between locations. "The primary ingots are carried to the machine shop in a covered box. After scalping, the ingots are returned to the melting area in a covered box. The second melt ingots are delivered to the machine shop in a covered box," noted one confidential security memo.

Despite vigilance while handling classified materials, accidents did happen. Later that year, head security officer/librarian Eleanor Abshire issued a suggestion after a fire broke out in the classified thorium melting room on the "northeast end of the east wing of the hafnium purification building." Around lunchtime on October 27, 1955, a jar of metal thorium shavings was awaiting transfer to another building when the sound of shattering glass echoed through the room. "Q" clearance employees rushed in to find the jar, wooden table, and doorframe ablaze. After making a hurried emergency call, the employees extinguished the flames before the fire department arrived. While nobody was injured, a notebook regarding thorium melting was partially burned, and all security badges and temporary passes had been reduced to ash. Worst of all, two weeks' worth of work was lost when classified notes regarding a "C-13 Savannah River" project were utterly destroyed. "There was no evidence of sabotage on the part of any employee," Eleanor concluded, and spontaneous combustion was ultimately to blame. In the future, she suggested that "ignitable" material such as shavings should not be placed anywhere near classified notebooks. Understandably, this incident stayed out of the newspapers.

The reference to "C-13 Savannah River" was regarding the Savannah River Site. The massive facility, located in South Carolina, was the nation's "largest building project since the construction of the Panama Canal," stated a *Post and Courier* history on the site, and its purpose was to produce tritium and plutonium-239 for the nation's nuclear weapon arsenal. Savannah River also had a robust research and development department to support the work performed on the 310-square mile site.

One known collaboration involving the Albany Bureau was the creation of a thorium electrode for a reactor operated by Savannah River at Oak Ridge, Tennessee. One technical paper, which may have been related to the electrode production, described how electrolytic thorium powder provided by Horizons Inc. was melted at the Albany Bureau, with supplemental melts being made at Battelle Memorial Institute and at Horizon's own facilities.

Creating the thorium electrode was unexpectedly problematic at first. The thorium powder that had been compacted into an electrode proved to have too much resistance to serve its intended purpose. Bureau technicians devised a way to lessen the electrode's resistance by running a weld bead down the length of the electrode. That technique solved the problem, and thorium melting was on its way. The paper concluded that "conversations with the scientists at that station [Albany] have indicated that no difficulties were encountered in using the consumable arc melting techniques in a water-cooled copper hearth furnace once a suitable electrode was formed," noted a 1957 technical paper on thorium research and development.

Uranium work at the Bureau seemed to be even more hush-hush than thorium work. In March of 1955,

R.H. Roberson and E.T. Hayes were involved with the investigation of uranium-niobium-ternary alloys that the Bureau had proposed the prior fall. The $60,000 "Uranium Project" was authorized through the Bureau of Ships and the Westinghouse Atomic Power Division to test corrosion behavior. Two-hundred pounds of natural uranium were received the prior year in rolled-strip form, then secured in a padlocked concrete vault at the Albany laboratory. Five separate work areas were utilized during the project, all of which were in the Physical Metallurgy building, which included an alloying section, a melting section, and a metallographic section. Each specimen was inscribed with a code number which followed the uranium through its testing phases. As with so many nuclear-related investigations of this era, the ultimate outcome of the project is unknown.

Another mystery surrounds a comment made by an early Bureau employee when he was interviewed by the Department of Reclamation in the mid-1990s. When asked about what Bureau employees did once zirconium production came to a halt, former station security monitor Glenn Kenagy remarked, "The AEC was doing lots of explosions, [both] underground and at Bikini and various places. Some shapes [which were classified] were poured here and shipped to Livermore [then University of California Radiation Laboratory, or UCRL]... [the United States] went into big competition with the Russians over bombs, how to make bigger or smaller."

Kenagy's commentary about post-zirconium projects raises questions about what work could have been done in collaboration with UCRL in terms of atomic tests. In 1952, the University of California Radiation Laboratory was established with no clearly defined mission other than to assist Los Alamos scientists with designing thermonuclear weapons, as well as component and instrumentation testing of those weapons. With relatively few employees and with little experience, the laboratory was seen as a weak rival to Los Alamos, but that didn't deter its newly hired crew.

In the mid-1950s, two young scientists at the University of California Radiation Laboratory were working to find innovative ways to make thermonuclear weapons smaller and light enough to fit on submarines or be attached to warheads. After a few embarrassing failures (which Los Alamos scientists mercilessly poked fun at), successful thermonuclear bombs tested in the Marshall Islands and at Bikini Atolls proved that the newly-established Radiation Laboratory had made considerable progress.

As to what "shapes" could have been poured in Albany—and of what material—one can only speculate. Former Deputy Director Howard Poppleton insisted that no enriched material was ever handled at the Albany Bureau, so the possibility of natural uranium work is a possibility, although it's likely a variety of different metals were worked on for UCRL. Beryllium oxide tampers were used in shots during Operation Teapot (a series of nuclear tests in Nevada) in May 1955; the tamper was a jacket around the fissionable material that reflected neutrons back into the fissionable material, creating a more efficient detonation.

Beryllium—with its deadly health hazards—was worked with at the Albany Bureau, but intimate details have been lost to history, with one exception: it was publicly revealed that the Bureau made trigger mechanisms for weapons during a classified project for the AEC. The only physical proof of its existence was in the form of contamination that was found in 2005, as eight of the 44 buildings on campus were found to have surfaces tainted by trace amounts of beryllium dust. In

February 2005, employees were surprised to find a sample of beryllium oxide hidden away in a storage cabinet, a relic from a forgotten era of metallurgy. "Research projects involving beryllium have not been conducted at the center since the 1970's," noted an article about the find.

Thorium-232 was another possible material the Bureau worked on for UCRL. In *The Traveler's Guide to Nuclear Weapons*, authors James M. Maroncelli and Timothy L. Karpin claim, "In 1953, the laboratory constructed the Mold Shop (Building 3)[8] and soon began to cast thorium there into various classified test shapes. The Radiation Laboratory in Livermore [UCRL] then took the thorium shapes and machined them to final specifications for eventual use in nuclear test detonations." This claim correlates to Kenagy's comment about the Bureau casting shapes for UCRL.

While thorium-232 isn't a fissionable material, it could be used to make a thermonuclear device more efficient. "The yield of a nuclear weapon can be increased by surrounding the device with uranium 238, in the form of either natural or depleted uranium, or with thorium-232, in the form of natural thorium. This approach is particularly advantageous in a thermonuclear weapon in which uranium-238 or thorium-232 in the outer shell of the secondary capsule is used to absorb an abundance of fast neutrons from fusion reactions produced within the secondary," noted Britannica.com.

In 1955, the Radiation Laboratory had its first successful thermonuclear detonation when Operation Teapot was initiated at the Nevada Test Site. After two and a half years of failures, the smaller facility that was always second fiddle to Los Alamos was proving itself with smaller, more useful nuclear weapons.

Collaboration between the Albany Bureau and the Radiation Laboratory continued throughout the decade—and possibly longer, with one source stating that the Bureau provided thorium to the facility into the 1960s. The only known code-named project occurred at the Bureau two years later; the secret Hummingbird Project, or simply "UCRL Project," spanned most of 1957 and may have continued into 1958. Security memos reveal that the project was a "preliminary study of several alloy systems . . . included will be the effects of heat treatment on microstructure and physical properties . . . the composition of these alloys are classified . . ." Fabrication of shapes, casting, and pattern work would be performed in different areas of the facility.

Whatever Albany employees were making for the Radiation Laboratory, it was deeply shrouded in secrecy. Security measures included key-card access to off-limits areas for badged, Q-clearance employees. Almost eighty Bureau workers had the appropriate clearance for the Hummingbird Project, though details were on a "need-to-know" basis. Around-the-clock shifts worked behind locked doors and blacked-out windows. The vault where classified notes and samples were stored was alarmed with a direct connection to the Albany Police Department. Three employees were chosen to serve as security monitors, in addition to the station security monitor, who oversaw all restricted areas.

Much care was taken when the alloys and shapes were ready for shipping. "Secret pieces will receive the highest level of protection during transfer," insisted one security memo, and ground shipments needed Armed Surveillance Service, while air shipments required an Armed Guard Service. Shipping containers needed to be "sturdy, built either of heavy plywood or steel and the Bureau of Mines' lead seals will be placed at all joined edges," noted the same security memo. The shipments were radioactive and had to be labeled "Metal NOIBN," (Not Otherwise Indicated By Name).

As one of the enduring mysteries of the Albany Bureau, details surrounding the Hummingbird Project may be lost to time. Freedom of Information Act requests have yielded no further information.

By 1956, there was so much going on at the Albany Bureau that the monthly newsletter had swelled to a twelve-page tome and morale was soaring with new projects and developments. "Last year about this time, about half of use *[sic]* were wondering whether or not we would still have a job after July 1 and the gloom and doom people had plenty of feed on which to fatten the worry bird," Joe Thom mused in the January 1956 *Bugle* editorial. But "stable and possibly increased employment" was anticipated in the next eighteen months, which buoyed the hopes of the remaining Bureau staff.

As employees saw new life being breathed into the laboratory, those in Federal employ made the move to establish a credit union. Space was cleared out in the conference room in the Operations Building as a temporary office space. Five directors, three members, and three committee members were elected. Edward Knakal—who was only known as "Heavy" around the lab, due to his imposing 300-pound stature— was elected president of the newly formed Linn Government Employees Credit Union. Any Civil Service employee was encouraged to join.

The jovial Heavy Knakal had earned his nickname during his employment at the Boulder City Bureau before transferring to a new alloying and refining plant in Redding, California. The nickname followed him to Albany when he moved with his family in 1951 to work in the Ferrous Metals Branch. By 1956 Heavy was serving as the foreman of the zirconium pilot plant and it was clear those under him appreciated his leadership. "*!$#* What in the &*$ can you say?" exclaimed one coworker, when interviewed by *Bugle* reporter Doris Wells. "Everybody knows that he goes to bat for the boys more than any other foreman. He always is looking out for our interests. He's the best *&$%$ foreman on the base!"

The neighborhood surrounding the Albany Bureau was experiencing a surge of growth and development as well; Albany Union High School had recently been built directly to the east of Building 1 and students streamed past the Bureau on their daily trek to school. By the end of the year, the school was growing fast enough that a five-room addition had to be constructed; the new building included a music room and a new wing with a drama and physics space, and a classroom.

The Fir Oaks addition neighborhood ("Mortgage Row") was growing and there were plans for a new tennis club to be established. Founders Rod Tripp and William (Bill) O'Hearn lamented that only two locations in Albany had tennis courts—the old college courts lovingly kept up by Bureau tennis enthusiasts, and Burkhart Park. For the next two years, the men scoured the town for land that would be suitable (and cheap enough) to establish a club.

The two men repeatedly scoped out the land behind the Bureau of Mines, noting how much empty, unused space there was in the southern field. They figured it would be useless to approach the government about purchasing the land, but after many failed attempts at securing other locations, they were desperate. Director Mark Wright was a friend of Tripp and O'Hearn, so the two approached Wright. "Is there a way to buy this property, or lease the property, or use this land to make it beneficial to the people of Albany?" Bill O'Hearn recalled asking Wright. Director Wright inquired with his contacts in Washington, D.C. "who knew the ins and outs of the property."

Tripp and O'Hearn had a pitch that was hard to turn down; their main focus of their planned tennis club was to provide a place to teach the game to Albany youth. Along with a recreational pool for summer swimming, the club would be sure to attract families. Because of Wright's connection, the pair was able to lease a skinny strip of land—just wide enough for regulation tennis courts—for $60 a year from the Federal government, "which was exactly the right price for our budget," said O'Hearn. The lease was to be available for a decade or more, though Tripp recalled the government alluded they could have the lease extend "*probably* forever," which made Tripp and O'Hearn slightly nervous, considering the amount of money that would be needed to construct tennis courts, a clubhouse, and a pool.

After the lease was secured, the drive for membership was on. Construction of the club began on the southernmost end of the "Back Forty" field in the late 1950s, and by 1960 or 1961, the new Albany Tennis Club was ready to host the first youth tournament. The pool was frequented by members and their families before and after matches, though O'Hearn recalled some pool tomfoolery in the early days. "We had a few incidents happen around the club . . . we started to experience some vandalism; chairs being thrown into the pool and things like that." Mischievous pranks persisted until adult club members decided to hold an overnight stakeout to catch vandals in the act. "People would volunteer to stay up until midnight," O'Hearn said.

O'Hearn was playing doubles one night when the surprised players heard a tremendous *ka-duhnk!* coming from the closed pool area. He shot out of the tennis court area to find two youths sauntering away. After confronting the boys, O'Hearn took them back to the pool, where he found a ten-pound rock sitting at the bottom of the (thankfully undamaged) pool. The boys were instructed to immediately retrieve the rock—by diving in fully clothed.

While the area around the Albany Bureau was growing both in population and status, the town itself was on the cusp of an entirely new private industry. Early in January 1956, Albany mayor Charles McCormack announced that plans for Oregon Metallurgical titanium plant were moving ahead. It was hoped that the plant would employ 60–100 people— many of which would be former Bureau employees. Prominent Eugene lumberman Dale Fischer would head up the new venture. Though a location hadn't been finalized, a 60-acre tract of land on the southernmost end of town was being considered. There were hopes that once the location had been secured, construction could start within 45 days, with operations beginning by the first of July.

February brought more heartening news by way of a telegram from Senator Richard Neuberger, who reported that the Atomic Energy Commission was once again starving for zirconium, and for an emergency period of eighteen months, the AEC would be using every possible resource to produce more zirconium. Carborundum's production couldn't keep up with the

AEC's projected appetite for the nuclear-age metal, so there was talk of restarting the shuttered zirconium plant at the Bureau, though at this point, it was unsure if private industry or the government would be leading the effort, though the Albany Chamber was angling toward attracting a private operator.

"A resolution calling for private operation of the zirconium pilot plant at the Albany station of the U.S. Bureau of Mines was passed today by the Board of Directors of the Albany Chamber of Commerce and telegraphed to Oregon congressmen and key Interior Department and atomic energy officials in Washington, D.C.," noted the *Albany Democrat-Herald.* The Albany Chamber of Commerce president stated that there were several private firms vying to operate the plant for the production of zirconium sponge.

On the exact day that the *Greater Oregon* newspaper made the announcement, the rival *Albany Democrat-Herald* reported that Bureau Director Shelton would be retiring after 27 years of service with the government to become to general manager of the new Oregon Metallurgical corporation, resignation effective March 15.

Shelton's looming departure signaled the end of an era for the Albany Bureau of Mines. Since replacing first director Bruce A. Rogers in 1946, the laboratory under Shelton's guidance had achieved a whirlwind of metallurgical successes. From the ramp-up of Kroll's zirconium experiments to the creation of the world's first commercial zirconium plant, to the world's only hafnium-producing facility, the site had seen a lot of firsts in a relatively short amount of time. A decade of pioneering work that contributed to the creation of the world's first nuclear submarine would be a legacy of Shelton's leadership.

On the evening of March 14, 1956, over 100 employees and their spouses attended a farewell gala for Shelton at the distinguished Cascade Room at the Hotel Albany. During the social hour, ladies in formal dresses and men in suits drank and mingled. The swish of off-the-shoulder satin gowns accompanied the electric organ music played by employee Betty Webber, providing ambiance. After dinner was served, an awards ceremony revealed the level of devotion and respect Shelton had fostered among his employees during his decade in charge, as gifts and kind words were showered on the director.

Acting Director Mark Wright was toastmaster for the night. Letters had flowed in from Bureau dignitaries and past employees all over the country for the event and Wright read them aloud. Wing Agnew, former Albany employee and director of the Spokane station, declared that "this is the first time in my 20 years with the Bureau that I have seen no friction," a true testament to Shelton's leadership abilities, especially considering the breakneck pace at which *Nautilus* research and production had to be performed. In Joe Thom's *Bureau Bugle* editorial, he added that with Shelton, "We didn't have our ideas forced into the background by officious mannerisms and the old desire to kill . . . Shelton has directed the group which supervised the growth of our laboratory from a small college campus to a multi-million-dollar metallurgical laboratory," added Thom.

During the after-dinner presentation, Mrs. Shelton was presented with an orchid corsage and bracelet; Stephen was given golf clubs and a matching bag, a zirconium plaque declaring a lifetime membership to the Bureau Associates, a zirconium desk name plate and letter opener, a titanium cigarette lighter, and a bracelet bejeweled with titanium oxide gems. All these items were carefully handcrafted by Bureau employees during their off-hours.

The feelings of admiration between boss and staff were mutual. "I have never before been where there was so much willingness to cooperate," Shelton declared during his speech. "In thanking his associates Shelton returned praise, asserting that any success he may have attained here was due to their eagerness to accomplish their assignments," wrote the *Albany Democrat-Herald*.

When Shelton had replaced director Dr. Rogers in 1946, he had a plethora of education, experience, and leadership ability—just the right combination to guide the young laboratory to success. While navigating the challenges of working with Rickover (a challenge all unto itself) to create nuclear-grade zirconium and hafnium, Shelton had submitted a total of two additional patents in his name and was in the midst of submitting his fourth patent, the "Method of Manufacturing Titanium and Titanium Alloys" was granted and published in 1959. As the new general manager for the up-and-coming Oregon Metallurgical, Shelton was once again the perfect fit.

By mid-March 1956, Oregon Metallurgical, (now referred to as Oremet) founders had purchased the tract of land on the southernmost edge of town and preparations were being made to start construction. The foundation area was being prepped and bids would begin soon. The first work would focus on outside utilities and drainage, and specs for the plant were being drawn up by Cornell, Howland, Hayes, and Merryfield, a Corvallis-area engineering company. Investments for the business had grown to $500,000 in capital, with $1 million in stock authorization. More Bureau employees were signing up to work at Oremet by the day. Joe Thom, the voice of positivity and optimism in the *Bugle*, urged those staying behind to have "wisdom and tact," and to not count out the dwindling government laboratory.

CHAPTER FIFTEEN

A NEW HOPE AND A NEW ERA

May 1956–December 1956

"May 2 marked the dawn of a new industrial era in Albany."
—Albany Democrat-Herald, Jan 1 1957

"As old means of livelihood failed to meet the needs, Albany—probably more than any other Oregon city—found new fields. Timber and agriculture aren't dead, and they will continue to be basic to the area's economy, but the new industries will make the difference between getting by and prospering."
—Albany Democrat-Herald *editorial, December 31, 1956*

The four buildings involved in zirconium production at the Albany Bureau (the zirconium plant, reduction plant, chlorination building and purification tower) had been sitting idle and silent for exactly a year. The gleaming white purification tower no longer held bubbling solutions in its five-story high Pyrex columns; inside the collegiate-looking zirconium pilot plant and reduction plant, light from the expansive windows settled on dismantled spaces dulled by layers of dust. The hustle of round-the-clock production had been replaced by an unsettled stillness, broken only by occasional drips and leaks caused by the wetter-than-usual spring weather. The cold buildings no longer hummed with electricity; all the furnaces had been dismantled and removed upon closure, and building doors remained tightly locked—until a sudden order from the Atomic Energy Commission sent a ripple through campus early that May: the zirconium plant needed to be reopened within 90 days.

Earlier in the year, a number of companies responded to a proposal to operate the Bureau's facilities. Among those who responded were the Wah Chang Corporation, Harvey Aluminum Division, and Olin Matheson Chemical Corporation. The proposal from the Harvey Aluminum Corporation was most favorable, but negotiations faltered and Harvey failed to produce a signed contract.

Local papers' headlines soon blazed with the good news that New York–based Wah Chang Corporation had been selected as the operating entity and it was hoped 130 (mostly) local people would find employment with the venture. A representative from the Pittsburgh AEC office visited Albany to meet with Wah Chang officials to secure a 2-year contract for 300,000 pounds of zirconium a year, with a renewal clause in case more was needed. The AEC had already ordered construction of three more zirconium plants in three different states, plus had arranged to acquire 200,000 pounds of zirconium from the Commodity Credit Corporation of Japan, with deliveries expected soon.

Shanghai native Stephen Yih was named general manager of the zirconium plant. Yi had been hired by Wah Chang in 1953 and was a strong candidate for the position, as he had recently volunteered to head Wah Chang's titanium project at the Boulder City, Nevada, Bureau station.

In the early 1950s titanium from Japan was considered the finest in the world. Wah Chang founder Dr. K. C. Li sent two people to Nevada to learn how to use the Kroll process to create high-purity titanium sponge. Stephen Yih and C. L. Lo volunteered to make the move to the southwest. Within a year of his arrival Yih had led his team in making titanium that surpassed the quality of Japanese titanium. With his recent experience in Nevada, reviving Albany's mothballed zirconium plant wouldn't prove to be much of a challenge for the ambitious thirty-seven-year-old Yih.

  Work began right away as a "reactivation team" was brought in to start reassembling furnaces and replace broken or worn out equipment. Chemical engineer James McClain had just resigned from his 14-year career at the Bureau to head up Wah Chang's reactivation efforts. It was hoped that the entire zirconium plant would be up and ready within two weeks' time, though when the reactivation crew assessed the buildings, news was grim: the asbestos gaskets holding together the slender Pyrex tubes in the Purification tower had decayed from disuse. When water was poured through them, the tubes spurted and dribbled at the gaskets. More than fifty pumps that regulated liquid within the tubes were completely broken. Instead of two weeks, repairs in the Purification tower took four months to complete.

  Wah Chang's presence at the Bureau was welcomed warmly by Bureau employees in the *Bugle*. "We have some new neighbors here to run our zirconium plant for us," wrote the newsletter. "The world-famous Wah Chang Corporation should prove to be very stimulating company. They have already enjoyed considerable success in producing other metals and it will no doubt prove interesting to watch them apply their knowledge to zirconium. Welcome, Neighbors! We hope you will like us and that your efforts will be profitable."

Stephen Yih needed to establish temporary office spaces for Wah Chang, preferably somewhere quite close by. One wonders why space couldn't be made in an empty Bureau office, but if the newly-established credit union had to be operated out of a conference room, it's highly likely that there was simply no available space in any of the Bureau buildings. So a Wah Chang scout began knocking on neighbor's doors along Broadway Street to the west.

One of the first homes approached was 1840 SW Broadway, a 1700-square-foot house located directly across from the back of the Bureau's administration building and its Persian walnut tree with enormous branches. The home was owned by Joseph Ficq, a school teacher at Liberty Elementary who was single at the time. The Wah Chang scout offered to lease the house from Ficq, which meant he would need to find another living arrangement and move out in just a few weeks' time. Incredibly, Ficq agreed.

Quick changes were made to the home's interior. "The kitchen cabinets and appliances were removed and stored, and the kitchen area became the office of Stephen Yih," wrote Frederick Ficq, Joseph's son. "Additional wiring and lighting was installed, and a telephone switchboard was placed upstairs. The lease was to run for just over two years. The house and garage thus served as office space for that time, until the summer of 1958. Beginning in January of 1957, an additional small office building also on the property was leased by the company as well. The house looked much the same as it does [now]. The 'Wah Chang' sign hung just to the left of the front porch archway." The "sign" that was hung on the house was a crude wooden plank with the words "Wah Chang Corp.," plus the home's address, hastily written in black handwriting, attesting to the lightning-fast transition and temporary nature of the arrangements.

As unseasonably wet spring weather began to turn to drier skies in early May, there were hopes that the zirconium plant would be operational by mid-month. In a quick 24-hour trip, two Wah Chang assistant treasurers flew in from corporate headquarters in New York to assess progress. All plant Manager James "Jim" McClain needed were replacement parts (most likely for the Purification plant) and enough staff to start the operation.

Just as Wah Chang was establishing itself at the Albany Bureau, Oremet's foundations were being poured and walls were being erected. Word had spread about the titanium venture throughout Oregon; a Portland company, Electric Steel Foundry Co., purchased 100 shares of stock in Oremet. Electric Steel was involved in the processing, sale, and distribution of metals and its sales connections would be advantageous to the new company. Oremet stockholders were well pleased with the way things were progressing.

The wealth of knowledge that had blossomed from the Albany Bureau was spreading by way of dedicated employees who shared their metallurgical insight in the U.S. and beyond. The spring and summer of 1956 were particularly poignant; at the 109th meeting of the Electrochemical Society in San Francisco in early May, Stephen Shelton was the keynote speaker. Three of eight papers presented to the Society were from the Bureau alone. That same month at Iowa State University in Ames, the Bureau's Frank Block of the

Photo: *Bureau Bugle*
Haruo Kato was at the helm of the Bureau's Physical Metallurgy Fabrication section.

Photo: *Bureau Bugle*
Frank Block oversaw all chemical research in the Process Metallurgy department.

Process Development Unit, and Haruo Kato of Physical Metallurgy attended an invitation-only Metallurgical Information meeting, which was attended only by those who were directly involved with AEC-sponsored work. About three hundred scientists were in attendance.

Haruo Kato and Frank Block were two top-notch metallurgists at the Bureau. Kato, a Seattle native, was a sophomore in college when he was imprisoned by the government at two separate internment camps for people of Japanese descent, during World War II. He later served in the U.S. Army in the 442nd Combat Team, serving mostly in Italy and France. After the war he returned to his studies at the University of Washington, where he earned a degree in Metallurgical Engineering. Kato spent a year working for Boeing, but "decided routine physical testing just wasn't for a man looking for a future," noted the *Bureau Bugle*. Kato, his wife Kei, and their two sons and two daughters found greener pastures in Albany. Kato was an active Toastmasters member and taught judo at Oregon State College. He headed up the Bureau's Physical Metallurgy Fabrication section.

Oregon born-and-bred Frank Block earned his degree in chemical engineering at Oregon State College after serving during World War II. Before his graduation, Block was hired by the Bureau and became involved in research spanning the rare earths, cobalt, and nickel, plus zirconium, hafnium, magnesium, and chromium. By the time he and Kato were invited to the AEC's exclusive informational meeting, Block oversaw all the chemical research in the Process Metallurgy department.

At the Pacific Northwest regional conference of the American Institute of Mining, Metallurgical and Petroleum Engineers held in Seattle, three Albany Bureau papers were presented. In June, Mr. Holmes, a zirconium plant employee, was granted two months' leave to travel to France, where he would act as a consultant for metallurgical plants hoping to produce malleable zirconium.

The next month, Robert Beall traveled across the globe with his family, also on two months' leave, to help set up a titanium melting facility in Avesta, Sweden. Beall wrote back to the *Bugle*, stating that his family had lodged in a small hotel overlooking a harbor. The weather was often good enough so the family could enjoy swimming, and working with the Swedes was pleasant, although Beall found the language barrier difficult.

As summer was ripening in Oregon, A. H. Roberson departed on a "world metallurgical tour" when he went to Europe to attend a meeting of the Institute of Metals, where he presented a paper on titanium and zirconium casting. In Paris, he attended the Organization for European Economic Cooperation—a group that had been guests at the Albany Bureau a year prior. Roberson continued on to Germany to visit firms interested in zirconium, titanium, tantalum, and columbium (niobium). Roberson commented that Germany was in a vast phase of rebuilding; plants he visited had brand-new equipment because everything had been utterly destroyed during the war. "Stuttgart was about 80 percent destroyed and many of the fine buildings have never been restored," he reported to the *Bugle.* "The former New Palace on the public square is a gaunt skeleton of a fabulously beautiful structure. The Germans rebuilt their factories first and are gradually rebuilding the cities. For this reason their economic comeback is far ahead of England where the whole hearted effort for going ahead seems to be lacking," he mused.

Oremet began titanium ingot production in July 1956. Albany had jumped into full-fledged titanium production at just the right time; on Independence Day that year, the U-2 spy plane flew over the USSR for the first time. Birthed under extreme secrecy at Lockheed's SkunkWorks and radar-tested at infamous Area 51, the "Dragon Lady" was designed to fly at unheard-of altitudes to avoid detection—and any land-based missiles that might be launched at her.

But flying at such an extreme altitude meant the aircraft would be operating in an oxygen-starved atmosphere. "Even the thrust of the best jet in the world would be reduced to a fraction of what it would be at sea level," noted Kathleen Housley in *Black Sand*. Any measure to reduce the weight of the aircraft was taken; the aluminum skin was a mere 0.02 inches thick, "…which meant the aircraft was both fragile on the ground and extremely delicate to fly. If a pilot flew the U-2 too slow, the airplane could stall. If he flew too fast, the wings could literally come off," wrote Annie Jacobson in *Area 51: An Uncensored History of America's Top Secret Military Base*.

Pratt & Whitney's J-57 engine was of particular concern, being one of the heaviest single components of the aircraft, so during the two years of development, special consideration was given to its structural materials. Titanium was a front-runner metal, but just as with zirconium and the *Nautilus* reactor, nobody was quite sure which alloy would be the best to use. Fortunately, Watertown Arsenal (later the Army Research Laboratory) had been toying with different combinations and settled upon a titanium-aluminum-vanadium alloy called Ti-6Al-4V (now known just as Ti-6-4). The aircraft was a success and its flights over Russia gained valuable intel as it skimmed the stratosphere with its on-board cameras clicking away continuously. More U-2s were ordered, and the demand for titanium was increasing.

By fall 1956, Oremet had begun operations and employed about 70 people. Mayor McCormack, who had secured financing at the outset, was pleased with the new corporation. Oremet made headlines in October when the largest single batch of titanium ingots left the plant on a truck, bound for a cross-country trek to Pittsburgh Firth Sterling, Inc. The $45,000 order was bound to be forged into "bars, rods, and such other forms as are required in the construction of jet airplane engines. Ultimate destination of this consignment is the Ford Aircraft Corporation, a subsidiary of the Ford Motor Co." The 7,000 pound order had taken several weeks to produce, but General Manager Stephen Shelton revealed that Oremet had gained additional equipment that would allow the plant to churn out future orders of that size in about four days.

The Albany Bureau was still involved with ilmenite (titanium) smelting as well, which attracted a flood of visitors from all over the country from places like Battelle Memorial Institute, the National Lead Co., Metal Chlorides Co., the Columbia-Southern Chemical Corp, and the Lincoln Electric Co., just to name a few. "The popularity of our lab is due probably to the fact that ilmenite currently is being run in the smelter," noted the *Bureau Bugle*.

For those lucky individuals who were able to see ilmenite smelting firsthand, the fiery experience was not soon forgotten. "When this writer went down to the Smelter to see if the boys had any *Bugle* news, she was lucky enough to get there just as they were tapping the furnace," wrote Doris Wells. "If you've never seen an ilmenite run being tapped for titanium slag, then you haven't lived. Smoke, flames, heat, and dust fly all over the place. The men tapping the furnace look like men from Mars in the aluminized chaps, coats, and helmets. It looked very exciting and dangerous to this layman."

Danger was never far from reactive metal production; toward the end of 1956, Bureau neighbors once again got front row seats to not one, but two, blazes at the plant. One fire started in the back of the smelter building when a pile of bagasse (sugar cane fibers used as biofuel) caught on fire. Thankfully, damage was slight. Not long after, tragedy was averted when the Wah Chang–operated zirconium plant caught on fire again. This time, the fire was caused by a hairline crack that had splintered along a pipe containing a solvent. The pressure caused the chemicals to squirt directly onto an electrical outlet, resulting in a fire. Wiring, glass equipment, and the roof were (once again) damaged. Plant operators leapt into action to quell the blaze, which was finished off by the Albany Fire Department. Luckily, the plant escaped with only about $2,000 worth of damage.

Across from the machine shop, Wah Chang had transformed the idle zirconium plant into a bustling beehive of production, but operating the Bureau's facility was just the beginning for the New York–based corporation. Just north of Albany, on the banks of swampy Murder Creek, Wah Chang executives had been eyeing a suitable plot of land to build a titanium plant and a second zirconium facility, but there was a setback: they needed permission to obtain a right-of-way to the Willamette River. Unsure of the outcome, Wah Chang started considering Boise, Idaho as a possible location for one or both plants. But the landowners, brothers Carl and Oscar Nygren, with "loyalty and civic pride," gave their blessing to Wah Chang so that construction could begin right away.

Portland general contractor George A. Moore, who had just recently finished Albany Union High

School's 5-room addition, was in the Willamette Valley once again to transform an empty space between the Oregon Electric and Southern Pacific Railroad lines into Wah Chang's newest plant, but unseasonably bad October weather was already hampering efforts. Drenching rains produced dangerously slick mud that beleaguered workers who were hustling to finish the zirconium plant and smaller titanium plant by the end of November, with production expected by the beginning of the new year. The million-dollar facility was expected to employ 1,000 people by the time it was in operation.

    Between the old Bureau furnaces firing up, a row of new furnaces being used at Oremet, and even more new furnaces at two Wah Chang plants, Albany leaders realized that securing another power source would be necessary. The establishment of the Northwest Electro-development Laboratory had been born out of the desire to wisely utilize the abundant energy produced by the Northwest's hydroelectric power, but now it was clear the power grid was about to be taxed far beyond prior usage. At the end of 1956, BPA administrator William A. Pearl proposed transferring non-federal power over BPA transmission lines; Albany realized this would be a good call since their new plants were, of course, completely reliant on electricity. Pacific Power & Light was the supplier of energy to the new industries, save the Bureau, which ran on an independent BPA line.

    Social activities and Bureau-sponsored events were blossoming again and growing to include members of Oremet and Wah Chang. The ladies' card clubs openly welcomed wives and employees of the two new industries in town. The nine-month old Linn Government Employees Credit Union had gained over 100 shareholders by December 1956, with $11,500 in shares. "The outlook so far for the shareholders is very bright and they should realize good dividends," insisted Edward "Heavy" Knakal, credit union president, in a *Bugle* article inviting people, "whether you are a member or not," to swing by the makeshift office in the Operations Building just to say hello.

As the laboratory's Christmas party rolled around, the *Bureau Bugle* wrote about Heavy's latest holiday-related predicament. Without overtly stating that Heavy was the Bureau's Santa Claus stand-in (lest children of a reading age peruse their parent's copy of the newsletter) the article noted that one of Heavy's favorite things was to grow beard and dress for colder weather, subtly hinting at his holiday role. Usually, the big man had trouble finding a costume. "I don't have to use any pillows but [I] have to find clothes big enough to fit," he confessed about his holiday-related side job. But by the end of 1956, Heavy had shed enough pounds that coworkers joked they'd have to change his moniker to "Slim."

Besides a jolly Santa and the traditional family holiday party at the Bureau, there was much to look forward to for Albany Bureau employees. The laboratory that had started as a small facility struggling to find qualified employees during the Second World War had exploded into a round-the-clock production facility, urged on by the brilliant and exacting Captain Rickover as he delivered on his promise to create the world's first nuclear submarine. The first significant amounts of nuclear-grade zirconium—and hafnium—had been produced in a quiet, unassuming neighborhood in southwest Albany. An undercurrent of other work, equally important but much less visible, some shrouded in total secrecy and lost to time, was performed concurrently. Political forces, World War II, the Korean War, and the Cold War directly influenced almost every facet of activity during the early years of Albany Bureau of Mines.

The wealth of knowledge gained from years of trial and error, educated guesses and lucky coincidences, had built a small army of the world's most informed metallurgists on the subjects of zirconium, titanium, and hafnium, plus others like molybdenum, tantalum, and niobium. That small army was now going out on a monthly basis to the corners of the developed world to consult, assist, and teach the new processes developed at the Albany Bureau. And now the small town of Albany was going to benefit from two new titanium plants, two zirconium plants, and in the near future, an entire specialty metals industry born from one laboratory.

As ruddy-faced children clambered onto jolly Heavy Knakal's lap that Christmas while whispering their wish list, Bureau employees mingled with old friends and new. Drinks in hand, foremen, secretaries, maintenance men and metallurgists all belted out carols and danced in celebration. A fresh energy had been infused into the Albany Bureau, with Wah Chang's revival of the zirconium plant, the Bureau's continued secret work with the Atomic Energy Commission, and ilmenite smelting. Although the Bureau's first era had come to a close, the future was bright for the little laboratory in Albany's southwest corner.

Photo: *Bureau Bugle*
Heavy Knakal took on the role as the Bureau's jolly St. Nick during annual Christmas parties.

Photo: Stephen T. Anderson Collection
A note about the photos: most of the photos that are credited to the Stephen T. Anderson collection, and are of the Bureau personnel or grounds, are attributed to Bureau photographer Robert (Bob) W. Nelson. Mr. Nelson was employed by the Bureau for 26 years, likely beginning around 1945. Of Mr. Nelson's photographic preferences, former technical photographer Stephen Anderson remarked, "He didn't like taking photos with anything smaller than a 4x5" format, as that just wasn't professional. In fact, every one of the official Albany photographic records I've gone through from the Bureau's very beginning until Bob's retirement in 1973 was done with large format cameras."

EPILOGUE

The end of zirconium production at the Albany Bureau is generally considered to be the conclusion of the laboratory's "golden age." With the hand-off of the zirconium production plant to the private sector, the all-consuming focus that had been a driving force since 1944 was no longer the backbone of the laboratory. Despite that, there was no lack of new work assigned to the Albany Bureau, and some of that work would make significant impacts in the areas of medicine, defense, and infrastructure. Classified work for the Atomic Energy Commission with uranium and thorium continued into the 1960s, carrying on the undercurrent of secrecy that had developed during the period when zirconium and hafnium were being produced for the *Nautilus*.

The Albany Bureau continued to be a cornerstone of community involvement and a supportive social hub for employees and their families. Many children of employees have fond recollections of being welcomed onto Bureau grounds during working hours to visit a parent, see the extensive rock collection in the Petrographic Laboratory, or to ride bikes on the paved driveways. The annual Easter egg hunts and holiday parties were the gems of social gatherings for all ages.

After his departure from the Bureau of Mines in 1951, Dr. Kroll joined the faculty at Oregon State University in Corvallis to teach metallurgy. During his years at Oregon State, he established the Metal Research Foundation, a non-profit grant and scholarship organization. Kroll left Corvallis in 1961 for Belgium, where he had a home built in close proximity to family. Of his time spent in Oregon, Kroll later said that "the years I spent in Albany were the happiest of my career." Kroll died on March 30, 1973, in Brussels, at the age of 83.

The influence of knowledge gained by Bureau employees (and not just the ones with advanced degrees) spread far and wide. Because of the laboratory's influence, an entirely new industry was established in Albany. Wah Chang opened their new site in January of 1957—just six months after construction began—and began producing reactor- and commercial-grade zirconium and hafnium while concurrently operating the Bureau's plant. The Space Race combined with the Cold War created an unprecedented need for never-before utilized metals and alloys, particularly pertaining to aircraft development.

Other successes at the site include superconducting alloys found in MRI machines and high-temperature, high-strength materials for the aerospace industry, including niobium components for the Apollo missions. Today, Wah Chang's successor, Allegheny Technologies Incorporated, produces components for SpaceX.

Oremet blossomed under Stephen Shelton's leadership, with former Bureau titanium and zirconium metallurgist Frank Caputo at his side. Titanium, the metal that Kroll had tried in vain to promote in America just twenty-five years earlier, was now in high demand, thanks in part to the development of the U-2 and SR-71 reconnaissance aircraft.

Shelton was promoted to president in 1959 and Oremet became one of two titanium sponge producers in the United States that created specialty alloys for electronics, medical, aerospace, military, and other applications, such as sponge destined to become golf clubs. The titanium industry experienced waves of booms and downturns, and Oremet weathered them all until the COVID-19 pandemic swept the globe, slowing airline activity to a crawl. Then owned by Allegheny Technologies Incorporated, the plant shut down after 64 years of operation and remains closed at the time of publication.

A number of other metals-related businesses emerged from the Bureau's influence, including Pacific Cast Technologies, Northwest Industries, Inc., Selmet, and Stack Metallurgical Group. The Linn Government Employee's Credit Union grew to the point where it took over the entire boiler-room building on the far northeast corner of the Bureau's campus and changed its name to Federal Metals Credit Union in 1957, opening up its membership to anyone in the Albany metals industry. In 1999 the name was changed to Central Willamette Credit Union, and today membership is open to anyone in western Oregon.

Later research at the Albany Bureau led to significant advances in mining safety. During the 1970s, employees worked on finding ways to reduce methane explosions in coal mines. Using high-speed photography, employees analyzed "the conditions in mining equipment that caused methane ignition, and how to prevent the explosion," retired employee Robert Blickensderfer recalled.

In the 1980s, Blickensderfer and his team established the world's leading wear-testing laboratory at the Albany Bureau. In that facility, mining tools were put through rigorous tests designed to simulate usage over extended periods of time. Test results prompted the development of more wear-resistant materials for the mining industry.

Local health concerns in the late 1970s and 1980s prompted the government to begin an extensive analysis of the Albany Bureau of Mines site, with the State of Oregon heading up an additional analysis of schools in the immediate area. Because of the nature of work performed at the Bureau during the 1940s through the 1970s, with radioactive materials uranium and thorium, plus hazardous beryllium, it was deemed that the site was eligible for cleanup under the Formerly Utilized Sites Remedial Action Program (FUSRAP). Locations inside buildings on campus were painstakingly tested for potentially unsafe conditions, as were grounds outside, and on surrounding properties. The Back Forty field became pockmarked with bore holes as surveyors from Argonne National Laboratory analyzed water flow, soil composition, and contaminants present.

A collection of 700-plus pages of findings outlined remedial actions; in the end, 18 buildings and 37 outdoor areas were decontaminated. For a period of two years, between 1987–1988, and then again in 1990–1991, researchers had to work among partially torn-up buildings, excavated outdoor areas, and cordoned-off spaces while suited-up workers hauled off contaminated building materials and topsoil. In the end, almost 3,000 cubic yards of soil were hauled off to the Hanford low-level radioactive waste area for disposal, along with 400 cubic yards of structural debris and almost 70 cubic yards of equipment. Because of the remediation, the campus today is considered compliant with decontamination criteria.

The Albany Bureau continued to function as the Albany Research Center as a part of the Department of Interior until the national Bureau of Mines was abolished in 1996, when operations transferred to the Department of Energy. Just prior to the transition, the Department of Reclamation conducted a study of the site and deemed most of the buildings to be historically contributing, with 40 buildings included in the Oregon Historic Sites database. In 2005 the facility was adopted into the National Energy Technology Laboratory complex, making it the only national laboratory in Oregon.

Current work at NETL focuses on emerging energy technologies. As in the early days, the site's analytical laboratories continue to allow researchers to thoroughly investigate material characteristics and properties, through state-of-the-art electron microscopes, X-ray diffraction, X-ray fluorescence, thermogravimetric analysis, and a metallographic laboratory. The Mechanical Testing Laboratory allows researchers to analyze a material's performance in response to stress, mimicking situations to assess how well the material will perform in a real-world setting, like in power plants.

NETL's Severe Environmental Corrosion Erosion Facility allows researchers to study the effects of extreme environments on surfaces. Within the facility, materials can safely be exposed to high or low temperatures, or in pure, mixed-gas, or mixed gas-liquid situations to emulate different situations. "Research . . . supports NETL's investigations into oxy-fuel combustion, oxidation, refractory materials stability, and fuels," notes one summary.

In the High-Pressure Immersion and Reactive Transport Laboratory, researchers study geologic and engineered media like cement, casings, or pipeline to recreate environments to mimic underground environments for oil and natural gas, unconventional resources, and carbon storage. In this laboratory, extensive corrosion and alloy work takes place in a myriad of high temperature, high-pressure autoclaves.

The Geosciences Laboratory focuses on natural and engineered materials collected from the field. The Geoscience Analysis, Interpretation, and Assessments (GAIA) Facilities is composed of high-end computing stations and advanced software that can create 3D visualizations, coupled with real world data to evaluate and interpret geological features, such as the depth of drilled wells.

A new area of study at NETL includes work performed in the Magnetohydrodynamic (MHD) Laboratory, where a decades-old concept, now better analyzed through computer-modeled concepts, has been tested and proven. "MHD is a scientific discipline interested in the interaction of an electrically conductive fluid with a magnetic field. In an 'MHD generator,' this interaction leads to useable electric power without any moving mechanical parts," notes one explanation. Also called direct power extraction, an MHD turbine can be used in much higher temperature applications and could be a key component in future energy production. "The MHD process can generate large amounts of power, is suitable for peak power generation with no pollution while the lack of moving parts ensures reliability," notes one NETL press release.

If one walks around the perimeter of the laboratory today, the buildings look very much the way they did in the early days. Some alterations have occurred because of expansion (as with several temporary buildings) but the historic look and feel has been carefully maintained through adherence to guidance from the Oregon State Historic Preservation Office. Even the iconic beach cruisers purchased in the late 1940s and early 50s are still used by employees to ride across the expansive campus, seventy some years after their introduction.

A team of dedicated employees keep building exteriors and interiors tidy and clean, and the grounds are expertly maintained. Mature trees are inspected annually and cared for by arborists. In the spring, the false horse chestnuts that line Broadway Street to the west bloom pink and white and rhododendrons form low blooming hedges along buildings. In the fall, the deciduous trees on campus turn brilliant shades of red and orange and the Persian walnut bursts forth with brilliant yellow leaves.

    The biggest change to the campus came after the tragic events of September 11, 2001, when a chain-link security fence was installed around the entire perimeter, ending decades of the public being allowed into the park-like setting. Round-the-clock security guards patrol the perimeter of the fence. Gone are the days of children laughing and playing on the giant Persian walnut, whose enormous, octopus-like branches rest on the ground.

    With each administration change comes budgetary uncertainty for Albany's historic laboratory, but just as in the past, employees and the community rally around the site, hoping to secure its future. With any luck, the site that has brought such positive change to the Willamette Valley will continue to thrive and endure.

"I am happy that a gracious fate has allowed me to carry, for a while, the flag of rare metals research, around which many young men have now gathered to carry on, where I have left off."

—WILLIAM J. KROLL

ENDNOTES

1. Some creative license was taken with this introduction, as no trip reports or official documentation has yet been found about Captain Rickover's visits to Albany. Rickover stated, "Dr. Kroll had worked on the development of a zirconium production process at the Bureau of Mines facility at Albany, Oregon. I made several hurried trips to see the work being done at that facility to furnish zirconium for the first naval reactors. Usually Dr. Kroll, then a consultant to the Bureau of Mines, and several senior officials of the Bureau of Mines met me at the Portland airport on Friday evenings. We would drive to Albany, inspect the equipment, and discuss the results of the production effort underway. Dr. Kroll always gave me straightforward answers. He was a scientist. I am an engineer. Our common interest was zirconium. I think we both understood the problems the other faced. I believe we had this understanding because we based our discussion on principles."

    It is not known when exactly Rickover made his first trip, but because of Kroll's progress with zirconium and the Atomic Energy Commission's interest in the metal, August 1949 is a likely date.

2. At her retirement from the Bureau, it was planned that a new technical library at the site would be named after Eleanor Abshire.

Unfortunately, the new library never came to pass and the extensive collection of periodicals, journals, and technical information was disassembled (and some pieces disposed of) when the Bureau was abolished in 1996.

3. In the 1970's Mae Jean—then known simply as Jean Gress—continued her career in journalism working for the *Longview Daily News* in Washington State as their staff artist.

4. There are varying viewpoints on why Kroll would have left at such a seemingly inopportune time. James Overby Shelton, youngest son of Stephen Mattheson Shelton, recalls "Kroll was stubborn and difficult to work with. When it came to adapting/fine tuning the process which was preventing finalizing the process . . . we were running out of time. The process for zirconium was very similar to [dad's] process for titanium. [Dad] had to get the project done and Kroll had to get out of the way."

Local news articles in later years noted, "Kroll, leader in the titanium processing field, is needed back in the laboratory. But since he left the Bureau of Mines at Albany, Oregon, in 1951, his creative work in metallurgy has stopped. This is because he has had to devote his time and energy to a battle with the U.S. Alien Property Custodian. His mental distress caused by the situation has seriously impaired his health, and already the suit has cost him an exorbitant amount of money." Close friend H. Andrew Johansen recalled that Kroll spent about a million dollars of his own money battling the government.

In his 1982 Kroll Award acceptance speech, Stephen Yih noted, "Stephen Shelton is the one who fired Dr. Kroll from the Bureau of Mines. He told me how he fired Dr. Kroll. He and Dr. Kroll had a hot argument about the equipment design for zirconium production. Kroll was so mad that he told Mr. Shelton that some people make a living with their brain but he did not know how Shelton made his living. Shelton told me he could not put up with that and he had to ask Dr. Kroll to resign."

Stephen T. Anderson, a longtime former Bureau employee, points out that "Kroll was not fired but reluctantly left because of legal patent issues…many of those who knew Kroll said he was a very kind but strongly focused man. He was married to his research and was a strong individualist which is why he didn't fit well into a government research atmosphere. And I am sure this is where there might have been some tension between him and Shelton as he preferred individual research verses a group effort. He was hired as a consultant and not a government employee."

Kroll's close friend H. Andrew Johansen suggested that Kroll left when he realized he couldn't sue the U.S. Government while being employed by them. Kroll's battle with the government began around 1947 and was still going when Kroll left in early 1951. The patent battle wouldn't be resolved until 1955, when Kroll received one half of one percent of the retail price of titanium made with the Kroll process.

5. During a phone conference with Naval Reactors Laboratory Field Office Chief Counsel Cliff Nunn, and Idaho National Laboratory Naval Reactors Facility Public Affairs Director Don Dahl, I was informed that while the Mark I prototype was still housed at the Naval Reactor Facility outside of Arco, Idaho (as of 2019), the historic reactor is completely off-limits to the public and is only accessible to Navy personnel. Further, documents regarding the development of the Nautilus are still classified, with no plans for future release. Mr. Nunn mentioned that while the technology is quite old, it is still relevant enough that it must remain classified.

6. Costing about a billion dollars, the Aircraft Nuclear Propulsion (ANP) program ran from 1946 to 1961, with the aim of creating nuclear propulsion systems for aircraft. The benefit of such a propulsion system would be similar as with a submarine, as the craft could stay aloft much longer than conventional aircraft. The project was scrapped by President Kennedy, citing too-high costs for fifteen years of development with no significant

progress. Two decommissioned reactors from the program can be seen displayed in the parking lot at the Experimental Breeder Reactor 1 facility in the desert outside of Arco, Idaho.

7. Says Stephen T. Anderson of the potential fire hazard of the Bureau of Mines during that era: "My father (Captain Tom Anderson of the Albany Fire Dept.) told me many times that the department was "extremely" concerned of the possibility of the fire moving into the west end of town because of the rare metals and gases that were on site. There was the huge possibility of an enormous explosion if the zirconium and magnesium had caught fire, and if any water spray hit the burning metal. And the hydrogen tanks in the same vicinity would add to its destructive force. And thank goodness that never occurred!

   After the fire a team was set up to develop a plan to keep a general record of the locations of reactive metal and other hazards that would assist in the departments strategy of what they were potentially up against before ever reaching the facility."

8. Skull furnaces developed by the Albany Bureau had a water-cooled crucible that has a "skull" of frozen metal inside, of the same kind as what is being melted (i.e., a lining of titanium for melting titanium). The amount of metal to be melted remains molten until it is poured from the water-cooled crucible into the mold.

9. Building 3, the Mold Shop, was built in the summer of 1953 and was originally used as raw material and sponge storage. After 1955 it was converted to the Mold Shop, where metals were cast into shapes. The briquet press was also located within. Despite being in good working condition, Building 3 was torn down sometime after the late 1990's.

QUOTE INDEX

CHAPTER ONE
"Through this substation, affordable electricity..."
"Electric Cooperative Gets Bonneville Juice," *Albany Democrat-Herald*, Nov 20, 1940, www.newspapers.com.

"Construction moved steadily along..."
"Roosevelt, Ickes Prepare Order to Tie Bonneville, Coulee Power," *Albany Democrat-Herald*, Aug 24, 1940, www.newspapers.com.

"In 1936, the Pacific Northwest Planning Commission..."
Report on the Northwest Electro-development Laboratory 1946 (Albany, Oregon: U.S. Department of the Interior, Bureau of Mines), 1946, PDF page 5.

"assist in the mineral industries."
"Schulein Sees Large Industry For Chromites," *The World Newspaper*, May 11, 1940, www.newspapers.com.

"conservation, production, sale, and distribution of helium..."
The U.S. Bureau of Mines, September 1976. https://ufdc.ufl.edu/AA00022529/00001/1j.

"After the United States entered World War II..."
Ibid.

"inside track..."
"Mine Laboratory for Corvallis," *The Capital Journal*, Aug 24, 1942, www.newspapers.com.

"Like hell it won't stop,"
"Bureau Turns Albany's Fortune," *Corvallis Gazette-Times*, Aug 31, 1984, www.newspapers.com.

"A bunch of us got out and blocked the tracks,"
Ibid.

"Now that you're here, we want you to look at the site,"

Ibid.

"Albany seemed to have just what the Bureau wanted..."
"Albany College Buildings Urged for Mines Laboratories Site; Curlee Leaves for Washington," *Albany Democrat-Herald,* Jan 8, 1943, www.newspapers.com.

"a great deal of horsemeat is served."
Ibid.

"two carloads of assorted Oregonians..."
Hurley, V.A. "Oregon Community of Tomorrow: Metals Industry: Teamwork to Initiate the Metallurgical Complex," (Corvallis, Oregon: Oregon State University, December 1971), 5

"At five minutes after 10, Secretry Ickes blasted..."
Ibid.

"Dr. Dean is the man upon whose recommendation..."
Ibid.

"one of seven accredited colleges in the west..."
"50 Sites Suggested For Location of Mines Laboratory," *Albany Democrat-Herald,* Jan 12, 1943, www.newspapers.com.

"On February 2 and 5, Secretary Ickes received telegrams..."
Ferguson, Bobbie, and Christine Pfaff. *An Evaluation of the Historic Significance of the Department of the Interior, Bureau of Mines, Northwest Electrodevelopment Laboratory/Albany Research Center, Albany, Oregon, Vol. 1* (Denver, Colorado, U.S. Department of the Interior Bureau of Reclamation Technical Services Center, 1998), 13.

"earnestly desirous"
Ibid.

"the worst spot I have been in..."
Ibid., 14.

"strong opposition to the location..."
Ibid., Appendix B, Memorandum from Secretary Ickes to President Roosevelt, March 10, 1943.

"On the whole, I believe that it will be most advantageous..."
Ibid.

"This will acknowledge with thanks your letter...."
Roosevelt, Franklin D. *Memorandum to Senator McNary*, March 17, 1943.

"The facilities available at Albany appear to be excellent..."
Ibid.

CHAPTER TWO
"...Secretary Harold L. Ickes' orders locating the project..."
"Raver Says Lab Important to War Industries," *Albany Democrat-Herald*, March 18, 1943, www.newspapers.com.

"pushed as rapidly as possible,"
"Northwest Gets Laboratory To Bolster War Production of Magnesium, Aluminum," *Nevada State Journal*, March 24, 1943, www.newspapers.com.

"The Bureau of Mines proceeded with plans for conversion..."
Report on the Northwest Electro-development Laboratory 1946. Albany, Oregon: U.S. Department of the Interior, Bureau of Mines, 1946.

"I told him that the existing buildings were structurally sound..."
Ferguson, Bobbie, and Christine Pfaff. *An Evaluation of the Historic Significance of the Department of the Interior, Bureau of Mines, Northwest*

Electrodevelopment Laboratory/Albany Research Center, Albany, Oregon, Vol. 1, (Denver, Colorado: U.S. Department of the Interior Bureau of Reclamation Technical Services Center, 1998), 16.

"...the Albany place is very inferior."
Ibid.

"Often children came to the Home..."
Haven, Beverly. *The "Home," Albany Orphans Home and Hospital.* November 2009. www. https://www.facebook.com/groups/651830194980931/files

Another article told about the four Flower...
"The Flower Children," *Albany Democrat,* March 29, 1901, www.newspapers.com.

"Frank Camp, November 17, 1890..."
"Carpenter's Note on Building Tells of Weather in 1890," *Albany Democrat-Herald,* May 2, 1929, www.newspapers.com.

"Once the Boiler building was not used..."
Stephen T. Anderson, note to the author, Jan 29 2022.

"The entire area is covered over,"
Ferguson, Bobbie, and Christine Pfaff. *An Evaluation of the Historic Significance of the Department of the Interior, Bureau of Mines, Northwest Electrodevelopment Laboratory/Albany Research Center, Albany, Oregon, Vol. II,* (Denver, Colorado: U.S. Department of the Interior Bureau of Reclamation Technical Services Center, 1998), Historic Building Inventory Record for Building #33, page 2.

"...The arrangement of laboratories, shops, and offices...
Report on the Northwest Electro-development Laboratory 1945 (Albany, Oregon: U.S. Department of the Interior, Bureau of Mines), 1946, PDF page 8.

"Dr. Rogers expects this laboratory to work..."
"Laboratory Officials, Contractors Arrive; Project Expected Utilize All Buildings on Former Campus," *Albany Democrat-Herald,* October 9, 1943, www.newspapers.com.

"very emphatically"
"Laboratory Not Out; Modification Of Plans Expected as War Measure," *Albany Democrat-Herald,* November 18, 1943, www.newspapers.com.

"Because of the shipyards in Portland..."
Report on the Northwest Electro-development *Laboratory 1946* (Albany, Oregon: U.S. Department of the Interior, Bureau of Mines), 1946, PDF page 17.

"how are you;"
"Frank Stellmacher to Be Retired," *The Bureau Bugle,* (Albany, Oregon: Bureau of Mines Associates, Inc. June-July 1954, Vol III, No. 10.), 1.

CHAPTER THREE

"A far away picture still remains in my mind..."
William J. Kroll, *A Luxembourg Scientist.* (Luxembourg: Fondation Nicolas Lanners, 1998), 13.

"Two years spent in building a metallurgical plant..."
Hayes, Earl T. "A Biographical Appreciation," *Metal Progress*, Vol. 70 #2, Aug 1956, p 86-88.

"In the beginning, my neighbors didn't trust me..."
Housley, Kathleen L. *Black Sand: The History of Titanium*, (Hartford, CT: Metal Management Aerospace, Inc., 2007), 12.

"Whoever in the thirties made his way..."
William J. Kroll, *A Luxembourg Scientist.* (Luxembourg: Fondation Nicolas Lanners, 1998), 13.

"an agreement with Siemens and Halske..."
Hayes, Earl T. "A Biographical Appreciation," *Metal Progress*, Vol. 70 #2, (Aug 1956), 86-88.

"With physical properties similar to those of..."
Housley, Kathleen L. *Black Sand: The History of Titanium*, (Hartford, CT: Metal Management Aerospace, Inc., 2007), 18.

"A critical survey and small-scale..." Baroch, C.T., T.B. Kaczmarek, W.D. Barnes, L.W. Galloway, W.M. Mark, and G.A. Lee, Titanium Plant at Boulder City, Nev.: Its Design and Operation, Reports of Investigation 5141 (Washington, D.C., United States Department of the Interior, Sept 1955), 2.

"However, for scale-up to occur..." Housley, Kathleen L. *Black Sand: The History of Titanium*, (Hartford, CT: Metal Management Aerospace, Inc., 2007), 18.

"In the summer of 1944 I made a call..."
Stephens, William. *Zirconium in the Nuclear Industry, Sixth International Symposium.* (Philadelphia, PA.: ASTM Special Technical Publication, 1982), 7.

"It would appear that the manufacture..."
R.S. Dean memorandum for B.A. Rogers, April 27, 1944.

"...one of the problems of considerable local interest..."
R.S. Dean letter to Dr. Kroll, April 27, 1944.

"It was primarily these rare metals..."
Silverman, Milton. "The Wonder Metal That Blows its Top," *Saturday Evening Post,* Nov 8, 1952, 124.

"three times as strong as the best armor plate," Ibid.

"They are pleased with the work..."
"Mines Bureau Officials View Laboratory Here," *Albany Democrat-Herald*, June 9,1944, www.newspapers.com.

"with which investigations are being made..."
"Libbey Heads State Mines Office; Dr. Schlechten Joins Lab Staff," *Albany Democrat-Herald*, July 29, 1944, www.newspapers.com.

"Dr. Rogers regards him as a valuable..."
Ibid.

CHAPTER FOUR
"concentration of the products in the black sands..."
Report on the Northwest Electro-development Laboratory 1945 (Albany, Oregon: U.S. Department of the Interior, Bureau of Mines), 1946, PDF page 8.

"the hope that some improvement in procedure..."
Ibid.

"work on equipment for producing metallic..."
"Pullman Laboratory of Mines Bureau Closed," *Albany Democrat-Herald*, October 26, 1944, www.newspapers.com.

"any ideas I have regarding processes..."
Letter from Kroll to Dean, Oct. 12, 1944.

"making malleable zirconium within six months..."
Ibid.

"...I did however work practically full time,"
Ibid.

"most anxious to begin the work..."
Kroll letter to Dean, Nov. 18, 1944.

"I am glad to inform you that..."
Dean letter to Kroll, Dec. 22, 1944.

"travel order, book of transportation..."
Ibid.

"on the type of vacuum gauges..."
B.A. Rogers letter to Kroll, Jan. 2, 1944.

"the extraction of several millions of dollars,"
Twenhofel, W.H. *Origin of the Black Sands of the Coast of Southwest Oregon, Bulletin No. 24,* (Portland, Oregon: State of Oregon Department of Geology and Mineral Industries, 1943), 3.

"concluded the troublesome black sand..."
Richards, Robert H. *Black Sand of the Pacific Coast.* Technology Quarterly and Proceedings of the Society of Arts, Vol. 19, (Boston: The Institute, 1906), 163.

"as novel as any instrument..."
Ibid., 165.

"boundless enthusiasm,"
Ibid.

"white-hot steel was tapped from it."
Ibid.

"The atmosphere when he [Dr. Kroll] was here..."
H. Andrew Johansen video recorded presentation, 2005.

"inadequate capacity of the condenser."
Kroll, William, A.W. Schlecten and L. Yerkes, **Ductile Zirconium from Zircon Sand. 1946,** https://vdocuments.net/ductile-zirconium-from-zircon-sand.html

CHAPTER FIVE
"zirconium metal adheres tightly to the inside..."
Ibid.

"...if fires are started, a snuffer is placed..."
Ibid.

"...he just brushed it off as one of the hazards..."
Stephen T. Anderson, note to the author, Jan 29, 2022.

"It is expected that future work..."
Kroll, William, A.W. Schlecten and L. Yerkes, **Ductile Zirconium from Zircon Sand. 1946,**
https://vdocuments.net/ductile-zirconium-from-zircon-sand.html

CHAPTER SIX
"It is the purpose of the Bureau..."
"Mines Laboratory Making Progress, Chamber is Told," *Albany Democrat-Herald*, February 22, 1945, www.newspapers.com.

"I am greatly worried over the problem..."
"All Bureau of Mines Northwest Work to be Directed Through Albany," *Albany Democrat-Herald*, May 22, 1945, www.newspapers.com.

"Much of Union Carbide's involvement in the Manhattan Project..."
"Manhattan, NY." Atomic Heritage Foundation. https://www.atomicheritage.org/location/manhattan-ny#:~:text=Much%20of%20Union%20Carbide's%20involvement,uranium%20ore%20from%20domestic%20sources

"...he played a vital part in perfecting..."
"Age of Science Only Dawning, Says Former German University Savant," *Albany Democrat-Herald*, Aug. 31, 1945, www.newspapers.com.

"Metallurgical properties of uranium..."
"Linking Legacies: Connecting the Cold War Nuclear Weapons Production Processes to Their Environmental Consequences," (Washington, D.C., The U.S. Department of Energy Office of Environmental Management, 1997), 150.

"ornamental plants and shrubs..."
"Landscaping Progress at Laboratory Seen," *Albany Democrat-Herald,* Sept. 8 1945, www.newspapers.com.

"fruit trees, shade and ornamental trees..."
Ferguson, Bobbie, and Christine Pfaff. *An Evaluation of the Historic Significance of the Department of the Interior, Bureau of Mines, Northwest Electrodevelopment Laboratory/Albany Research Center, Albany, Oregon, Vol. 1,* (Denver, Colorado: U.S. Department of the Interior Bureau of Reclamation Technical Services Center, 1998), 52.

"Speaker Says Atomic Power May Be Harnessed..."
"Speaker Says Atomic Power May Be Harnessed for Industrial Use Soon," *Albany Democrat-Herald,* Sept. 22 1945, www.newspapers.com.

"a long time in the making,"
Ibid.

"I can find no excuse for the regional office..."
"Wants Mines Laboratory Taken From This City," *Albany Democrat-Herald,* March 13, 1946, www.newspapers.com.

"Senator Mitchell, who never misses a chance..."
"An Ill-Founded Attack," *Albany Democrat-Herald,* March 14, 1946, www.newspapers.com.

"This laboratory was built during the war..."
"Assistant Mines Director Tours Local Laboratory, Praises Work," *Albany Democrat-Herald,* March 13, 1946, www.newspapers.com.

"...while this metal was discussed only..."
Ibid.

"There is more than a possibility..."
Hornish, Harrison P. "Zirconium, Metal of Numerous Uses Made From Chrome Waste," Coos Bay Times, Oct 25 1946, www.newspapers.com.

"origin, composition, and economics of black sand"
"Mines Laboratory is Studying Beach Sands," *Albany Democrat-Herald*, May 18, 1946, www.newspapers.com.

"headquarters is just as effective in Albany..."
"Albany Delegation Discusses Bureau of Mine Lab With Sec. J.A. Krug," *Albany Democrat-Herald*, June 15, 1946, www.newspapers.com.

"made life rather unpleasant for him."
"Dr. Dean Resigns," *Albany Democrat-Herald*, Sept 9, 1946, www.newspapers.com.

"...under [his] direction, the Bureau's laboratory..."
Ibid.

"Dr. Dean maintained an intimate knowledge..."
Ibid.

"Places were marked for 42..."
"Dr. Rogers Entertains Employes At Dinner," *Albany Democrat-Herald*, Dec 7, 1946, www.newspapers.com.

"grew up on a farm in Nebraska..."
Mary Perry, email to the author, June 9, 2019.

CHAPTER SEVEN

"...So much energy had been released..."
"The Manhattan Project: An Interactive History," https://www.osti.gov/opennet/manhattan-project-history/index.htm

"One of the most obvious potential uses..."
Hewlett, Richard G. and Francis Duncan, *Nuclear Navy 1946-1962*. (Chicago and London: The University of Chicago Press, 1974), pg. 23

"experimental power reactor"
Ibid.

"...By making this a cooperative effort involving..."
Ibid.

"He had assembled in his section a group..."
Ibid, pg. 33

"He personally sifted through battle reports..."
Ibid.

"He could speak with devastating frankness,"
Ibid., pg. 34

"His passage leaves a boiling wake of lacerated egos..."
"The Man in Tempo 3," Time Magazine, Jan 11 1954,
http://content.time.com/time/subscriber/article/0,33009,8
19338-9,00.html

"Our purpose was to see how nuclear energy..."
Rickover, H.G., L.D. Geiger, and B. Lustman. *History of the Development of Zirconium Alloys for Use in Nuclear Reactors* (Washington, D.C., Energy Research and Development Administration, Div. of Naval Reactors, 1975), 4.
https://www.osti.gov/servlets/purl/4240391

"It was obvious that a nuclear-powered..."
Ibid.

"It had to be compact so that it would fit..."
Ibid.

"Metals that would withstand high..."
Hewlett, Richard G. and Francis Duncan, *Nuclear Navy 1946-1962.* (Chicago and London: The University of Chicago Press, 1974), pg. 38

"began what was to become an increasingly..."
Ferguson, Bobbie, and Christine Pfaff. *An Evaluation of the Historic Significance of the Department of the Interior, Bureau of Mines, Northwest Electrodevelopment Laboratory/Albany Research Center, Albany, Oregon, Vol.1,* (Denver, Colorado: U.S.

Department of the Interior Bureau of Reclamation Technical Services Center, 1998), 29.

"fundamental alloy studies."
Letter from Ralston to the Navy, April 28, 1947.

"...give the Armed Forces top priority on all shipments..."
Ibid.

"he was a cowboy with a degree in Chemical Engineering,"
William Gilbert email to the author, November 2, 2021.

"Hint of a New Super-Metal,"
"Black Sands in Spotlight Again," *The World,* Sept 16, 1947, www.newspapers.com.

"next step in the zirconium process..."
Ibid.

"withstand corrosion at high temperatures..."
Rickover, H.G., L.D. Geiger, and B. Lustman. *History of the Development of Zirconium Alloys for Use in Nuclear Reactors* (Washington, D.C., Energy Research and Development Administration, Div. of Naval Reactors, 1975), 5.
https://www.osti.gov/servlets/purl/4240391

"just enough to ruin it,"
"Stockpile and Accessibility of Strategic and Critical Materials to the United States in Time of War, Part 9," (Washington: United States Government Printing Office 1955), 65.

"...there was no known way of separating this hafnium and zirconium,"
Ibid, pg. 65

"so intimate is the association of these two..."
Hess, Harold Dewitt. *"Hafnium Content of Domestic and Foreign Zirconium Minerals."* Report of

Investigations #5856. (Washington: Department of the Interior, Bureau of Mines, 1962), 2.

"...was responsible for determining how to extract..."
Atomic Heritage Foundation: Glenn Seaborg.
https://www.atomicheritage.org/profile/glenn-seaborg

"applicability of the method to produce significant..."
Street, Kenneth Jr., and Glenn T. Seaborg. "The Ion-Exchange Separation of Zirconium and Hafnium," (Berkeley, California: University of California Radiation Laboratory, Oct. 11, 1948), 3.*
*Cover page of this report states the year 1943, though on page 3, the date is written correctly as 1948.

"Why haven't we heard about this before?"
Rockwell, Theodore. *The Rickover Effect.* (Annapolis, Maryland: United States Naval Institute, 1992), 87.

"At once I decided to choose zirconium..."
Rickover, H.G., L.D. Geiger, and B. Lustman. *History of the Development of Zirconium Alloys for Use in Nuclear Reactors* (Washington, D.C., Energy Research and Development Administration, Div. of Naval Reactors, 1975), 6.
https://www.osti.gov/servlets/purl/4240391

"At the time of the decision,"
Ibid.

"So at that time I would say that the zirconium..."
"Stockpile and Accessibility of Strategic and Critical Materials to the United States in Time of War, Part 9," (Washington: United States Government Printing Office, 1955), 65.

"President Truman cautioned Congress today..."
"$119,635 For Albany Plant," *The Capital Journal,* Jan 12, 1948, www.newspapers.com.

"A.R. Kaufman, J.E. Glen, and Frank J. Graceio,"
"Visitors in Albany," *Albany Democrat-Herald,* Feb 24 1948, www.newspapers.com.

"With normal sources of supply unavailable..."
Rickover, H.G., L.D. Geiger, and B. Lustman. *History of the Development of Zirconium Alloys for Use in Nuclear Reactors* (Washington, D.C., Energy Research and Development Administration, Div. of Naval Reactors, 1975), 18.
https://www.osti.gov/servlets/purl/4240391

"...to permit development of a pilot plant..."
"Power Lines in Western Oregon So Overloaded New Ones are Due," *Corvallis Gazette-Times,* April 13 1948, www.newspapers.com.

"It is ironic to reflect that, of...titanium..."
Rickover, H.G., L.D. Geiger, and B. Lustman. *History of the Development of Zirconium Alloys for Use in Nuclear Reactors* (Washington, D.C., Energy Research and Development Administration, Div. of Naval Reactors, 1975), 51.
https://www.osti.gov/servlets/purl/4240391

"...no general review of zirconium and its compounds..."
Skinner, G.B., C.W. Beckett, and H.L. Johnston, "Thermal, Structural, Electrical, Magnetic, and Other Physical Properties of Titanium, Zirconium, Hafnium, and Thorium and Some of their Simple Compounds, Technical Report No. 102-AC49/2-100-2," (Ohio: Ohio State University, 1950), 1.

"The use of Zr in industry..."
Ibid.

"We are soon to be favored..."
Ferguson, Bobbie, and Christine Pfaff. *An Evaluation of the Historic Significance of the Department of the Interior, Bureau of Mines, Northwest Electrodevelopment Laboratory/Albany Research*

Center, Albany, Oregon, Vol. I.* (Denver, Colorado: U.S. Department of the Interior Bureau of Reclamation Technical Services Center, 1998), 32.

"If we receive the requested..."
Ferguson, Bobbie, and Christine Pfaff. *An Evaluation of the Historic Significance of the Department of the Interior, Bureau of Mines, Northwest Electrodevelopment Laboratory/Albany Research Center, Albany, Oregon, Vol I.* (Denver, Colorado: U.S. Department of the Interior Bureau of Reclamation Technical Services Center, 1998), 60.

"The building was constructed by..."
Ibid.

"high temperature strength properties..."
Ibid.

"branches so wide you could walk out..."
Monika Niebuhr-Sims comment on Facebook group The Historic Significance of the Albany Research Center, Nov. 13, 2020.

"A metal of princely price is being reduced..."
White, Vernon S. "Industrial, Medical and Military Importance of Albany Lab's Zirconium Work Described." *Albany Democrat-Herald,* June 22, 1948, www.newspapers.com.

"None of the Albany-produced metal..."
Ibid.

"undiminished vigor."
"Good News of the Black Sands," *The World,* June 25, 1948, www.newspapers.com.

"...We may be on the verge..."
Ibid.

"The final window pane had been..."
Ferguson, Bobbie, and Christine Pfaff. *An Evaluation of the Historic Significance of the Department of the Interior, Bureau of Mines, Northwest Electrodevelopment Laboratory/Albany Research Center, Albany, Oregon, Vol. I.* (Denver, Colorado: U.S. Department of the Interior Bureau of Reclamation Technical Services Center, 1998), 32.

"reinforce the overloaded circuit..."
"New Power Line to Serve Albany," *Albany Democrat-Herald,* Aug 5, 1948, www.newspapers.com.

"The zirconium project..."
"Production Rushed Here on Atomic Research Metal," *Albany Democrat-Herald,* Dec 12, 1950, www.newspapers.com.

"undoubtedly lost forever,"
"Black Sands Information Publication Is Planned; California Firm Carries on Study," *The World,* Oct 8, 1948, www.newspapers.com.

"I walked over and looked at the bulletin board..."
Robert L. Govro phone conversation with the author, March 2021.

"Would you kindly prepare for demonstration..."
Ferguson, Bobbie, and Christine Pfaff. *An Evaluation of the Historic Significance of the Department of the Interior, Bureau of Mines, Northwest Electrodevelopment Laboratory/Albany Research Center, Albany, Oregon, Vol. I.* (Denver, Colorado: U.S. Department of the Interior Bureau of Reclamation Technical Services Center, 1998), 33.

"EXPEDITE PREPARATION OF DEMONSTRATION..."
Ibid.

"How to extract titanium from its ore..."
"New Strong, Light Metal Is Extracted," *Popular Science*, Vol. 153: No. 6. (Dec 1948), 105.

CHAPTER EIGHT
"A multimillion-dollar atomic plant..."
"Big Atom Plant to Test Devices," *Albany Democrat-Herald*, Feb 10, 1949, www.newspapers.com.

"One of them will be a..."
Ibid.

"saw the complete operation..."
"Open House Held At Albany Plant," *Albany Democrat-Herald*, Mar 4, 1949, www.newspapers.com.

"The melting and casting of zirconium..."
Kroll, W.J., and H.L. Gilbert, *Melting and Casting Zirconium Metal*, (Sept 1949), 158. https://citeseerx.ist.psu.edu/viewdoc/download?doi=10.1.1.832.9642&rep=rep1&type=pdf

"...the discovery made at the Albany Station..."
Ibid., 159.

"it is rather expensive and now..."
Ibid.

"permit fusion of ingots up to..."
Ibid., 161.

"...tungsten electrodes may have to be bundled,"
Ibid.

"This very successful and cheap..."
Ibid, 163.

"Experiments indicate that all..."
Ibid, 169.

"Some of the early products..."
"The Development of a Melting Method for Conversion of Zirconium Sponge to Corrosion Resistant Ingot," (May 4, 1950), 4.
https://digital.library.unt.edu/ark:/67531/metadc172827/

"Until the coolant had been selected..."
Rockwell, Theodore. *The Rickover Effect.* (Annapolis, Maryland: the United States Naval Institute, 1992), 91.

"Even though it was impossible..."
Rickover, H.G., L.D. Geiger, and B. Lustman. *History of the Development of Zirconium Alloys for Use in Nuclear Reactors* (Washington, D.C., Energy Research and Development Administration, Div. of Naval Reactors, 1975), 18.
https://www.osti.gov/servlets/purl/4240391

"If I may be so bold as to venture..."
Rockwell, Theodore. *The Rickover Effect.* (Annapolis, Maryland: United States Naval Institute, 1992), 60.

"ambiguous promise"
Ibid, 61.

"The decision was a logical choice..."
Rickover, H.G., L.D. Geiger, and B. Lustman. *History of the Development of Zirconium Alloys for Use in Nuclear Reactors* (Washington, D.C., Energy Research and Development Administration, Div. of Naval Reactors, 1975), 6.
https://www.osti.gov/servlets/purl/4240391

"would be a full-scale prototype,"
Allen, Thomas B. and Normal Polmar. Rickover: Controversy and Genius—A Biography (New York City: Holiday House, 1982), 143.

"reactor testing station"
"AEC Officials Begin Touring Station Area," *The Post-Register,* April 21, 1949, www.newspapers.com.

"an atomic engine for naval ships."
"Idaho Location 'Definite' for West Atomic Plant, Montana's Push Reveals," *The Times-News,* March 22, 1949, www.newspapers.com.

"atomic unit"
"News Thrills Arco Citizens; Lost River Area Residents Call Quick Celebration," *The Post-Register,* March 23, 1949, www.newspapers.com.

"thrilled"
Ibid.

"The winter of 1949 was a dinger,"
Letter from Robert Beall to Stephen O'Hare, December 21, 1982.

"be ready for installation..."
Allen, Thomas B. and Norman Polmar, "Rickover: Controversy and Genius—A Biography," (New York City: Holiday House, 1982), 146.

"...Congressmen, surprised by and concerned..."
Ibid, 147.

"several hurried trips"
Rickover, H.G., L.D. Geiger, and B. Lustman. *History of the Development of Zirconium Alloys for Use in Nuclear Reactors* (Washington, D.C., Energy Research and Development Administration, Div. of Naval Reactors, 1975), 3.
https://www.osti.gov/servlets/purl/4240391

"Usually Dr. Kroll, then a consultant..."
Ibid.

"When Dr. Kroll and I met at Albany,"
Ibid., 13.

"We urgently needed zirconium..."
Ibid., 6.

"...the successful tests being done..."
Ferguson, Bobbie, and Christine Pfaff. *An Evaluation of the Historic Significance of the Department of the Interior, Bureau of Mines, Northwest Electrodevelopment Laboratory/Albany Research Center, Albany, Oregon, Vol. I.* (Denver, Colorado: U.S. Department of the Interior Bureau of Reclamation Technical Services Center, 1998), 61.

"I had been assigned the job..."
Rickover, H.G., L.D. Geiger, and B. Lustman. *History of the Development of Zirconium Alloys for Use in Nuclear Reactors* (Washington, D.C., Energy Research and Development Administration, Div. of Naval Reactors, 1975), 7.
https://www.osti.gov/servlets/purl/4240391

"The Navy and Center people..."
Ferguson, Bobbie, and Christine Pfaff. *An Evaluation of the Historic Significance of the Department of the Interior, Bureau of Mines, Northwest Electrodevelopment Laboratory/Albany Research Center, Albany, Oregon, Vol. I.* (Denver, Colorado: U.S. Department of the Interior Bureau of Reclamation Technical Services Center, 1998), 38-39.

"hurry-up order,"
"Completion of Metals Plant Due by Aug. 15," *Albany Democrat-Herald,* Jul 11, 1950, www.newspapers.com.

"vital non-corrosive defensive metal"
Ibid.

"considered most unlikely to succeed"
"Personnelities," The Bureau Bugle, Vol III No. 2, (Albany, Oregon: Bureau of Mines Associates, Inc., August 1953, Vol III, No. 10.) page 3,7.

"Most of his engineering skill,"
Ibid.

"'I consider myself fortunate that I worked..."
Ibid.

"Three shifts of about seven men..."
De Ganahl, Charles. "Albany Produced Zirconium Plays Vital U.S. Defense Role, Plant Expansion Begins; Kroll Process Described," *Albany Democrat-Herald,* June 8 1950, www.newspapers.com.

"Even now, equipment is being installed..."
"Zirconium Already Produced in Still Unfinished Building," *Albany Democrat-Herald,* Aug 17 1950, www.newspapers.com.

"...the land prototype in Idaho offered..."
Rockwell, Theodore. *The Rickover Effect.* (Annapolis, Maryland: the United States Naval Institute, 1992), 69.

"Construction of the Mark I..."
Roddis Jr., Commander L.H., and J.W. Simpson. *The Nuclear Propulsion Plant of the USS Nautilus SSN-571 (Nov. 1954),* 495.

"'When America's first atomic engine..."
"Metal With a Future; Meet Little-Known Zirconium—it Looms Large in Rocket and Atomic Research," *Science and Mechanics Magazine,* (April 1950), 95.

CHAPTER NINE

"'One of the U.S. government's research agencies..."
Ibid.

"Seems that zirconium lets in radiation..."
Gilbert, Henry L. "Melting of Zirconium," (December 1951 Bureau Bugle, Vol. 1 No. 4) 1,4-7

"Called the 'Bureau of Mines' by the man..."
Production Rushed Here on Atomic Research Metal, *Albany Democrat-Herald,* Dec 12 1950, www.newspapers.com.

"...Northwest ores of iron and the ferroalloy..."
"Albany Regional Headquarters for U.S. Bureau of Mines," *Albany Democrat-Herald,* Dec 12 1950, www.newspapers.com.

"This furnace operates at a bright red..."
Ibid.

"A large and well-equipped shop..."
Ibid.

"...the construction staff designs and build..."
Ibid.

...by use of microscopes, spectroscopes..."
Ibid.

"By the end of 1950 Captain Rickover..."
Rockwell, Theodore. *The Rickover Effect.* (Annapolis, Maryland: United States Naval Institute, 1992), 117.

"While corrosion resistance improved tremendously..."
Rickover, H.G., L.D. Geiger, and B. Lustman. *History of the Development of Zirconium Alloys for Use in Nuclear Reactors* (Washington, D.C., Energy Research and Development Administration, Div. of Naval Reactors, 1975), 55.
https://www.osti.gov/servlets/purl/4240391

"...there is no guarantee any of this will work out..."
Rockwell, Theodore. *The Rickover Effect.* (Annapolis, Maryland: the United States Naval Institute 1992), 118.

"The corrosion resistance of the material..."
Rickover, H.G., L.D. Geiger, and B. Lustman. *History of the Development of Zirconium Alloys for Use in Nuclear Reactors* (Washington, D.C., Energy Research and Development Administration, Div. of Naval Reactors, 1975), 51.
https://www.osti.gov/servlets/purl/4240391

"teetered on a razor's edge of acceptability,"
Ibid, 58.

"It was rumored to have been…"
Ferguson, Bobbie, and Christine Pfaff. *An Evaluation of the Historic Significance of the Department of the Interior, Bureau of Mines, Northwest Electrodevelopment Laboratory/Albany Research Center, Albany, Oregon, Vol. II.* (Denver, Colorado: U.S. Department of the Interior Bureau of Reclamation Technical Services Center, 1998), PDF page 216

"grown increasingly perplexed and bitter…"
Teal, Marion. *Off the Beat. Corvallis Gazette-Times,* Nov 21 1952, www.newspapers.com.

"had to get out of the way,"
Stephen Mattheson Shelton II message to the author, November 2, 2021.

"Some people make a living with their brain…"
Stephen Yih award acceptance speech, Date,

CHAPTER TEN
"The new plant, fourth major addition…"
Excavation Work Starts At Site of Zirconium Plant. *Albany Democrat-Herald,* Apr 17, 1951
www.newspapers.com.

"To extract the metal,"
"New Strong, Light Metal is Extracted," *Popular Science Monthly,* (Dec 1948), 105.

"The Atomic Energy Commission requires…"
The Development of a Melting Method for Conversion of Zirconium Sponge to Corrosion Resistant Ingot. (May 4, 1950), 1.
https://digital.library.unt.edu/ark:/67531/metadc172827/

"Since zirconium is badly needed,"
Ibid.

"It would be expected on the basis..."
Ibid, 5.

"...to recover the tin and copper from...the material..."
Howard Poppleton interview with the author, April 20, 2017.

"Beall's development of consumable electrode..."
Ferguson, Bobbie, and Christine Pfaff. *An Evaluation of the Historic Significance of the Department of the Interior, Bureau of Mines, Northwest Electrodevelopment Laboratory/Albany Research Center, Albany, Oregon, Vol. I.* (Denver, Colorado: U.S. Department of the Interior Bureau of Reclamation Technical Services Center, 1998) 37.

"Much of the success of the Bureau's..."
"Successful Research at the Albany Research Center,"

(Albany, Oregon: Bureau of Mines, 1977), 36.

"All the companies were interested..."
Rickover, H.G., L.D. Geiger, and B. Lustman. *History of the Development of Zirconium Alloys for Use in Nuclear Reactors* (Washington, D.C., Energy Research and Development Administration, Div. of Naval Reactors, 1975), 51.
https://www.osti.gov/servlets/purl/4240391

"...considered one of the most difficult..."
Higbie, K.B., and J.R. Werning. "Separation of Tantalum-Columbium by Solvent Extraction Reports of Investigation 5239," (Washington, D.C., United States Department of the Interior, July 1956), 36.

"When they got the building finished,"
Robert L. Govro phone conversation with the author, March 2021.

"Those big glass columns..."
Ibid.

"...a growing dissatisfaction with the continued..."
Rickover, H.G., L.D. Geiger, and B. Lustman. *History of the Development of Zirconium Alloys for Use in Nuclear Reactors* (Washington, D.C., Energy Research and Development Administration, Div. of Naval Reactors, 1975), 59.
https://www.osti.gov/servlets/purl/4240391

"The '828' process demonstrated..."
Westinghouse Elec. Corp. v. Titanium Metals Corp. Oct 1969, 3. https://casetext.com/case/westinghouse-elec-corp-v-titanium-metals-corp

"The pass-word [sic] in the production..."
Gilbert, Henry L. "Melting of Zirconium," (December 1951 Bureau Bugle, Vol. 1 No. 4) 1,4-7

"...two tenths of one percent graphite..."
Ibid.

"which look like small gray lumps of bread,"
Ibid.

"twelve welding machines"
Ibid.

"Thus with our little water cooled..."
Ibid.

"On the basis of experimental work..."
Westinghouse Elec. Corp. v. Titanium Metals Corp. Oct 1969, 3. https://casetext.com/case/westinghouse-elec-corp-v-titanium-metals-corp

"Those experienced in the art and science..."
Rickover, H.G., L.D. Geiger, and B. Lustman. *History of the Development of Zirconium Alloys for Use in Nuclear Reactors* (Washington, D.C., Energy Research and Development Administration, Div. of Naval Reactors, 1975), 56.
https://www.osti.gov/servlets/purl/4240391

"A better name for the world's first..."
Hewlett, Richard G. and Francis Duncan, *Nuclear Navy 1946-1962*. (Chicago and London: The University of Chicago Press, 1974), pg. 177

"Choice of the name had been..."
Ibid.

"The Navy practice was to..."
Ibid.

"BUREAU OF MINES BLACK SHEEP?"
"Bureau of Mines Black Sheep? It's a fact!! That's How We Rate in the National Safety program of the Bureau of Mines," Bureau Bugle, Vol. 1 No. 4 (Albany, Oregon: Bureau of Mines Associates, Inc. (December 1951), 1.

"registration room,"
Wright, M.L., *New Deal on Visitors,* Bureau Bugle, Vol. II No. 1 (Albany, Oregon: Bureau of Mines Associates, Inc. (Jan-Feb 1952), 1

"despite the tremendous number..."
Ibid.

"You were tired all the time,"
Robert L. Govro phone conversation with the author, March 2021.

'Get Dilling' was always expected,"
Dilling New Head, Bureau Bugle, Vol. II No. 7 (Albany, Oregon: Bureau of Mines Associates, Inc. (Sept 1952), 1,6.

"determining radiation intensities..."
"Leader of Linn Atomic Monitoring Team Attends Civil Defense Meet," *Albany Democrat-Herald,* Jan 29, 1952
www.newspapers.com

"It seems that on occasion, there appeared in a reduction retort..."
Letter from Robert Beall to Stephen O'Hare, December 21, 1982.

"The building in which the hafnium..."
Ferguson, Bobbie, and Christine Pfaff. *An Evaluation of the Historic Significance of the Department of the Interior, Bureau of Mines, Northwest Electrodevelopment Laboratory/Albany Research Center, Albany, Oregon, Vol. II.* (Denver, Colorado: U.S. Department of the Interior Bureau of Reclamation Technical Services Center, 1998), PDF page 245.

"The Submarine Thermal Reactor (STR) for the Nautilus..."
Ferguson, Bobbie, and Christine Pfaff. *An Evaluation of the Historic Significance of the Department of the Interior, Bureau of Mines, Northwest Electrodevelopment Laboratory/Albany Research Center, Albany, Oregon, Vol. I.* (Denver, Colorado: U.S. Department of the Interior Bureau of Reclamation Technical Services Center, 1998), 37.

CHAPTER ELEVEN
"Despite the adoption of crystal bar..."
Rickover, H.G., L.D. Geiger, and B. Lustman. *History of the Development of Zirconium Alloys for Use in Nuclear Reactors* (Washington, D.C., Energy Research and Development Administration, Div. of Naval Reactors, 1975), 60.
https://www.osti.gov/servlets/purl/4240391

"Fortunately, Bettis already had underway..."
Ibid, pg. 8

"...a good compromise between corrosion resistance,"
Ibid.

"I always thought I found the tin addition first but..."
Ferguson, Bobbie, and Christine Pfaff. *An Evaluation of the Historic Significance of the Department of the*

Interior, Bureau of Mines, Northwest Electrodevelopment Laboratory/Albany Research Center, Albany, Oregon, Vol. I.* (Denver, Colorado: U.S. Department of the Interior Bureau of Reclamation Technical Services Center, 1998), 37.

"I remember one year sitting down on the ground,"
Barbara Snow recollection posted on *The Historic Significance of the Albany Research Center* Facebook page, June 8, 2021.
https://www.facebook.com/photo/?fbid=10158176815013085&set=gm.1874063879424217

"Bureau officials explained that because..."
"3 Nearby Cities Prepare to Act on DST Question," *Albany Democrat-Herald,* May 6, 1952
www.newspapers.com.

"The winning party, known as the Early Birds..."
"Summer Hours—May 19," *Bureau Bugle*, Vol. II No. 3 (Albany, Oregon: Bureau of Mines Associates, Inc. (May 1952), 4

"when I worked in the separations department,"
Robert L. Govro phone conversation with the author, May 2021.

"When anyone had the opportunity, they'd go down..."
Ibid.

"very, very valuable."
Ibid.

"The work was undertaken because both..."
"Successful Research at the Albany Research Center," (Albany, Oregon: Bureau of Mines, 1977), 19.

"...the AEC assured us..."
Howard Poppleton interview with the author, April 20, 2017.

"...picked up a huge bright yellow keel..."
Hewlett, Richard G. and Francis Duncan, *Nuclear Navy 1946-1962*. (Chicago and London: The University of Chicago Press, 1974), pg. 179

"Bureau of Mines building,"
Youths Sight Saucer Over Albany; Air Force Notified. *Albany Democrat-Herald,* July 7, 1952
www.newspapers.com.

"shot back into the sky,"
Ibid.

"We passed the object as it stood..."
The UFO Evidence (Unidentified Flying Objects) Washington, D.C., The National Investigations Committee on Aerial Phenomena (NICAP), 1964, PDF page 78.

"like the tentacles of an octopus"
Ibid.

"stood still at first..."
Official declassified UFO Report to JEPHQ/USAF Director of Intel, Wright Patterson AFT Ohio. July 8, 1952, 2.

"All of us have been flying a number..."
"4 Report 'Saucer' Over Atom Plant," Cleveland Plain Dealer, July 6 1952.

"These airborne oddities were taken..."
Paul Dean message to the author, June 14, 2021.

"tight-lipped silence"
"Albany Lab Tests Rich Uranium Ore; Site of Deposit Withheld," *Albany Democrat-Herald,* July 23, 1952
www.newspapers.com.

"If these samples are representative..."
Ibid.

"...Since remelting costs money..."
Westinghouse Elec. Corp. v. Titanium Metals Corp. Oct 1969, 3. https://casetext.com/case/westinghouse-elec-corp-v-titanium-metals-corp

"By the summer and fall of 1952..."
Rockwell, Theodore. *The Rickover Effect.* (Annapolis, Maryland: the United States Naval Institute, 1992), 123.

"We can barely make the fuel elements..."
Ibid, 124.

"About this time, the reactor at the Idaho test site..."
Letter from Robert Beall to Stephen O'Hare, December 21, 1982.

"Do we throw it all away?" Rockwell, Theodore. *The Rickover Effect.* (Annapolis, Maryland: United States Naval Institute, 1992), 124.

"the Mark I equals Mark II"
Ibid., 125.

"Mark Two does not equal Mark One"
Ibid.

"The first equation says we won't..."
Ibid.

"And amid further cries of protest..."
Ibid.

"It is a tribute to the vision of Admiral Rickover..."
Rickover, H.G., L.D. Geiger, and B. Lustman. *History of the Development of Zirconium Alloys for Use in Nuclear Reactors* (Washington, D.C., Energy Research and Development Administration, Div. of Naval Reactors, 1975), 59.
https://www.osti.gov/servlets/purl/4240391

"tall, lovely tower"
Sellard, Dan. [Unreadable] Research at Albany Boasts Wealth of Northwest. *The Eugene Guard,* Aug 3, 1952 www.newspapers.com.

"little is known to the public but vital…"
Ibid.

"The bureau seems to operate on…"
Ibid.

"spud flakes,"
"Food and Games Draw 600," *Bureau Bugle*, Vol. II No. 6 (Albany, Oregon: Bureau of Mines Associates, Inc. (Aug 1952), 1.

"oodles of baked ham"
Ibid.

"…that committee either knows how…"
Ibid.

"The pop was flowing like water,"
Ibid.

"by far the finest picnic we have had to date."
Ibid.

"Unfortunately, as happens so frequently in…"
Rickover, H.G., L.D. Geiger, and B. Lustman. *History of the Development of Zirconium Alloys for Use in Nuclear Reactors* (Washington, D.C., Energy Research and Development Administration, Div. of Naval Reactors, 1975), 61.
https://www.osti.gov/servlets/purl/4240391

"An immediate halt was called to the further…"
Ibid.

"It was widely suspected that the error was less..."
Ibid., 62.

"I selected it for the Nautilus reactor..."
Ibid., 9.

"Damage was confined to the wooden electrode..."
"Small Fire Flares at Bureau of Mines Plant," *Albany Democrat-Herald,* Aug 28, 1952, www.newspapers.com.

"BUREAU LOSES KEY MEN"
Wells, Doris. "Bureau Loses Key Men," *Bureau Bugle,* Vol. II No. 7 (Albany, Oregon: Bureau of Mines Associates, Inc. (Sept 1952), 1.

"develop improvements on the present..."
Ibid.

"The processes, research, and patents developed..."
Ibid.

"'My new position will be in the development..."
Ibid.

"I regret leaving the many good friends..."
Ibid.

"If any one of those three..."
Letter from Robert Beall to Stephen O'Hare, December 21, 1982.

"Repairs are being made as soon..."
"Fire Sweeps Zirconium Plant," *Bureau Bugle,* Vol. II No. 8 (Albany, Oregon: Bureau of Mines Associates, Inc., Nov 1952), 1.

"Apparently the silence concerning the uses..."
"Odds n' Ends," *Albany Democrat-Herald,* Nov 11, 1952 www.newspapers.com.

"...So many have expressed a desire..."
"Public Invited to Open House; Bureau of Mines to Show Lab Work," *The Eugene Guard,* Nov 17, 1952 www.newspapers.com.

"I can't pretend to understand it,"
"700 Inspect Many Displays," *Albany Democrat-Herald,* Nov 22, 1952 www.newspapers.com.

"When AEC scientists bumped into..."
"The Wonder Metal That Blows its Top," *The Saturday Evening Post,* Nov 8 1952, 34.

"To many observers, the future of the fiery..."
Ibid, 128.

"The fears of those working..."
Rickover, H.G., L.D. Geiger, and B. Lustman. *History of the Development of Zirconium Alloys for Use in Nuclear Reactors* (Washington, D.C., Energy Research and Development Administration, Div. of Naval Reactors, 1975), 72.
https://www.osti.gov/servlets/purl/4240391

"The experience on reduction..."
Ibid., 73.

CHAPTER TWELVE
"Explosion of a "bomb"
"Blast Set Off at Laboratory," *Albany Democrat-Herald,* Feb 25, 1953 www.newspapers.com.

"Consequently...no one was injured..."
Ibid.

"The first atomic power plant..."
Smith, Delos. "Increased Know-How Obtained From First Atomic Power Plant," *Corvallis Gazette-Times,* Jan 9, 1953 www.newspapers.com.

"With the aid of tremendous efforts..."
Letter from Robert Beall to Stephen O'Hare, December 21, 1982.

"As Operation of Mark I was about..."
Kintner, E.E. "Admiral Rickover's Gamble," *The Atlantic,* Jan 1959.
https://www.theatlantic.com/magazine/archive/1959/01/admiral-rickovers-gamble/308436/?single_page=true

"The year 1953 was extremely busy for all persons..."
Gordon, Robert. "Miracle Metals Serving in war and Peace- A History of the Role Two Rare Metals Played in the Birth of Nuclear Power. Oct. 1, 2000.
https://www.power-eng.com/nuclear/miracle-metals-serving-in-war-and-peace151a-history-of-the-role-two-rare-metals-played-in-the-birth-of-nuclear-power/#gref

"The Chalk River results seemed to..."
Kintner, E.E. "Admiral Rickover's Gamble," *The Atlantic,* Jan 1959.
https://www.theatlantic.com/magazine/archive/1959/01/admiral-rickovers-gamble/308436/?single_page=true

"...until they were as nearly perfect..."
Ibid.

"That first operation was amazingly successful,"
Ibid.

"don't drive too far or you will end up in the lake,"
Galloway, Jack and Doris Wells, "Hobo Party Planned," *The Bureau Bugle,* (Albany, Oregon: Bureau of Mines Associates, Inc. April 1953. Vol II, No. 11), 1, 4.

"pot luck midnight lunch"
Ibid.

"...it is hard for me to put it into words..."
Wells, Doris and Jack Galloway. "Hobo Party Smash Hit," *The Bureau Bugle,* (Albany, Oregon: Bureau of

Mines Associates, Inc. May-June 1953. Vol II, No. 12), 1, 2.

"The official Bureau hobo is..."
Ibid.

"a teaser of tango..."
Wells, Doris. "Dance Club News," *The Bureau Bugle,* (Albany, Oregon: Bureau of Mines Associates, Inc. May-June 1953. Vol II, No. 12), 8.

"Murray...understood and backed Rickover's..."
Rockwell, Theodore. *The Rickover Effect,* (Annapolis, Maryland: United States Naval Institute, 1992), 140.

"...there were many happy people in the Idaho..."
Kintner, E.E. "Admiral Rickover's Gamble," *The Atlantic,* Jan 1959.
https://www.theatlantic.com/magazine/archive/1959/01/admiral-rickovers-gamble/308436/?single_page=true

"calm and stable machine..."
Ibid.

"He had visualized that if the forty-eight-hour..."
Ibid.

"Rickover's reply was firm and calm,"
Rockwell, Theodore. *The Rickover Effect.* (Annapolis, Maryland: United States Naval Institute, 1992), 115.

"Now there could be no mistaking..."
Ibid.

"To those of us who had participated..."
Kintner, E.E. "Admiral Rickover's Gamble," *The Atlantic,* Jan 1959.
https://www.theatlantic.com/magazine/archive/1959/01/admiral-rickovers-gamble/308436/?single_page=true

"I have an important announcement to make."
Rockwell, Theodore. *The Rickover Effect.* (Annapolis, Maryland: United States Naval Institute, 1992), 160.

If we never get to build an..."
Ibid., 161.

"Apparatus for melting and casting metals..."
"New G.E. Laboratory For Metal Research," *The New York Times,* Aug. 23, 1953
www.timesmachine.nytimes.com.

"'surrounded by a fog of 'security' so thick..."
Millis, Walter, "New Weapon," *Newport Daily News,* Oct 28 1953. www.newspapers.com.

"There is, of course, the mysterious compartment..."
Ibid.

CHAPTER THIRTEEN
"Nautilus is a symbol of man's dreaming,"
Abel, Elie. "Atomic Submarine Launched by U.S.; Summer Tests Set, First Nuclear Ship Christened by Mrs. Eisenhoser—Can Outrun Most Destroyers," *The New York Times,* Jan 22, 1954
www.timesmachine.nytimes.com.

"The launching of the Nautilus marked..."
Metal for Atomic Sub Engine Made At Mines Bureau," *Greater Oregon,* Jan 22 1954, www.newspapers.com.

"Since no data is available,"
"Guinea Pigs Living on Station," *Bureau Bugle*, Vol. IV No. 2 (Albany, Oregon: Bureau of Mines Associates, Inc., Aug 1954), 3.

"If the pigs must die it should be by natural causes,"
Ibid.

"This is an American age..."
"Mines Lab Viewed by Survey Team," *Albany Democrat-Herald*, Feb 2, 1954 www.newspapers.com.

"Here Russia knows what is done..."
"450 Employed Here Now at Bureau of Mines," *Greater Oregon*, Feb 26 1954 www.newspapers.com.

"One call from a civilian plane spotter could sound the alarm..."
"Importance of GOC in National Defense Stressed at Meeting," *Greater Oregon*, Feb 22, 1955 www.newspapers.com.

"Operation Skywatch,"
"Observers Have First Anniversary," *Greater Oregon*, Oct 15, 1954 www.newspapers.com.

"...more of a factory than a laboratory-experiment..."
Myers, Bruce K. "Off the Beat," *Corvallis Gazette-Times*, Jan 25, 1954, www.newspapers.com.

"Our hackles rose the other day..."
"Unwise to Move the Mineral Lab," *Albany Democrat-Herald*, Mar 12, 1954 www.newspapers.com.

"...Oregon should serve notice..."
Ibid.

"difficult to conceive how such action..."
"No Idea of Removing Plant," *Albany Democrat-Herald*, Mar 27, 1954, www.newspapers.com.

"These reductions are not consistent..."
"Mines Bureau Budget Cut Under Attack," *Albany Democrat-Herald*, Apr 19, 1954, www.newspapers.com.

"I can make them grow,"
"Bureau of Mines Employee Honored Upon Retirement," *Albany Democrat-Herald*, Jun 29, 1954, www.newspapers.com.

"The men who have worked under him..."
Higbie, Ken. "Frank Stellmacher to be Retired," *Bureau Bugle*, Vol. III No. 10 (Albany, Oregon: Bureau of Mines Associates, Inc. (June-July 1954), 1,3.

"Perhaps his last great service to the..."
Ibid.

"...and the smog is deadly,"
"Letter from Hank," *Bureau Bugle*, Vol. IV No. 15 (Albany, Oregon: Bureau of Mines Associates, Inc. (Nov 1954), 8.

"What have you got against this pig..."
"That you May Live," *Bureau Bugle*, Vol. IV No. 3 (Albany, Oregon: Bureau of Mines Associates, Inc. (Sept 1954), 3.

"It is the first time in history that a project..."
Holmes, Henry. "Zr Plant Turns Out Millionth Pound," *Bureau Bugle*, Vol. IV No. 3 (Albany, Oregon: Bureau of Mines Associates, Inc., Sept 1954), 1, 5.

"...perhaps, titanium will become almost..."
Block, Frank. "Titanium," *Bureau Bugle*, Vol. III No. 9 (Albany, Oregon: Bureau of Mines Associates, Inc., May 1954), 6.

"Time Magazine reported that scientists..."
Housley, Kathleen L. *Black Sand: The History of Titanium*. Hartford, CT: Metal Management Aerospace, Inc., 2007, pg 47.

"deleterious contamination."
Beall, R.A., F.W. Wood, J.O. Borg, H.L. Gilbert, "Production of Titanium Castings," Report of Investigations #5265 (Washington, D.C.,: Department of the Interior, Bureau of Mines, August 1956). Pg. 1

"The solution is, of course..."
Ibid.

"...[Melting] techniques once acceptable..."
Beall, R.A., "Cold Mold Arc Melting and Casting," Bulletin 646, "Washington, D.C.,: Department of the Interior, Bureau of Mines, 1968), 25.

"...especially if the containers are stored under summer sun,"
Ibid., 29.

"My job on that I was to go over..."
Robert Govro phone conversation with the author, Sept. 2021.

"Once the metal was..."
Ibid.

"...the Bureau of Mines assembled, adapted..."
"Thorium Group Gets Unit Citation," *Bureau Bugle*, Vol. VI No. 6 (Albany, Oregon: Bureau of Mines Associates, Inc. (January 1957) 1,4.

"Their enthusiasm, cooperation, and teamwork..."
Ibid.

"Cooperative work for the Atomic Energy Commission..."
Lowery, Ronald R., "Radiation Hazards Encountered in Arc Melting Thorium," Reports of Investigation #5969, (Washington, D.C.,: Department of the Interior, Bureau of Mines, 1960), 1.

"hard nut to crack,"
Johansen, Herman. "Ductile Chromium," *Bureau Bugle*, Vol. III No. 7 (Albany, Oregon: Bureau of Mines Associates, Inc. (March 1954) 3,5.

"Such a simple solution after so many years of work!"
Ibid.

"The production of uniformly ductile molybdenum..."
Campbell, Tom. "Molybdenum," *Bureau Bugle*, Vol. IV No. 6 (Albany, Oregon: Bureau of Mines Associates, Inc. (Dec 1954) 7.

"As many of my readers know, this type of research..."
Ibid.

"effective dissemination of both scientific and industrial information."
"Seventeenth Semiannual Report of the Atomic Energy Commission," (Washington, D.C., United States Government Printing Office, Jan 1955), VII.

"...This beautiful building full of the very finest equipment..."
McClain, Jim. "Another Million," *Bureau Bugle*, Vol. IV No. 6 (Albany, Oregon: Bureau of Mines Associates, Inc. (Dec 1954) 4.

"However, because of its nature, utility, and flexibility,"
Ibid.

"Oh, how glad we are that the tension has been lifted..."
Wells, Doris. "Editor's Comments," *Bureau Bugle*, Vol. IV No. 5 (Albany, Oregon: Bureau of Mines Associates, Inc. (Nov 1954) 2.

"The crew had never seen any other propulsion system..."
Rockwell, Theodore. *The Rickover Effect.* (Annapolis, Maryland: the United States Naval Institute), 191.

CHAPTER FOURTEEN
"For more than five years, the big deal here..."
Thom, Joe. "Editorial," *Bureau Bugle*, Vol. IV No. 7 (Albany, Oregon: Bureau of Mines Associates, Inc. (June 1955) 2.

"confer with scientists of government and private industry..."
Ibid.

"What the hell is a titanium plant?" Oregon Metallurgical Company History, http://www.fundinguniverse.com/company-histories/oregon-metallurgical-corporation-history/

"...armed with shotguns or wearing six-guns strapped to their waists"
"Prospectors Throng into Lakeview Area," *Corvallis Gazette-Times*, Jul 21, 1955 www.newspapers.com.

"The uranium-bearing rock so far found in Oregon..."
"Uranium Ore Found; Mountain Areas in this Area Look Good Too, Say Experts," *Greater Oregon*, Jul 22, 1955 www.newspapers.com.

"The uranium was reported to be in the form..."
Uranium is Found in New-Type Rock," *Corvallis Gazette-Times*, Jul 22, 1955 www.newspapers.com.

"Iron ore supplies in the Midwest are dwindling..."
"Test Alaska Iron Ore at Mines Lab," *Greater Oregon*, Apr 22, 1955 www.newspapers.com.

"We quit melting sponge for zirc,"
Ferguson, Bobbie, and Christine Pfaff. *An Evaluation of the Historic Significance of the Department of the Interior, Bureau of Mines, Northwest Electrodevelopment Laboratory/Albany Research Center, Albany, Oregon, Vol. I.* (Denver, Colorado: U.S. Department of the Interior Bureau of Reclamation Technical Services Center, 1998), 44.

"Melting stayed same or bigger,"
Ibid.

"The primary ingots are carried to the machine shop..."
Security memo from Robert Beall to Eleanor Abshire, March 2 1955.

"northeast end of the east wing of the hafnium purification building."
Security memo from Eleanor Abshire, October 1955.

"There was no evidence of sabotage on the part of any employee,"
Ibid.

"ignitable"
Ibid.

"...conversations with the scientists at that station..."
Abraham, Lothar, Edward L. Thellmann, James L. Wyatt. "Research and Development in the Field of Thorium Chemistry and Metallurgy, Final Report. Pilot Scale Production of Thorium Metal by Fused Salt Electrolysis, Volume 2." (Cleveland, Ohio: Horizons, Incorporated, 1957), 190.

"The AEC was doing lots of explosions, underground and at Bikini..."
Ferguson, Bobbie, and Christine Pfaff. *An Evaluation of the Historic Significance of the Department of the Interior, Bureau of Mines, Northwest Electrodevelopment Laboratory/Albany Research Center, Albany, Oregon, Vol. I.* Denver, (Colorado: U.S. Department of the Interior Bureau of Reclamation Technical Services Center, 1998), 44.

"...Research projects involving beryllium have..."
Paul, Alex. "Traces of Beryllium Found," *Corvallis Gazette-Times*, Oct 20, 2005 www.newspapers.com.

"In 1953, the laboratory constructed the Mold Shop..."
Maroncelli, James M. and Timothy L. Karpin, "The Traveler's Guide to Nuclear Weapons," Kindle edition. (Lacey, Washington: Historical Odysseys Publishers, 2002). 477.

"...The yield of a nuclear weapon can be increased..."

"Basic two-stage design," Britannica.com, https://www.britannica.com/technology/nuclear-weapon/Basic-two-stage-design

"preliminary study of several alloy systems..."
"Areas of Activity relating to the UCRL Project Security Memo," undated, 1.

"Secret pieces will receive the highest level of protection during transfer,"
Abshire, Eleanor. Security Memo No. 60, April 26, 1957, 1.

"sturdy, built either of heavy plywood or steel..."
Ibid.

"Metal NOIBN,"
Ibid., 2.

"Last year about this time,"
Thom, Joe. "Editorial," *Bureau Bugle*, Vol. V No. 11 (Albany, Oregon: Bureau of Mines Associates, Inc. (June 1955), 2.

"stable and possibly increased employment"
Ibid.

"!$#* What in the &*$ can you say?"*
Wells, Doris. "Personnelities; Edward "Heavy" Knakal," *Bureau Bugle*, Vol. VI No. 3 (Albany, Oregon: Bureau of Mines Associates, Inc. (Oct 1956), 3,5.

"Everybody knows that he goes to bat..."
Ibid.

"Is there a way to buy this property,"
William O'Hearn, recorded interview of the Albany Tennis Club history, undated.

"who knew the ins and outs,"
Ibid.

"...which was exactly the right price for our budget,"
Ibid.

"probably forever,"
Ibid.

"We had a few incidents happen,"
Ibid.

"A resolution calling for private operation..."
"Private Operation of Albany Zirconium Plant Advocated," *Albany Democrat-Herald*, Feb 24, 1956 www.newspapers.com.

"...this is the first time in my 20 years..."
"Workers Fete Bureau Chief," *Albany Democrat-Herald*, Feb 24, 1956 www.newspapers.com.

"We didn't have our ideas..."
Thom, Joe. "Editorial," *Bureau Bugle*, Vol. V No. 12 (Albany, Oregon: Bureau of Mines Associates, Inc. (Mar 1956), 1,2.

"I have never before been where..."
"Workers Fete Bureau Chief," *Albany Democrat-Herald*, Feb 24, 1956 www.newspapers.com.

CHAPTER FIFTEEN

"...We have some new neighbors here..."
Thom, Joe. "Editorial," *Bureau Bugle*, Vol. V No. 14 (Albany, Oregon: Bureau of Mines Associates, Inc. (May 1956) 2.

"The kitchen cabinets and appliances were removed..."
Ficq, Frederick. Written recollection of his home's history, undated.

"Stuttgart was about 80 percent destroyed and many of the fine..."
"Roberson Returns from Europe," *Bureau Bugle*, Vol. VI No. 4 (Albany, Oregon: Bureau of Mines Associates, Inc. (Nov 1956) 3.

"...Even the thrust of the best jet in the world..."
Housley, Kathleen L. *Black Sand: The History of Titanium*. (Hartford, CT: Metal Management Aerospace, Inc., 2007), 55.

"...which meant the aircraft was both fragile..."
Jacobson, Annie. *Area 51: An Uncensored History of America's Top Secret Military Base*. (New York, NY: Back Bay Books, 2012), 5.

"bars, rods, and such other forms..."
"Albany Titanium Plant Ships $45,000 Order," *Albany Democrat-Herald*, Oct 9, 1956 www.newspapers.com.

"The popularity of our lab..."
Wells, Doris, "Pyrometallurgy," *Bureau Bugle*, Vol. VI No. 3 (Albany, Oregon: Bureau of Mines Associates, Inc., Oct 1956), 8.

"When this writer went down to the Smelter..."
Ibid., 9.

"loyalty and civic pride,"
"Loyal Citizens," *Greater Oregon*, Dec 7, 1956 www.newspapers.com.

"The outlook so far for the shareholders..."
Knakel, Edward. "The Facts About Your Credit Union," *Bureau Bugle*, Vol. VI No. 5 (Albany, Oregon: Bureau of Mines Associates, Inc. (Dec 1956) 4.

"I don't have to use any pillows..."
Wells, Doris. "Personnelities," *Bureau Bugle*, Vol. VI No. 3 (Albany, Oregon: Bureau of Mines Associates, Inc., Oct 1956) 3, 5

Epilogue

"the conditions in mining equipment that caused methane ignition..."
Robert Blickensderfer email to the author, Dec 3 2021.

"Research...supports NETL's investigations..."

"Research Facilities & Resources," (http://www.albanyresearchcenter.org/research.html).

"MHD is a scientific discipline interested in…"
"NETL Leading in Magnetohydrodynamic Power Generation Research," www.netl.doe.gov, June 17, 2020.

SELECTED BIBLIOGRAPHY

2018. *Atoms on the Grid! - Shippingport, 1957.* Dec 18. https://www.ans.org/news/article-2093/atoms-on-the-grid-shippingport-1957/.

Day, David T., Ph.D. 1902. "Platnium." *Mines and Quarries 1902*, 661-662.

deWeese, R.W., and R.S. Mason. 1967. "A is for Albany, Z is for Zirconium." *The Ore Bin*, October.

Duncan, Francis. 1990. *Rickover and the Nuclear Navy.* Annapolis, Maryland: Naval Institute Press.

Energy, U.S. Department of. n.d. *The Manhattan Project: An Interactive History.* https://www.osti.gov/opennet/manhattan-project-history/.

Ferguson, Bobbie, and Christine Pfaff. June 1997. *Albany Research Center Volume II Inventory Forms.* Denver, Colorado: U.S. Department of the Interior, Bureau of Reclamation.

February 1998. *An Evaluation of the Historic Significance of the Department of the Interior, Bureau of Mines, Northwest Electrodevelopment Laboratory/Albany Research Center, Albany, Oregon VOLUME 1.* Denver, Colorado: U.S. Department of the Interior, Bureau of Reclamation.

Fortune Magazine. 1949. "Titanium: The New Metal." May 121-128.

Gordon, Robert, Sc. D. 2000. *Miracle Metals Serving in War and Peace—A History of the Role Two Rare*

Metals Played in the Birth of Nuclear Power. Oct 1. Miracle Metals Serving in War and Peace—A History of the Role Two Rare Metals Played in the Birth of Nuclear Power.

Helwett, Richard G. and Francis Duncan. 1974. *Nuclear Navy 1946-1962.* Chicago and London: University of Chicago Press.

Hopkins, Henry Powell. September 15, 1943. *Specifications for Alterations to Existing Buildings at Albany, Oregon for an Electrodevelopment Laboratory.* Baltimore, Maryland: Henry Powell Hopkins.

Housley, Kathleen L. 2007. *Black Sand: The History of Titanium.* Hartford, CT: Metal Management Aerospace, Inc. .

Jablonski, Paul D. and Paul C. Turner. 2005. *Liquid Metal Processing and Casting Experiences at the US Department of Energy's Albany Research Center.* Report, Albany, Oregon: U.S. Department of Energy.

Kintner, Commander E.E. 1959. "Admiral Rickover's Gamble." *The Atlantic*, Jan.

January 1997. *Linking Legacies Connecting the Cold War Nuclear Weapons Production Processes to Their Environmental Consequences.* Washington, D.C.: U.S. Department of Energy Office of Environmental Management.

Meyer, Robinson. 2014. "What It Felt Like to Test the First Submarine Nuclear Reactor." *The Atlantic*, Oct 8.

Nininger, Robert D. 1954. *Minerals for Atomic Energy.* Toronto, New York, London: D. Van Nostrand Company, Inc.

Plastino, Ben J. 1998. *Coming of Age: Idaho Falls and the Idaho National Engineering Laboratory 1949-1990.* Chelsea, Michigan: BookCrafters.

Polmar, Norman, and Thomas B. Allen. 1982. *Rickover: Controversy and Genius, A Biography.* New York: Simon and Schuster.

1946. *Report on the Northwest Electrodevelopment Laboratory.* Report, Albany, Oregon: United States Department of the Interior Bureau of Mines.

Richards, Robert H. December 14, 1905. "Black Sands of the Pacific Coast, 1905." *Technology Quarterly and Proceedings of the Society of Arts, Vol 19* 163-166.

Rickover, H.G., L.D. Geiger, B. Lustman. 1975. *History of the Development of Zirconium Alloys for Use in Nuclear Reactors.* Washington, D.C.: United States Energy Research and Development Administration Division of Naval Reactors.

Rockwell, Theodore. 1992. *The Rickover Effect: How One Man Made a Difference.* Annapolis, Maryland: Naval Institute Press.

Shelton, Stephen M. 1951. "Zirconium." *Scientific American*, June: 18-21.

Silverman, Milton. 1952. "The Wonder Metal that Blows its Top." *The Saturday Evening Post*, Nov 8: 124.

The Mining World, Vol XXIII. 1905. "The Portland Exposition." Aug 5: 1.

2014. *They Harnessed the ATOM - the first Navy prototype nuclear plant.* Oct 10. https://www.ans.org/news/article-1635/they-harnessed-the-atom-the-first-navy-prototype-nuclear-plant/.

Thomas, D.E., E.T. Hayes. n.d. *The Metallurgy of Hafnium.* Report, Washington, D.C.: Naval Reactors, Division of Reactor Development, United States Atomic Energy Commission.

Twenhofel, W.H. 1946. *Mineralogical and Physical Composition of the Sands of the Oregon Coast from Coos Bay to the Mouth of the Columbia River.* Bulletin No. 30, Portland, Oregon: State of Oregon Department of Geology and Mineral Industries.

Westinghouse Elec. Corp. V. Titanium Metals Corp. 1969. Civ. A. No. 792 (United States District Court, D. Nevada, Oct 1).

1998. *William J. Kroll: A Luxembourg Scientist.* Luxembourg: Fondation Nicolas Lanners.

Yih, Stephen W.H. June 30, 1982. "Colorful Figures in Zirconium Industry ." *ASTM Zirconium Conference.* 9.

MORE INFORMATION

Interested in more in-depth information? Try the following resources:

• Scan this QR code to visit our history community at the **Historic Significance of the Albany Research Center (U.S. Bureau of Mines)** Facebook Page for more photos, memories, and discussions.

• Visit the complete online Bibliography webpage at https://historyofalbanyresearchcenter.wordpress.com/

• Contact the author at RocketshipGD@yahoo.com

Thank you for reading this book! Help get the word out by leaving a review on Amazon.com or Goodreads.com. Reviews are immensely helpful to independent authors like myself.

OTHER BOOKS BY TAI STITH

The Incredible Secrets of Hadley Hill

The Heart of Abshire House

The Legacy of the St. Alodia Hotel

The Fulbeck Six

The Alpha Prototype

The Wugawanda

The Wugawanda's Not-So-Silent Night

Made in the USA
Las Vegas, NV
20 March 2022